Real estate appraisal in a nutshell

Real estate appraisal in a nutshell

A restatement and simplification of theory and practice

SECOND EDITION

JAMES INNES STEWART, Q.C.

A.A.C.I., M.B.A., M.A., Barrister-at-Law

University of Toronto Press

First edition 1962
Copyright, Canada, 1962
by J. Innes Stewart
© University of Toronto Press 1967

Second edition 1972
© University of Toronto Press 1972
Toronto and Buffalo
Printed in Canada

ISBN 0-8020-1861-0 (cloth)
ISBN 0-8020-6136-2 (paper)
LC 79-186283

This second edition is dedicated to all my friends,
dear and remote, old and new.

Acknowledgements

This book is not one of the Nutshell series published by Sweet and Maxwell Limited, London, and I appreciate the agreement of that firm to this effect.

The Appraisal Institute of Canada for permission to extract from articles written by myself in A.I.M.

Southam-MacLean Publications Limited for permission to extract briefly from Engineering and Contract Record.

I appreciate the kindness of the following authors and publishers to quote brief excerpts from the indicated books:

A.W. Currie, *Canadian Economic Development* (Thomas Nelson & Sons [Canada] Limited)

B.S. Keirstead, *Essay on Profit & Income Distribution* (Basil Blackwell, Oxford)

B.S. Keirstead, *Capital, Interest & Profits* (The Macmillan Co. of Canada Limited)

Alfred Marshall, *Principles of Economics,* 8th Edition (The Macmillan Company, London)

George L. Schmutz, *The Appraisal Process* (George T. Schmutz)

Paul Wendt, *Real Estate Appraisal* (Holt, Rinehard and Winston, Inc, New York)

Prefaces

PREFACE TO THE SECOND EDITION

Reception accorded the first edition of 'Nutshell' in the nine years since its publication has been gratifying, as has been the clarification of several of the inconsistencies of accepted appraisal theory mentioned therein, although credit for this latter matter is not claimed. Also additional concepts have been incorporated into the texts and programmes of the Appraisal Institute of Canada, the Society of Real Estate Appraisers, and the American Institute of Real Estate and Appraisers. The first two named have introduced the study of economic theory into their curricula, together with an extension of the vocational aspects of their programmes to include evolving techniques; A.I.R.E.A. has developed new and advanced courses on these techniques.

Two of the seemingly popular features of the first edition were its simplicity of expression and example and its brevity. In this new edition the simplicity has been retained as the text itself, while updated to 1971, is basically the same; the brevity has been to some extent eroded, however, by the addition of three new chapters. These appear at the end of the original text as their subject matter does not yet form part of the accepted theory; to introduce them earlier could break the flow of the presentation of this theory.

Chapter 14 discusses the Ellwood concept and related aspects of mortgage-equity analysis and capitalization; Chapter 15 presents a largely narrative analysis of the economics of real property, while Chapter 16 is an adaptation of a paper 'An Economist Looks at Appraisal Theory' which originally appeared in the Journal of the Canadian Institute of Realtors of March 1964 and was reprinted in the July, 1966 issue of The Real Estate Appraiser published by the Society of Real Estate Appraisers.

I am indebted to all the individuals who over the years have commented on the first edition; their help has been considerable. But in particular my thanks go to the principals of Stewart, Young and Mason Limited, Gerry Young, Dave Mason, and Al Williams; they have been most generous in sharing their time and experience with me. Ray Hillesheim and Hugh McPherson of Stewart, Young and Mason have also provided invaluable help in reworking and updating various examples and analyses, while Frank Helyar of the quantity surveying firm of Helyar, Vermeulen, Rae and Mauhan Limited has made available information on current costs and construction. John Griggs of Georgian College of Applied Arts and Technology, Barrie, Ontario, has helped me clarify the explanation of the compound interest techniques of capitalization, while Dave Crawford of A.E. LePage Limited permitted the use of extracts from an analysis presented at the 1970 seminar of the Association of Ontario Land Economists, which appears in Chapter 14, Reference 1.

J.I. STEWART

Preface to the first edition

This book is meant to be a simplified restatement of the theory and practice of appraising with particular reference to the Canadian scene. It is hoped that it will be of assistance not only to the professional and salaried appraiser, but also to teachers and students of the subject, the lawyer, accountant, and real estate broker or salesman, and the interested property owner or user. For this reason the material is presented largely in narrative terms and the arithmetic examples are confined to the final three chapters. Considerable use is made of footnotes so that the basic argument is not interrupted unduly.

There is nothing original in the work except perhaps that the ideas of others may have been combined in original ways. This means that I am obliged to every other economist and appraiser. I have also been fortunate in being associated with many members of the legal profession and the real estate vocation not only in all the provinces of Canada, but also in the United States, and with members of the Appraisal Institute of Canada, the American Institute of Real Estate Appraisers and the Royal Institution of Chartered Surveyors; the comprehensive training in real property matters of members of this British Institution should be the envy of all American and Canadian practitioners. All these individuals have had a part in forming the thoughts which are repeated in this book.

My particular thanks are due to my partners and associates in the firm of Stewart, Young and Mason. Florence Cali, Mary Holliday and Kathleen Macdonald struggled through endless drafts and revisions to finally produce the finished manuscript; David Mason and Gerald Young have been of great help with their practical and theoretical comments, while Alan Williams has helped not only in this way but also with the diagrams.

Naturally I can't place the blame for any errors in either content or connotation on anyone but myself.

J. I. STEWART

Contents

✳ – N.B.

✓ – Brief

Real estate appraisal in a nutshell

Introduction

The problem of the use of land and of its value have become progressively more complex as Canada has changed from an agricultural and primary production nation to one in which manufacturing industries are the most important single economic sector. This change has been accompanied by a coincident shifting of people to the cities and the Gordon Commission estimates that 79% of the population will reside in urban areas by 1980.[1]

Similar problems have plagued planners and others interested in the question of land use in the United States, Britain and elsewhere. It is inevitable that many solutions developed in and by our neighbour to the south and our forebears across the ocean should be adopted in Canada. But the economic beginnings of Canada and the United States were very different, and of course the contrast is even greater between Canada and the United Kingdom or France and so later economic social and political developments are also very different. Therefore adaptation not adoption of American and other ideas is required.

In defiance of geography, two economic entities emerged in North America, namely Canada and the United States, and contrasts between the two appear from the very beginning of their development.[2] What is now Canada was from the start caught up in the problem of trans-continental economic growth involving large transport and administrative costs.

That two economic entities developed is due in large measure to a combination of geographic and topographic conditions. Fertile glacier soil covers a large part of the United States: the same glaciers scattered Canada's soil badly and left the rocks of the Canadian Shield as a barrier to the north and west. The soil of the central States was a major factor in the maintenance of a rapidly growing population and the development of communities, whereas to the north the Canadian Shield encouraged such industries as timber, fur and mining, but did not foster large settlements. Canadian development has been in a series of 'pockets' and only over relatively short distances do we find even a continuous ribbon or belt of intensive land use.

Eastern North America has four arteries leading to its centre, two in Canadian territory and two in the United States. The Canadian arteries (the St Lawrence River and Hudson Bay-James Bay) both lead directly to the centre, but both are unusable for several months of each year; also the St Lawrence-Great Lakes route is very long and was for centuries tortuous and difficult owing to rapids, waterfalls and hostile Indians. The American arteries (the Hudson and Mississippi Rivers) provide relatively ice-free transportation and the ocean ports serving them are not dependent on weather to the same extent as are those in Canada. True, both required technological developments to make them fully usable, but the low heights of land between the Hudson and the St Lawrence-Great Lakes system did not prove too serious an obstacle, and the coming of steam made it possible to defeat the problems of current, shifting sand and snags along the Mississippi.

The importance of France in the development of Canada is tremendous, and the writer feels that this early influence, continuing to the present day, has safeguarded Canada and prevented her from going 'haywire' in ways which appear in the history of the United States. Quebec is a bastion of solidarity and resistance to precipitate and unreasoned change. France, as a self sufficient continental power, desired colonies which could provide the luxuries demanded for a higher standard of living in the mother country. Instead along the St Lawrence, which from the earliest European occupation was a continental trade route and a means of access to the interior, she had sprawling scattered colonies with a simple basic economy: France was faced with major problems of communication and supply from weak bases on the river and coast. On the other hand, Britain, an island power with trans-oceanic interests and a modern economic organization, looked to her colonies as suppliers of staple goods and as markets for the products of her industries; her North American colonies up to 1776 were populous and compact geographically, and their chief drawback was that as time went on they developed relatively diversified economies and became 'active' instead of remaining 'passive' as did the colonies in Canada and those in the southern United States and the West Indies. Currie comments – 'The general pattern of Canadian economic history lies in the theory of the staple and arises out of the fact that throughout most of her history, Canada has been in the pioneer colonial stage of development.'[3]

Politically the two countries (and the predecessor colonies) developed quite differently. Canada under French rule had a feudalistic land system, a powerful church and an emphasis on centralization of control. But feudalism is an inadequate system of land tenure for agricultural development and without this industrial and commercial progress is difficult.

The British (i.e. American) colonies stressed trade, shipping and settlement and the English costs of colonial government were much less than those of France, while political institutions of England were more favourable to colonization. The American colonies were a growth of the Protestant Reformation with its stress on individualism and its recognition that the individual has the right to 'get ahead'; there was no condemnation of trade or of the workings of interest on invested capital.

American growth tended to centre in urban areas along the coast with rapid expansion westward being blocked by the Appalachian range. Bitter inter-community rivalry grew up for the control of the hinterland and transportation to it, and decisions tended to be made in the individual rival communities. In contrast the two major communities of early Canada, Montreal and Quebec, lie in the same transportation and economic system and no such rivalry or competition developed. Since their interests coincided, decisions once made were acceptable to both.

Until the 1830s the American colonies (and nation), with population and communities concentrated along the Atlantic coast, saw their future in and across that ocean. On the other hand, Canada had to concern itself with continental growth for which centralization of control was essential. Centralized institutions emerged early and these continually dampened initiative. Such centralization was unavoidable because of the heavy fixed developmental costs and the inevitable excess capacity; as a result a weak 'lop-sided' economy emerged.

Religious and social mixtures made continent-wide 'nationalism' impossible and this was accentuated by geographic barriers. The French Canadians were a homogeneous block and the Roman Catholic Church had an important influence on Canadian development. It checked the growth of the free equity which was developing in the American colonies; it also discouraged mortgaging the future for rapid exploitation. These factors plus geographic features tended to minimize speculation in land in the eastern part of what is now Canada, and hence this very important driving force, so prominent in American tradition, was of minor importance in early Canadian history. Even after Confederation the Federal government retained control of the public domain in the Prairie provinces and used it for the National Policy, and not until 1930 did these provinces have a 'public domain.'

After the Conquest, the French colonies became British, but great differences persisted between the colonies north and south of the Bay of Fundy. Those to the north were on marginal land and dependent on staples shipped to Britain and Europe; they relied on Britain for continuing life. Far to the north the Hudson's Bay Company had deep roots in Britain so that in general the colonies of what is now Canada looked to Britain.

On the other hand, the communities to the south resented British control as it constituted a tremendous strain on these capital-hungry colonies. They had developed a triangular trade with the West Indies and England and trade with the colonies to the north was not too attractive for them, particularly as these, having French origins, did not recognize English law of debt and contract.

American growth featured repeated 'bursts' of migration, settlement and consolidation and physical barriers reinforced this pattern. Before settlements were established in the trans-Appalachian area, a very strong base had developed along the Atlantic coastal plain from which migrants moved to the west supported by investment from the coast. A similar build-up occurred before the push across the Mississippi, before the occupation of the Great Plains, and before the eastern movement from the Pacific Coast across and beyond the Sierras. There has been no such 'build up' and 'burst out' in Canadian development, although the completion of the C.P.R. had an analogous effect, at a later date.

Such a pattern of growth tended to exaggerate sectionalism in America, but it also encouraged the development of those basic tenets of American life, that growth shall come from the free competition of small units and that there shall be no control over economic life. The diversity of the American social environment from early days has been perpetuated by liberal immigration policies through much of the history of that nation and also by social and other barriers created between the 'debtor' (at least in the early years) inland areas and the 'creditor' coastal communities. Such an environment favours changes in the status quo and the only resistance to economic progress arises out of inertia, prejudice or the power of vested interests. The importance of the individual emerges early in the history of the United States, and there has been a premium on aggressiveness, a belief in the right of every man to exploit the resources of the country and a distrust of centralized power and government, which is seen in the checks and balances forming part of the Constitution. The American Government until the 1930s was a 'passive' one; in Canada, on the other hand, Government has always been 'positive,' and has had to participate in the economic life of the nation right from the start.

The 'frontier' too was very different as between Canada and the United States. Turner states that the free lands of the United States have been the most important single factor in explaining the development of that country.[4] In the United States there was a free frontier, whereas in Canada it was always controlled; not that land was not 'free' (in fact Canada introduced the principle of the Homestead Act, a generation before its enactment in the States), but development was 'planned'; also in Canada there was not a 'settlement' frontier (as in the States), but rather a 'trading' frontier which continued to the late nineteenth century to hold its grip against any breakthrough.

Man can, by his technological skills, adapt his environment to suit his purposes and the Canadian colonists proved adept at developing overland techniques which were later formalized through the organization of the Hudson's Bay Company. The American colonists developed maritime techniques which, in time, made them the greatest carrying power in the world. In the American colonies the advance of all sorts of technology was favoured and the promise of large profits was held out for the discovery and development of the natural

resources of the country. The great distances involved tended to increase costs
and so transportation technology was particularly encouraged. Also the American colonies provided the stage for empirical experimentation and the techniques of mass production and interchangeable parts were the outgrowth of
the drive to technical achievement.

A well-organized credit and money system is almost essential and the north-
ern colonies, after becoming British North America, were able to rely on the
system already set up in Britain, whereas the American colonies after the Revolution had no such continuing influence. The demand for large supplies of
money was constant and insistent and led to many individual banks being
established; there was also a fear of having a centralized bank governing the
supply of money. The unit banking system developed and there was an absence from the American scene of any form of central banking from about
1836 to 1913, and even today there is no counterpart of the Bank of England
or the Bank of Canada. On the other hand, in Canada there has been almost
from the start strong relatively centralized banking control and although there
was no central bank as such until the mid 1930s the chartered banks and other
financial institutions have been very large with many branches in contrast to
the American system of individual unit banks.

The reason an understanding is needed of why Canada and the United States
have developed differently can be illustrated by considering a common appraisal problem. In the analysis of a city or neighbourhood, the appraiser is search-
ing for reasons why the community originally came into being to see whether
the same forces exist at the time of appraisal. If they do, he can draw certain
conclusions about the stability of the community; if they don't, he is faced
with that difficult appraisal problem, the neighbourhood or city in transition.[5]

So also we can consider the formative forces affecting two nations and analyse
these to see if they are still present; if they are the nations will continue to be
guided economically, socially and politically along the lines indicated. Contrast-
ing present day Canada with the United States, one cannot help but be struck
with the great differences between our institutions; this is bound to have a pro-
found effect on our everyday lives and attitudes; a few examples will, it is
hoped, make this clear.

Mention has been made of the different banking systems in the two countries:
one result has been the legal incapacity until 1967 of Canadian banks to lend
on real estate mortgages except in a limited way – a great contrast to the American situation with an effect on real property value and use in the two countries.
Another significant side effect of importance to appraisers has been the influence of the central bank upon the level of the rate of interest.

Another way of illustrating the differences is through the fundamental principles of government and here it will be helpful to expand the analysis to include the United Kingdom.

In Britain there is no 'Constitution' as such: Parliament is supreme and may legislate on any matter, so that a lawyer in examining legislation need only ascertain what the law means and not bother as to whether Parliament has power to so legislate. Legislation affecting land use must affect value and Britain has very sweeping legislation of this type.[6]

In contrast, the American constitutional picture is complex. There was from the start a distrust of central government and the formal constitution awards wide local and state powers and limits federal ones. In general, much power is constitutionally divorced from the federal sphere and the ultimate of protection for the individual and his property is guaranteed. When legislation is enacted it must stand both the test of judicial interpretation and scrutiny to decide whether the enacting level of government acted in the words of the lawyer, 'intra vires' or 'ultra vires.'

Canada is a 'half-way house' constitutionally. The British North America Act of 1867 (a statute of the United Kingdom) defines relative powers of the Federal Parliament and Provincial Legislatures. Section 91 specified exclusive Federal jurisdictions while Section 92 gives Provinces exclusive authority in other matters including: property and civil rights, local or private matters within a province, municipal institutions and education (Section 93). Residual powers are with Parliament. Since 1948 the Act can be amended by Canadian legislation in matters of sole federal jurisdiction; the Constitutional Conference in Victoria in 1971 may make full patriation possible.

Conflicts between Federal and Provincial powers continue to affect our lives and in passing it must be noted that included in the Federal powers are those to legislate on 'Interest.' Clearly 'Interest' (i.e. the cost of borrowing money) has a major effect on land use and development and yet 'Property' is largely a matter of provincial jurisdiction. Perhaps not so clear is the problem concerning Provincial Boards and Tribunals. For instance, some or all provinces have Boards which rule on planning and zoning matters, such as the Ontario Municipal Board whose jurisdiction extends to hearing assessment appeals and until 1970 also covered arbitration of claims in some classes of expropriation. The Ontario Expropriation Act, S.O., 1968-69, Ch. 36 provides for a Land Compensation Board to hear such claims. Such tribunals are not classified as 'Courts' and their decisions and awards do not constitute 'legal decisions' (in the strict sense). Another conflict which plagues planners and appraisers is that property used by either Federal or Provincial Governments (or their offshoots, some of which are of course industries) is not subject to local planning controls, or municipal taxation; this may make valuation more complex.

While thinking of courts the reader should also note another great distinction between American and Canadian practice. Arbitrations and trials are conducted in a less emotional atmosphere in Canada; many hearings to assess compensation for expropriated property in the United States are heard by a judge and jury and this forum lends itself to the development of techniques of presentation which will appeal to the typical juror.

There are many other major and countless minor ways in which Canada and the United States differ. For instance when we consider the railways we find that whereas in Canada there are two transcontinental systems operating, in the United States there are none. This difference has had a major effect upon the prevailing pattern of land use and development in the two nations and upon the location and economic health of towns and cities.

In no field is it more important to recognize the difference between the United Kingdom, the United States and Canada than in that of real estate appraisal. Most of the literature available in Canada is American or British, although the Appraisal Institute of Canada has recently made an important contribution.[7] The close ties with these countries and their advanced stage of development makes it inevitable that many of their legal decisions will be known to us. The influx of British appraisers to Canada and the free crossing of the American border add to the barrage of ideas which constantly batter us. We must open our minds to these ideas and concepts but must erect a mental sieve which will sort out the relevant from the irrelevant.

This book attempts to do a number of things within the limits imposed by the desire of the author to keep it as brief as possible. In the first place, the aim has been to simplify accepted appraisal theory. With this in mind, the examples used have been made minimal in number and basic in concept, while the subject matter of the text has been reduced to those phases of theory which are of practical importance.

Secondly, the order in which the various topics is taken up differs considerably from that in other texts. The author feels that the normal sequence of topics does not flow logically and that its use requires repeated repetition of explanations and examples. The most important changes in order are:

1 The Appraisal Process is covered prior to such topics as the nature and functions of appraisals and the nature of value. The reader thus can see how the appraiser attacks an assignment before he comes to a discussion of the way in which say the principle of substitution applies to the three 'approaches' to value.

2 The various 'principles' are discussed in a sequence which brings together those which are closely interrelated.

3 The market data approach is covered before site valuation and the cost and income approaches. Site valuation generally relies on market data: also gross and net income multipliers and the risk rate developed by analysis of market data are used in the cost and income approaches; estimates of accrued depreciation can also be made from market data. In practice the market data approach must be developed in whole or in part before the others can be completed and the order followed in this book reflects this practice. Contrast A.I.C. Text; the market data approach is treated last.

4 The cost approach to the value estimate is combined with the discussion on accrued depreciation in a single chapter.

5 In the income approach to the value estimate 'methods of capitalization' are covered in the same chapter as the 'Residual Techniques' and this also includes the discussion of 'lease interests.' The earlier comment about trying to simplify accepted theory is nowhere better illustrated than in the treatment afforded the income approach: if the result is confusion and not clarification, this too will also be most apparent in such treatment. It may be best to read Chapters 10, 11, and 12 through together before each is tackled alone. The evolving techniques based on Mortgage-Equity capitalization have been added as a separate Chapter 14.

6 Final correlation and the appraisal report are both covered in a single chapter which is supplemented by the reproduction of a synopsised appraisal report, extracts from which are used as examples in the text of the book. This report is based on an actual appraisal of a walk-up apartment; a number of simplifying assumptions have been made and the treatment has been aimed at explanation rather than elaboration of techniques. The author recognizes the risk entailed in reducing a real report to its bare essentials: the door is wide open to critics who can show shortcomings in both the assumption and the final result. This risk has been taken under the cover of the basic tenets on which this book is offered, namely brevity and simplicity. Preceding the report is a statement of the problem from which the reader or teacher can obtain the necessary data to work out his own solution for classroom use.

The third purpose of the present work is to point out certain apparent inconsistencies (or even errors) in accepted appraisal theory. The writer has been concerned for some years with the parrot-like repetitious platitudes which most writers, lecturers and speakers utter on various phases of the appraisal process. Advances in theory in most fields are largely made during periods of trial and tribulation, which for appraisal theory means depression periods. In prosperous periods, deficiencies in theory are concealed by rising prices or ignored through pressure of work. Accepted appraisal theory appears to have been formalized in the United States in the 1930s by the American Institute of Real Estate Appraisers and it has been adopted almost in its entirety by the Appraisal Institute of Canada and by individual appraisers, but not adapted.

There is serious doubt in the mind of the author whether some of the basic assumptions on which this theory rests ever had any validity, except of course in economic models where simplification is essential and justifiable. In most cases these questions are raised in footnotes and in Chapter 16 so that the continuity of the basic argument is not interrupted. In fact this basic argument is in general worked out around the accepted assumptions even though the author may question their validity. This has been done in the hope that the present book will be useful to teachers and students at various appraisal courses, the curricula and subject matter of which are based on these assumptions.

The author feels his criticisms are correct but realizes that many appraisers have considered the so-called 'inconsistencies' and found them not to be such. It is to be hoped that some of these appraisers will take the trouble to consider the questions raised and publish their comments.

This brings us to the fourth and final function of the book. By setting out the 'inconsistencies' which appear to be inherent in some techniques, it is hoped that other appraisers and academicians will consider the matter too so that this book will stimulate others to carry out their own analyses on both advanced and elementary levels. It seems that the basic theory as presently taught assumes that appraisers have a considerable theoretical and practical background in mathematics, economics, town planning, geography, law and sociology. This is certainly not valid in Canada and probably not in the United States, and so it is felt that the educational efforts of the professional Institutes should be extended both upwards and downward. This implies that not only should the concepts on which the theory rests be carefully re-examined, but also that a basic text on the social sciences as relied on by appraisers should be written: it should of course also be supported by a revision of the present curricula of courses to provide a more logical programme, not of trade-training, but of education. In Canada the first steps in this latter regard were taken in 1970 by A.I.C. in making a basic course in Economics a compulsory part of its curriculum.

Addendum

Reference has been made to the fact that under the American Constitution, major legislative powers are in the hands of the States and yet from reports in the daily press it is clear that the Federal Government and the President have much greater ability to effectively intervene in matters of state jurisdiction than is the case in Canada where provincial legislative rights, paralleling in many cases those of the States have been immune to federal threats and/or blandishments.

The reason for this is that a 'Bill of Rights' forms part of the Constitution of the United States, whereas in Canada it is a separate federal statute. Amendments 1 to 10 of the American Constitution were adopted by the Federal Congress in 1789 and by all State legislative assemblies by 1791. These amendments guarantee personal freedoms and have made it possible for Congress to enact a series of Civil Rights Acts, including the far-reaching one of 1964 which guarantees free and equal enjoyment ... without discrimination or segregation because of race, colour, religion, or national origin in any establishment which affects commerce or if the discrimination is supported by state action. Titles I to VII of the Act cover such matters as voting, public education, community life, and employment.

The Canadian Bill of Rights, 8-9 Elizabeth II Chapter 44, now R.S.C. 1970, Appendix III, protects the same areas of life and living but is not binding on the Provinces and can be expressly excluded from any other Federal statute. The British North America Act, the Canadian Constitution, has been amended in the past to give the Federal government exclusive powers in such areas as Unemployment Insurance and Old Age Pension which could have been handled under the Section 92 jurisdiction of the Provinces, but in the matter of civil rights this has not been done.

REFERENCES

1 / Royal Commission on Canada's Economic Prospects, 1957.

2 / W.T. Easterbrook and H.G.J. Aitken, *Canadian Economic History,* Macmillan 1966-7.

3 / A.W. Currie, *Canadian Economic Development,* Nelson, 4th Edition, 1963, p. 1.

4 / F.J. Turner, *The Frontier in American History,* Holt 1920.

5 / John Friedman and William Alonzo (Editors), *Regional Planning and Development,* M.I.T. 1964. Brian J.L. Berry shows that the size-distribution in Canada is based on a few primate cities whereas the United States has a rank-size distribution. This distinction has major implications.

6 / The Land Compensation Act, 1961, Ch. 33 also defines how compensation is to be determined in expropriation. The Ontario Expropriations Act, S.O., 1968-69, Ch. 36, sec. 13 and 14 (now R.S.O. 1970, Ch. 154) and Federal Expropriation Act, R.S.C., 1970, Ch. 16, 1st Supplement both require a market value estimate based on a willing buyer, willing seller concept.

7 / *The Appraisal Reference Manual,* and *Real Estate Appraising in Canada,* 1970. This latter work is referred to herein as 'A.I.C. Text.' The text of the American Institute of Real Estate Appraisers, The Appraisal of Real Estate – 5th Edition is referred to as 'A.I.R.E.A. Text.'

1

The appraiser and his work

General ideas on exchange

In paying a certain amount of money for something a purchaser must feel that
he is gaining more than he is giving up. Similarly a seller in accepting the money
must feel that he too is gaining more than he is giving up. Both parties must
feel that they are benefiting simultaneously; when this is so, we can speak of
the exchange as being 'efficient.'[1]

For an 'efficient' exchange, the parties must have adequate knowledge about
the object to be traded and its true worth. This implies that conditions of reasonably perfect competition exist, namely that there is a large number of sellers
of identical products, each selling at the same price and each conveniently
located and that simultaneously there are a large number of conveniently located buyers each adequately informed as to the prices asked by sellers and
the merits of the objects in question.

Such competition rarely exists, on the seller's side of the market. A store-
keeper, a manufacturer, or a farmer at the farmer's market can charge a small
premium and still retain most of his business, partly because customers have
loyalties or inertias, partly because of convenience, but largely because of
inadequate knowledge of the alternative opportunities. If we consider services
as opposed to goods, there is a clear difference in qualities between what individual buyers receive for their money and so rarely can an exchange of money
for services be 'efficient' in the economic sense.

Commodity exchanges illustrate efficient markets; identically graded and
classified items are exchanged in divisible quantities with many well informed
buyers and sellers present personally or by telephone at the same place. These
exchanges approach the ideal of perfect competition. But most other items
are not sold under such conditions and in fact advertising makes it impossible
for a customer to be fully informed as to the true merits of the seemingly

similar items which compete for his money. Most markets are in general a mixture of competition and monopoly.[2]

The real estate market is most imperfect and is in direct contrast, say, to the Winnipeg grain exchange. Every property differs to some extent from every other; the asking price is a point for starting negotiations to arrive at the final price; prospective purchasers can rarely be adequately informed as to comparative prices or values. Also, purchases may be based on mixed economic and emotional reasons.

The first level of appraisal activity

Whenever a person buys or sells anything he 'appraises' it. The general public in the real estate market makes up the first level of appraisal activity and from what was said above it is clear that this will be a rather poorly informed group of 'appraisers.' Yet, we must not underestimate the average citizen; it is because of his reasonably high level of general skills that reliance can be placed on transactions in the real estate market.

The second level of appraisal activity

Mention has been made of the increase in the use of urban land which characterizes Canadian development. This combined with the fact that the real property market is imperfect has led to the emergence of a large body of quasi-specialists; imagine the confusion in say Halifax, Vancouver or any community if there were no real estate brokers or salesmen, no mortgage brokers or lending agencies; (of course there might be no assessors and hence no taxes to pay!)

Our society is characterized by the growth of a vast army of specialized service organizations and businesses. That the need for such services will increase as more and more Canadians become residents of urban areas is indicated by the forecast of the Gordon Commission that whereas in 1955 'service' of various sorts comprised 46.6% of the national labour force, this will have increased to 55.3% by 1980.

The second level of appraisal activity then is carried on by the real estate broker and salesman, the mortgage lenders, brokers and appraisers, the municipal and governmental assessors and appraisers, the subdividers, builders and property managers and by all those other specialists who make the complex parts of the real property market fit together and function as an imperfect whole. They know more about the problems involved in real property use and value than the members of the general public. Among them are many highly trained appraisers and property managers who in a different context could adequately discharge the responsibility of giving professional advice on any property problem. This second echelon is secondary not in ability but rather in experience and the opportunity to display such ability. They are specialists in some specific section of the real property complex. As such they must and do express opinions as to value and optimum use of property; but many problems lie outside the sphere of their specialties.

The third level of appraisal activity

Just as the complexities of our society led to the evolution of the above noted specialties, so has this in turn led to the appearance of professional real estate consultants, property managers and appraisers. These are the 'specialist's specialists' to whom the members of the 'second level' can refer problems which are beyond either their competence or their inclinations; they are to a greater or lesser degree highly trained both through experience and education to handle a wide range of real property problems. They probably devote the major part of their earning capacity to assignments for which they are paid a fee or a salary (as compared to a commission) although many of them may engage in a general brokerage practice.

Many major users of real property employ such specialists in matters which differ from, or are more all-embracing than those normally handled by their own property departments. Also, with the growing complexity of our economy, public bodies are returning to the status of their medieval counterparts as major land owners; their ownership must not only be able to stand public scrutiny, but often necessitates compulsory acquisition of property so they employ salaried or independent professional appraisers. Also expropriation and municipal assessment being two-way streets, affected owners often need similar services. In fact, the growing demand of the citizens of Canada for more adequate public facilities and services is probably the single most important source of the increasing demand for professional appraisers.

Definitions and functions of appraisal

Webster's Collegiate Dictionary says 'appraisal; "Act of appraising esp. by one authorized; also an estimated value set upon a property."' This is quite inadequate; it also illustrates a fallacy, namely that appraisers 'set' values. It is the market which 'sets' the value; the appraiser tries to interpret the market.

We can think of an appraisal as having five essential parts.[3] It is:

1 a written, signed opinion of the value of an
2 adequately described property made as of
3 a specified date, which evaluates the
4 property rights involved according to
5 a defined concept of value.

We can also divide appraisals into two major overlapping categories, namely risk reducing and fair treatment appraisals.[4] Another matter which must concern us is the definition of the word 'value.' This has plagued people from the beginning of time and even economists are not unanimous in their conclusions. Webster gives 11 different meanings; A.I.R.E.A. lists 40 different varieties.[5]

II THE SCOPE OF AN APPRAISER'S WORK

The major part of an appraiser's responsibility lies in the area of estimating the value of real property. However a professional appraiser will find that he must help clients solve a wide variety of problems. The author has reviewed his own experience in this regard and has found that over the ten years immediately preceding the publication of this book, the 'non valuation' work which he and his associates have done can be classified as follows:[6]

Use of land and buildings

In advising on the optimum use of property the problem is to balance alternative opportunities and costs. The appraiser must recognize what the alternatives are and a well-rounded practical and educational background is the classroom in which the ability to so recognize is acquired.

Location

The location of a residence or enterprise is a 'one time' choice which once made is hard to change: real property is fixed in space and durable physically. Hence every decision about location is vital not only to the individual or enterprise concerned, but also to the community and nation.

Matters of internal business

Appraisers may be required to estimate value for purposes of accounting, allocation of rents between departments of an owner-occupied enterprise, income tax and succession duties. Special concepts of value may be involved and either the appraiser must know the applicable law or the client's lawyer should outline the requirements to the appraiser. Most lawyers assume that an appraiser who is a member of a recognized appraisal institute can interpret the word 'value' according to the concept applicable in each situation and so give no terms of reference: this may result in erroneous conclusions based on interpretations by an appraiser who did not know all the alternatives.

Real property management

Highly trained professional property managers are often retained by the owners of rented properties held as investments; these specialists and the practising appraiser may also be asked for advice on owner-occupied properties. As owners rely on accountants for advice on financial matters the appraiser must understand accounting and taxation methods of depreciation and replacement and recognize the basic distinctions between these and the analogous appraisal concepts.

Ownership, tenancy and financing

The appraiser may be asked the most favourable way in which real property should be acquired and/or occupied; for instance ownership by tenancy in common as contrasted with joint tenancy. Also the mortgage-equity position has an effect on values as explained later in Chapter 14 which is devoted to the Ellwood analysis. The appraiser must understand the ramifications of the above and, as noted, lawyers, accountants and clients may well assume that by his very membership in professional appraisal bodies, he has such understanding. Appraisal assignments often interlock with those of lawyers and accountants, so the appraiser should have a knowledge of the theories which form part of these disciplines.

Miscellaneous matters

Other appraisal problems include the valuation of machinery, goodwill, a going concern, a professional practice or small business, and the reproduction or replacement cost of a structure, building or installation. It is important that the appraiser realize his own limitations, both those imposed by his personal knowledge and background, and those imposed by custom and law.

III   THE APPRAISER IN TODAY'S ECONOMY

In the free-enterprise type of economy there is a gradual alienation of individual rights and responsibilities by government; our society is leaning more and more on socialistic concepts.
 Every type of society must answer four basic economic questions:

> For whom will the economy produce?
> How much will it produce?
> What will it produce?
> How will it produce?

 Mankind, from his earliest history has always had to allocate scarce resources among alternative uses. Many natural resources abound but rarely either in the form or the place for direct use; man must transport and convert them into usable forms and hence the above four questions. The assumption of the free-enterprise system is that allocation of resources (land, labour and capital) can best be effected in free markets and the economies of the western world have been built on this premise for the past two centuries. The system assumes that individuals try to get the greatest utility out of things they buy with their money and to suffer the least 'disutility' or 'sacrifice' at the tasks they perform to earn that money. Consumers will bid for those goods and services which they prize most highly and will not bid for others: these 'bids' when accepted by sellers become market prices.

The suppliers of the goods and services (be they manufacturers, wholesalers, retailers or individuals) observe the bidding and adjust their supplies upwards or downwards to meet the demand: such adjustment results in heavier or lighter employment and hence in workers earning greater or smaller wages to spend as consumers. The markets for each good and service will always be tending towards equilibrium positions where the supply of and demand for products and services will balance.

For the system to function effectively certain conditions must be fulfilled; (also see Chapter 15).

First, both suppliers and consumers must have adequate knowledge of total supply and demand at every instant and at every price.

Secondly, no supplier or consumer may be so powerful as to influence supply and demand; if he can, then by withholding supply or by not bidding, he could influence prices.

Thirdly, in each segment of each market, each good and service offered or purchased must be identical with each other good and service – i.e. there must be homogeneity.

The real estate market doesn't fit these requirements: 'knowledge' about sales, rentals, potential use of properties and so on, is far from perfect and each parcel is unique and not homogeneous. While no individual buyer or seller can influence overall supply and demand, the supply of real property cannot be increased or decreased quickly in answer to changing prices; the market for real property can never be 'perfect.' The very nature of the commodity and market implies that the assistance of experts is essential in a society the functioning of which is becoming more and more complex.[7]

Each individual allocates his resources, in an economically rational way. To him, these 'resources' are the dollars which he earns, but to society as a whole they are machines, water power, raw materials, trucks, planes – all those things both produced and natural which our complex world needs and uses, including three basic necessities, food, clothing and shelter.

All resources are 'scarce' in an economic sense and so individuals (including of course governments and corporations) must allocate them to maximize satisfaction. Real property is both scarce and an absolute necessity; every human being uses it every minute of every day. And as real property cannot be physically moved to meet demand, the need has existed since time immemorial to 'control' the use of land and to sacrifice the right of the individual to the needs of society as a whole. This narrowing of the rights of ownership proceeded slowly for many centuries, but in the past 50 years the trend has gained momentum. Today we can rarely use any land without thinking about restrictions, and the use of urban land is hemmed in by zoning, building, health and other by-laws and regulations. We must even consider the effect of uses or changes of use on taxes and succession duties; truly real property development has repercussions from the cradle to the grave!

To sum up, the market for real property being imperfect, qualified advisors on value and use are almost indispensable. Also the market cannot operate freely due both to the nature of the commodity, land, and to the very long physical life of buildings. Also, government intervention has on the one hand reduced the variety of uses for which property can be developed and on the other has increased the number of land uses which fall directly under public control and/or ownership.

The individual owner and user of real property requires advice. Often the Realtor and his salesmen can give such advice: often too the mortgagee, the assessor and the government appraiser can, within the field of his own specialty, be able to advise. But, inevitably, independent and impartial expert advice will be required and this is where the professional appraiser enters the picture.

What is the professional appraiser? He must be a mixture of realtor, lawyer, economist, geographer, sociologist, accountant, engineer – and above all he must be a human being who operates not so much with fixed notions as with flexibility.

The appraiser must realize that real property, the most basic of all our resources, is a heritage for the use of the individual, subject to the needs of society. He will then see his duty as being to offer impartial and unprejudiced advice and counsel so that this irreplaceable resource will be so used as to answer the four basic economic questions, For whom?; What?; How Much?; and How? Only by answering these questions optimally can the free enterprise economy best perform.

In North America the vocation of appraising is very young. It is too early to judge whether it will be willing and able to accept its responsibilities: whether it and its individual members will accept the dictum of discipline which is the sine qua non of a profession. It is by this, not by professional designations that the land-owning public, the courts and the other professions will or will not recognize appraisers as professional men.

From the observations of the author, a background in some phase of the real estate vocation is a prerequisite to successful appraising and if the phase happens to be selling so much the better. But the old cliché of experience being the best teacher has little validity in this or any other field unless the experience is combined with an understanding of the principles involved. These principles are becoming increasingly available through various educational courses, meetings and books.

REFERENCES

1 / Tibor Scitovsky, *Welfare and Competition,* Irwin 1951, Chapter XVI.

2 / Joan Robinson, *The Economics of Imperfect Competition,* Macmillan, London, 1933.

E.H. Chamberlin, *The Theory of Monopolistic Competition,* 7th Ed., Harvard 1958.

3 / A.I.C. and A.I.R.E.A. texts do not include 'property rights' as part of the minimum contents and do include 'contingent or limiting conditions.' Surely the former is and the latter is not an essential part of any appraisal.

4 / This is inherent in the analysis in A.I.C. text, p. 2.

5 / *Appraisal Terminology and Handbook,* A.I.R.E.A.

6 / A.I.M. Appraisal Institute of Canada, May 1959.

7 / An economic analysis of the real property market appears in Chapter 15.

2

The appraisal process
and the three approaches

I THE APPRAISAL PROCESS

The appraisal process is a formal framework under which the implication is
that the three 'approaches' (Cost, Market and Income) to the value estimate
will result in equivalent answers. The full framework is rarely used in Canada,
largely owing to the limitations inherent in the cost approach which are pointed
out later. But the idea of a series of steps is useful; it should become automatic
in the appraiser's attack in every assignment.

Definition of the problem

The subject matter of the five essential parts of an appraisal noted in Chapter
1 must be clearly understood by the appraiser: he identifies the property and
the rights involved, outlines the purposes and defines the value concepts to be
used and the effective date.

Identification of the property

Every appraisal should contain at least an abbreviated legal description to un-
equivocally identify the property. This is found in the registry or similar title
office. Legal descriptions in Canada were originally under various survey systems based on townships, sections, concessions and lots, which in urban areas
were then sometimes subdivided into smaller plans showing individual building
lots; in many jurisdictions it is mandatory to register such subdivision plans
before disposing of property.[1]

Every appraiser should learn to search titles particularly since his evidence
in court must be based on personal inspection of the instruments under which
comparable sales were consumated;[2] but the appraiser will generally assume
that the owner's title to the subject property itself is valid.

Property rights involved

A title search may disclose that the owner has disposed of some of his rights. Appraising a property subject to a lease which restricts alternative uses of the property differs from appraising a freehold.

The purpose of the appraisal

The appraiser must clarify the 'purpose' with his client, to be sure of the types of data required, the form his report will take and special types of information which he will need. For instance:

In an insurance appraisal, market sales have little relevance in a partial loss but the indemnity of an insurer is legally limited to the market value in a total loss unless extended by special rider.

In a partial expropriation a survey of the whole property and a plan of the expropriation are needed; relevant sales data should if possible include properties with a similar type of impediment, namely, say, a railway track running through them.

Value concept

The applicable concept of value relates closely to the purpose of the appraisal: it may be market value, 'fair' market value,[3] value to the owner, insurable value. The appraiser should clearly define or describe the value concept to be applied.

The effective date

The principle of change shows that appraisals are not made in a temporal vacuum; an opinion of value can be given only as of a specified date. Generally the current date applies but even then it is wise to use a date at least a day earlier than when the sales of comparable properties were checked at the registry office: then a new comparable sale registered between the times of search and the typing of the report can justifiably be omitted; of course when the appraiser learns of it he must consider it and may prepare a supplementary report. If there is any doubt as to the date or any of his terms of reference, the appraiser should request specific instructions from the client's lawyer.

In expropriations the effective date is usually either when the expropriating body took certain actions (such as passing a by-law) or the date of registration or of notice to the owner.

The preliminary survey

Breaking the problem down into its essentials enables the appraiser to determine what is involved. He can then quote a fee and a delivery date for the report. For instance if a court appearance may be necessary the appraiser must be able, under his terms of reference and the fee quoted, to make a thorough investigation and prepare a full report, particularly if this report

must be given to the other party as required by the Ontario Expropriation Act.
If consideration must be given to special value to the owner, conferences may
be involved so the appraisal fee must be flexible enough to allow for this.

An appraisal must be prepared within certain time limits, so a programme
must be followed. The appraiser should develop proformae to assist in pre-
paring reports and in recording his rough work. He may also delegate some
phases of the work to associates or outside specialists. Division of labour has
long been recognized as an important source of economies and while such
opportunities are limited in professions and vocations, where the knowledge
of the individual is the commodity he sells, still they do exist. For instance
it is often best to use an outside contractor or quantity surveyor to estimate
costs. Also in most communities specialists carry out registry office searches
for a fee; if this is not feasible every appraiser should think of employing
someone to specialize in digging out data. A lot of eventually usable data
becomes available and also the appraiser can use more of his talents and energies in research and investigation, talents and energies which can be dissipated
in the routine and frustrating work of the registry office.

General and specific data

Physical, social, economic and political matters beyond the physical limits of
the property being evaluated, affect its value; these include population, income
and employment trends and levels, zoning regulations, transportation and shopping facilities. An active appraisal practice produces much general data in the
normal course of business, and benefit can be gained by employing someone
to gather and arrange this. Such data are used over and over again so time and
effort are well spent in obtaining them and keeping them in usable form.

The specific data concerning the individual property include legal, physical,
and economic information.

Sources of data

The rule against 'hear-say evidence' is enforced before most courts, boards and
arbitrators and the appraiser should use sources of data which form a firm
basis for testimony. For instance, information on sales and leases obtained in
the registry or other title office is admitted while the same type of information
in a co-operative or multiple listing system may not be.

Municipal offices are good sources of data but again the 'hear-say rule' applies. The appraiser can probably give evidence as to the assessment of properties he has personally looked up in the rolls but not details, say, of the basis on
which the assessments were made. So also an appraiser can describe the existing zoning but cannot give evidence of, say, a proposed change in zoning which
he discussed with a municipal employee.

Of another character is information pertinent to the type, quality and cost
of construction of buildings. Appraisers rely on manuals and indices designed

to assist the laymen in costing and describing buildings. Estimates based on such methods may be inadmissible as evidence unless the individual giving it has some special background in construction or in cost estimating.

Another important source of data is the newspaper, as it keeps the appraiser abreast of happenings in the nation, community and neighbourhood: any court testimony based on such information should be given by outside specialists who are qualified to comment intelligently on the matter in question.

Data can therefore be classified as being general and specific and as being admissible and inadmissible. This latter classification does not mean that an appraiser cannot use inadmissible data in his appraisals but he must realize that 'hear-say' type data may be misleading both to his client and himself.

II   THE THREE APPROACHES

Alfred Marshall,[4] the great Cambridge economist formalized the idea of the equivalence of value estimates obtained in what the appraiser calls the Cost, Market Data and Income Approaches. But of course the ideas that value is determined by cost, saleability and income productivity go back much further than Marshall.

While the three approaches can be used in most appraisals the average appraiser is not competent in cost matters and so in expropriation appraisals an outside specialist generally prepares cost estimates from which the appraiser can estimate deductions for accrued depreciation.

Other types of appraisal in which the three approaches will rarely be used include valuations of vacant land, insurance valuations and those of special type buildings which neither sell nor rent on the market, and valuations of interests under leases.

The market data approach

This is the heart of the appraisal process since buyers and sellers are guided by the prices which obtain in the market. The appraiser uses data of sales, listings and offers for similar properties and analyses each in relation to the subject property. The more comparable are the properties the fewer adjustments will be required, and as the adjustments are of necessity subjective, this is important.

In litigious matters, details of each sale must be supported in court, and an appraiser giving evidence based on conversations with a vendor or a purchaser will be stopped under the hearsay rule. Nevertheless he must gather such information so the client's lawyer can decide whether the actual party to a comparable sale should be called as a witness. In appraisals which are not prepared for court purposes, such hearsay evidence can be used, but the implication should not be left that the appraiser has personal knowledge.

The cost approach

No informed buyer will pay more for an existing improved property than it would cost him to start with a similarly located parcel of vacant land and erect a new building thereon, assuming no undue time delay. But such a buyer would almost certainly pay less than new cost, as the existing building would have worn out somewhat or become outmoded: this wearing out is called accrued depreciation. From the viewpoint of the buyer accrued depreciation represents the difference between the current reproduction cost of the buildings and their value on the market as of the same date. It represents a 'loss in value' in all cases, but only where cost coincides with value will the amount of the accrued depreciation exactly coincide with the loss in value; this occurs only when the buildings develop the site to its highest use. See Chapter 9.

The Cost Approach is often called the 'summation' approach as it consists of an adding up process: the steps are as follows:

1 Evaluate the site as though vacant.
2 Compute the current cost of the improvements.
3 Deduct the estimated accrued depreciation.
4 Add the depreciated cost estimate to the land value.

The income approach

It has long been basic in economic theory that value is equal to the present worth of future benefits. The income approach estimates such present worth and in Britain and elsewhere it is generally the only approach used.

The Income Approach is the most cogent method of valuation of properties which are typically rented and when comparable sales and rentals indicate the appropriate capitalization rate. In Canada, the majority of properties are owner occupied although the tendency is to more and more rentals (particularly with the growing popularity of the lease-back type of tenure). Hence to use the income approach, the appraiser must often impute the rental which a property would earn if not owner occupied and must even in rented properties impute the expenses as most rentals are on a gross basis.

The key variable in the income approach is the selection of the capitalization rate. This rate should be obtained in the market[5] which implies that the appraiser can find sales of comparable properties for which the net rents are known or can be deduced. Secondary methods of finding the capitalization rate can be used if such market data are not available.

The Canadian appraiser must note that, while the rate of interest is described as being the price of money, it isn't only this, in Canada. As noted in the Introduction, the Canadian banking system is very different from the American. An important practical difference is that the rate of interest on high grade securities is much less a 'price' of loans (in the sense of being affected by the supply of and demand for loanable funds) than a rate determined by governmental fiscal and monetary policy.[6] Therefore in finding a risk rate, the use of the summation or the band of investment method (if the first mortgage rate is that on NHA or other government sponsored mortgages which is related to the 'determined' rate) may be even more theoretical than is the case in the United States. This is not to say that an overall rate cannot validly be built up by using a band of investment.[7]

III   CORRELATION AND THE FINAL ESTIMATE OF VALUE

In all phases of appraising, and in particular when using the three approaches to value, the appraiser is dealing with a series of related data and information which he must correlate with each other to arrive at supportable conclusions. This is so when he defines the problem, when he makes his preliminary survey, when he considers general, area and neighbourhood data and when he analyses the cost, market and income data. Appraising is a series of correlating steps, leading to a single estimate of value.

In some appraisals, only one approach is applicable and only one value estimate emerges, so no final correlation is needed. However, in most cases at least two estimates of value will have been developed, each based on different data and processed by different approaches: the final estimate depends upon correlating these individual approaches. On some occasions the client may wish to know the separate values of his property, say as a rental investment and if offered for sale: on other occasions he may want to know its worth for insurance purposes: still more commonly he (or in these cases generally his lawyer) may want separate estimates of the market value and the value to the owner. But while such individual estimates may be required, the client has retained the appraiser to estimate some concept of the value; he doesn't want to have to choose between two or three estimates, so these must be correlated. But a probability distribution of possible selling prices is often used as Dr Ratcliff has shown.

The appraisal report[8]

It has often been said that PhD theses are first weighed and then graded! Perhaps the same criticism could be levied against some appraisal reports as many inordinately long and detailed reports are submitted to clients along with a commensurate account for fees.

The report must be comprehensive enough to set out the procedures followed and the data considered in arriving at the final estimate, and while a lengthy report is usually unnecessary, it is always better to use a little more narrative than to omit some important features, particularly if the matter may be taken to court as an adequate report will put the lawyer[9] and the client in the picture. The report represents the appraiser in the eyes of the public: he should be sure that such representation is worthy of him.

REFERENCES

1 / In some provinces an owner cannot without the consent of some governmental body dispose of less, say, than 10 acres of land without subdividing it. A nice appraisal problem arises when a parcel of 15 acres is reduced by expropriation to say 9 acres in area, and so becomes less saleable. The Ontario Planning Act, R.S.O., 1960, Ch. 296 was amended to make a consent necessary even for parcels smaller than 10 acres; now R.S.O., 1970, Ch. 349.

2 / Peterkin v. H.E.P.C. of Ontario (1958) O.W.N., 225, as explained by Boland v. Minister of Highways, Ontario (1959) O.W.N., 261.

3 / Contrary to the opinion expressed in other texts, when a statute specifies 'fair' market value this may not necessarily be the same as 'market value.'

4 / Principles of Economics, Macmillan, London, 8th Ed. 1920, Reprinted 1957.

5 / The Appraisal Journal, January 1961, p. 19, 'The Capitalization Rate: Mirage or will-o'-the-wisp?,' Herbert R. Dorau.

6 / Capital, Interest and Profits, B.S. Keirstead, Macmillan, Toronto, p. 7 and Ch. IV. See also Chapters 15 and 16.

7 / See Chapter 14 on the Ellwood analysis and also Chapter 16.

8 / See Chapter 1 for the essentials of the appraisal report.

9 / Old lawyers never die; they just lose their appeal!

3

Real property and value

I THE NATURE OF REAL PROPERTY[1]

Appraisal theory distinguishes between land, real estate, real property. Law does not.

Land In law 'land' includes the soil and trees, flowers, posts, buildings, etc. attached to it; appraisal terminology excludes buildings. It extends downward to the centre of the earth and upward to the sky, but the ownership of air space above individual properties vests in the owners only insofar as they can or could effectively use it.[2]

Real estate In appraisal terminology this is *physical* land and/or buildings; i.e. tangibles.

Real property Implies the rights to use real estate; it is the total of all tangible and intangible benefits of ownership; physical land and real estate have value only because man has 'property rights' over them.

The above meanings are too finely divided in appraisal literature. In general we will use 'land' either generically or for property without buildings and 'real property' or 'real estate' for land on which buildings have been erected. A common link is the idea of fixity and immovability and so the above can be contrasted with:

Personal property These moveables or chattels if tangible may or may not form part of 'real' property; intangible chattels clearly are not 'real.'

II THE BUNDLE OF RIGHTS[3]

The rights

The difference between real property and real estate is that 'property' gives an owner or user the right to enjoy the benefits of a 'physical' estate. Writers have compared these rights to a bundle of sticks each labelled with a certain 'right'; the right to sell, to rent, to use and many others: and conversely the

right not to exercise any of these rights. But such rights are hemmed in by
legal, political, social and institutional limitations.

The limitations

Common limitations to property ownership include:
  Municipal taxation In all provinces, municipalities tax real property.
  Eminent domain All levels of government can expropriate property.
  Public restrictions on land use Municipalities can zone real property.
American texts call this the 'Police Power,' a meaningless term in Canada, but
note the use of it in A.I.C. Text, p. 18.
  Private restrictions on land use A vendor can by deed, impose restrictive
covenants governing future use of a property.
  Escheat Property of an owner dying without heirs or a will, or failing to
pay his property taxes for some statutory period, reverts to the Crown as does
that of a Corporation not holding a licence in mortmain.
  Miscellaneous limitations Such as easements, prescriptive, mineral, surface,
air, or riparian rights, party wall agreements and so on.
  It is the value of the rights in the bundle for each property, as limited by the
above which the appraiser estimates.

III   THE UNIQUENESS OF REAL PROPERTY

Land is one of the 'agents in production' but it differs from the others in
several ways:
  First, it is fixed in total supply although the supply for any given use can be
varied; competition will determine which of several alternative properties will
in fact be used for the purpose in question; the physical supply is fixed but the
economic supply is constantly shifting: this gives rise to the markets in which
appraisers function.
  Secondly, land must be used where it exists; competition sorts out the properties making up the physical community, and users who value certain locations will, by paying more, obtain them.
  Thirdly, land is permanent physically. This, compared with the lack of
permanence in buildings, is reflected in the various valuation techniques.

IV   THE NATURE OF VALUE[4]

General

The appraiser must estimate 'value' according to principles which are acceptable to competent courts. In both the United States and the United Kingdom
the applicable concept is, in general, 'market' value; in Canada, this is only
partly appropriate in expropriation appraisals; value to the owner may also

have to be considered and this has been defined as follows: '... the owner at the moment of expropriation is to be deemed as without title ... and the question is what would he, as a prudent man, at that moment pay for the property rather than be ejected (ed. note: in some cases "rather than fail to obtain it") from it.'[5]

Three major explanations of value have been developed by economists:

The cost of production theory: in the long run value tends to coincide with cost of production but in the short run, cost affects value only as it affects supply.

The labour theory: socially desirable human sweat and skill is the source of all value; any extra charges for investment in land, buildings, machinery or entrepreneurship represent exploitation of the labouring class. The extreme theorist is Marx.

The marginal utility theory: the value of *every* 'unit' is determined by the value of the *marginal* (i.e. 'next') unit; people pay more for the 'first' unit and the more they have of any thing the less they value the next unit.

Value is relative and cannot be considered in connection with one thing alone but must relate things as exchangeable items; in our society this relationship is between an object or service and money. Value must also relate to the utility and scarcity of the object or service and to the need and effective demand of one or more human beings. A famous statement as to these relationships is as follows: 'Nothing is more useful than water but it will purchase scarce anything ... a diamond on the contrary has scarce any value in use; but a very great quantity of goods can frequently be had in exchange for it.'[6]

In addition to utility, scarcity and demand, this quotation also refers to two important but misunderstood concepts of value, namely 'value in use' and 'value in exchange.' Adam Smith thought these were completely independent, and their connection was not clarified for nearly one hundred years. The clue is to consider the marginal utility of diamonds and of water; at what 'cost,' can the next diamond be obtained – and the next gallon of water. The 'utility' of each successive diamond is high while the 'utility' of successive gallons of water is under most circumstances reduced to zero and so the value of water will be zero whereas that of diamonds will be substantial.

Some appraisers feel that 'value in use' as used by the economist is equivalent to 'value to the owner' as used by the Courts. It is suggested that this is not so.

'Value in exchange' is based on assumed highest and best use on the market. 'Value in use' may also be based on highest and best use, in which case it is related to value in exchange by the concepts of marginal utility and price. But 'value in use' may also be related to present use as is the case when say an Assessment statute requires assessed values to be based on such use. 'Value to the owner' is quite different: it must be related to the highest and best use of a property, not only on the market, but also to the individual owner in question.

In Canada, the applicable value concept in many expropriations is value to the owner; there is considerable question as to how this is to be estimated. The appraiser will in most cases rely on sales or rentals of comparable properties. Special value to the owner can only arise in cases where a property has special features the owner can use to a greater extent than could a typical purchaser. The most clear-cut case is a unique, special purpose building, but uniqueness might also be due to location, the length of occupancy and any one of many things. The appraiser must ask himself whether these factors are such as would justify the owner, as a prudent man, in paying a premium 'rather than be ejected.' Some expropriation statutes require compensation to be based on market value; see Reference 6 of the Introduction.

Real property value

Real property yields its benefits over a long period of time and its potential uses cannot be realized at any one instant of time. Therefore, its value must be thought of as being the sum of the present worths imputed to all future uses of the property taking into account their differing positions in time.

Mention has already been made of the fact that the real estate market is imperfect as compared say to the market for wheat. Relating market imperfections to the long-run nature of an investment in real property, it is clear that even if it can be decided what the word 'value' means, it is still no simple matter to decide upon its amount in any given case. The appraiser must consider the utility and scarcity of a property from the viewpoint of a potential purchaser who needs the property and has the purchasing power to acquire it. This purchaser is not a professional trader or speculator in a 'perfect market'; he is an average prudent individual with imperfect knowledge who must ask himself: 'How much money should I pay for the right to receive the future benefits this property will produce?'

To answer this question the appraiser must consider the problem objectively. But, from what has been said about value, real property and its market, it is clear that every estimate of value is highly subjective and relies on the personal judgment of the appraiser; however, subjective bias can be reduced if three conditions exist:

first, if adequate sales, rental and other data for truly comparable properties are available.

secondly, if by experience the appraiser has acquired an innate sense by which he considers the differences between the subject property and the comparables.

thirdly, if by training and education he understands the tools of his trade and recognizes their limitations.

Market value

Any definition must be acceptable in Canadian courts and these merely use such comments as: 'The expression value in the open market is synonymous with the term 'market price or value' which has been defined as the price fixed by buyers and sellers in the open market, in the usual and ordinary course of lawful trade and competition ...'[7] Appraisers therefore generally rely on American definitions such as the following: 'Market value means "the highest price estimated in terms of money which the real property will bring if exposed for sale on the open market allowing a reasonable time to find a purchaser who buys with knowledge of all the uses to which it is adapted or for which it is capable of being put."'[8] Whatever definition is used it must visualize:

1 a willing, informed buyer and seller
2 a free, open market
3 exposure to the market for a reasonable time
4 'normal' terms of financing.[9]

Value to the owner

One would have expected that a series of tests for this would have been developed by appraisers but this is not so. The accepted test laid down by the courts is, on the face of it, not much help to owners, lawyers, appraisers or the judiciary. But appraisers should assist the courts in interpreting the test if applicable; 'special' value to a particular owner probably does not exist in measurable form in about 95% of all valuations. In the remaining 5% the appraiser must decide whether he can illustrate to a court the monetary equivalent of the special value. If he cannot, then perhaps either the owner himself or other experts can, but they (and the lawyers involved) anticipate that a qualified appraiser will be able to point the way for them.

Three ideas suggest themselves:

first, the key words in the test '... as a prudent man ...' can be considered in the light of market transactions.

secondly, it may be that owners of similar properties have indicated in the market place what they would pay for additional property contiguous to their own 'rather than fail to obtain it.'[10]

thirdly, when the property has been improved with buildings of unique utility to the owner, reliance may be placed on reproduction cost less physical deterioration. An owner in deciding how much he would pay rather than be ejected would consider the cost of erecting an equally usable special purpose building for the continuation of his business operations, and clearly he would not feel that any functional or economic obsolescence had accrued.[11]

Appraisers have the choice of either trying to estimate value to the owner or of having the courts conclude that their evidence is 'almost worthless.'[12] In our Criminal Courts every effort is made so that no innocent person is convicted; it should also be the aim of every appraiser to carefully consider first whether there is any special value to the owner and second, whether this can be measured in money terms. Market prices paid by prudent purchasers may not truly reflect value to an owner since a purchaser is not concerned with disturbance to the owner. Thus, an owner in deciding the price he would pay 'rather than be ejected' considers the extra expense and the inconvenience which may arise if he loses his property. Recent statutory provisions reflect this.

V   SOME IMPORTANT CONCEPTS AND PRINCIPLES

Supply and demand determine value

In a perfectly competitive market, production cost will coincide with selling price and the latter will equal value at least in equilibrium. But cost relates to selling price only by its effect on supply. Supply can be looked at as a schedule or curve showing how the quantity offered for sale increases as the selling price rises and vice versa. Apart from cost the key variable is scarcity.

On the demand side, desire, utility and ability to pay are the key variables. The demand schedule or curve shows that the lower the price of a thing the more of it will be demanded, and vice versa. We see that the supply curve slopes upward and the demand curve downward to the right.[13]

But, the unique characteristics of real property make it clear that its supply does not behave in the simple fashion of the diagram. The supply of land, say in Canada, is fixed and cannot be increased because of an increase in price; it is a 'stock.' Also, the supply of land in any individual parcel, is a stock and cannot be increased. Furthermore, supply and demand curves assume homogeneity which is inapplicable to real property. The idea of such curves is really invalid in the real estate market, but the concept is helpful when we think, not of the total supply of land in a country nor of the individual parcel of land, but rather of the multitude of parcels, each a relatively close substitute for many other pieces. An increase in price will not increase the supply of any given parcel, but rather will induce the owners of neighbouring or otherwise competing parcels to offer them on the market and builders to start new construction; this is a 'flow.'[14]

Alfred Marshall summed up the matter of the relative importance of supply and demand by comparing them to the blades of a pair of scissors;[15] cut a piece of paper and see if you can tell which blade does the work! It takes both blades to cut. However, the nature of real property implies that generally demand will be much more important in the market, since the supply of improved properties can only be increased over a considerable period of time; prices are set in the 'stock' part of the market. Decisions to improve or build are made by individuals who may be unaware of similar decisions by other developers. Consequently, the real estate market is typified by brief periods of under-supply and longish periods of over-supply and the easy-looking equilibrium of our diagrams may not be reached.

The principle of substitution

A synthesis of the cost of production theories of value of the English Classical economists with the marginal-utility theories of the Austrian School stresses the importance of both supply and demand, and shows that through the principle of substitution the estimates of value developed under the three 'Approaches' would be equivalent the one to the other. The principle affirms that when several properties, services or commodities provide the same utility, the one which can be bought at the lowest price will be acquired in preference to the others. It is a central part of each of the three approaches:

in the market data approach, a buyer of real property will compare properties offered for sale which provide equivalent utility and will acquire the one which can be purchased at the lowest price, assuming that the time element is favourable;

in the cost approach, a user of real property will pay no more for an existing improved property than what he would have to pay to acquire a suitable site and erect new improvements, providing his needs permit him to wait for the new property to be completed;

in the income approach, an investor will weigh the net income obtainable from any particular property against that obtainable from available substitutes.

The principle of substitution is constantly at work in all markets: certainly when the appraiser is concerned with the market value of a property, he must pay close attention to it; however, to be really effective, it requires relative perfection in the market. The real estate market is imperfect, and the principle is neither constant nor uniform in its effects.[16] In 'value to the owner,' the principle of substitution may not be operative at all or only to a limited extent; some properties do not sell on the market and consideration of substitutes must largely be confined to the question of reproduction costs.

Highest and best use

The principle of substitution has application only if we think in terms of properties having similar (strictly speaking 'identical') utilities and in appraisal theory such similarity is related to the central concept of highest and best use. Particularly when considering the value to an owner, the appraiser must think of the highest and best of the property to that owner.

Highest and best use is defined as being that use which is likely to result in the greatest net return over a specified period of time. The important points to note are:

'net return': i.e. what is left over after paying operating costs; this is generally expressed in terms of money or as a yield on investment but in the major segment of the real estate market, namely owner occupied residences, the return is measured in advantages and amenities.

'over a specified period of time': the appraiser must place himself in the shoes of the typical user or owner of the property and consider the duration of the stream of net returns in light of the behaviour of such individuals in the market. Such behaviour relates to the concepts of depreciation, recapture of capital and economic life,[17] which will be discussed later and is difficult to interpret. Therefore, the idea of highest and best use is, as are many other appraisal concepts, sometimes highly subjective.

In considering the highest and best use the appraiser must think of the physical, economic, social and political forces which affect the property. An easy trap to fall into is to assume that the permissible use under existing zoning and building by-laws is necessarily the highest and best use. Optimum use depends on the supply of and effective demand for property suited to various uses, and unless there is a reasonable equilibrium of these (or possibly even a noticeable excess of demand over supply) the highest permitted use will not be the highest actual use. Many Canadian communities have an over-supply of the land zoned for commercial and apartment development. To project such a use, say to estimate the value of a site in an expropriation, would require market evidence that such development is in fact being carried out.

On the other hand we must recognize that an owner may use his property as a permissible non-conforming use under the zoning regulations and therefore the highest and best use of that property will differ in his hands from that of neighbouring properties not enjoying such a legal exemption from conformity. Value to the owner estimates should relate to properties being similarly used or which are zoned to permit the type of use to which the owner is putting the property.[18] Further, the courts have permitted estimates of value to the owner to be based on assumed amendments in the zoning or other restrictions which might increase the value of the property in question: however, since the appraiser should only consider the present worth of such potential value, he must discount the estimate to reflect the risk and the period of time involved in obtaining the amendment; this is discussed in Chapter 12.

The importance of the concept of highest and best use cannot be over emphasized: it is the key to the whole appraisal process and careful attention to it will keep the appraiser from running onto the shoals of over-optimism or over-pessimism too frequently. The best use of most properties will be a continuation of the existing one (if for no other reason than that the buildings have many years of life remaining and have not been depreciated in full), but such properties generally do not require to be appraised by the professional. A practising appraiser earns most of his fees by appraising off-beat properties and in such assignments the opinion of highest and best use is both a difficult and an essential one to express.

The principle of change

The dynamic character of the concept of highest and best use is due largely to the fact that continuous change is the rule of life. Nowhere is this clearer than in man's efforts to adapt himself to his physical environment. He is no passive agent and has changed this environment itself and has also developed political, social and economic institutions to assist and regulate his use of nature's resources.

The clearest case of change concerning real property is the urban decay and blight which takes such a rapid and costly toll in Canadian cities. The question of highest and best use is compounded by the fact that redevelopment is required long before the actual structures have physically worn out: they are functionally and economically obsolete. This is an extreme illustration of the principle of change, but the appraiser is always observing land-use in a state of transition, not of permanence; his best guide to the direction and extent of such transition is the real estate market.

The principle of conformity

The writer was much tempted to modify the name of this principle from 'Conformity' to 'Compatibility' as he feels that the adherence to conformity of land use is not only undesirable but also that it lies at the root of the importance which the principle of change holds in our urban centres. However the word 'conformity' appears in the literature and in zoning terminology, so a change in terms might prove confusing. The principle affirms that property value is created and maintained by reasonable homogeneity of use and people. (If the word 'reasonable' implies that all compatible uses and people are included in the idea of conformity, then the choice of terms is unimportant.)

Even in the absence of formal regulations 'natural zoning' exerts its influence so that similar uses tend to group themselves in certain areas and districts. Planning controls are imposed to prevent individual land owners and users from developing their property in such a way that their private gain exceeds the social gain of the whole community. Such formal controls are only beneficial if they recognize the existence of the underlying social and economic forces which give rise to the natural zoning; if they do, we will have compatibility of land use; if they do not we will have conformity.

Strict conformity cannot possibly assist in maintaining values but instead will hasten the effects of the principle of change. Consider a young couple which gets married; in most cities they must seek accommodation in a different neighbourhood from that in which their parents live, largely because zoning by-laws have not permitted the erection of small apartments therein. They take an apartment, but when they have a child they must again move to a new neighbourhood where the zoning permits small single family dwellings. If they have say two more children, they will, if they can afford it, move to still an-

other neighbourhood where larger houses exist (perhaps they will go back to
the area from which they started in their parents' homes). Finally their children marry and leave home (to start a similar rotation) and the now-old couple
makes one more move to a neighbourhood which permits apartments or small
single family dwellings.

Post-war sales statistics show that the average family moves once every five
years: people, it has been truly said, do not wear their houses out – they tire
of them or outgrow them. Only a generation ago, the average family was estimated to occupy only about two houses during its entire life-stage. The speed-
up in moving has occurred in the period when zoning regulations have become
an accepted part of our way of life and coincides with emphasis on strict conformity, particularly of residential areas. People want compatible land uses
nearby and, if we have a change of owners of each property on the average of
once every five years, it is clear that the whole neighbourhood will see a 100%
change every generation. Every change introduces some variation in land use
and over a generation the cumulative effect may be so great as to completely
change the character of the neighbourhood. Deciding upon the highest and
best use under such circumstances is difficult if not impossible.

The principle of competition

This affirms that excess profit encourages competition which eliminates that
portion of profit over and above the amounts necessary to keep the agents in
production at work. The principle is well illustrated in the rash of shopping
centres, apartments and office buildings in the past two decades.

The agents in production

Even in a simple economy, production entails the combination of man's own
efforts with either natural resources and/or capital equipment. A subsistence
farmer works a farm with the aid of, say, a rough plough (probably pulled by
his wife!); he combines labour, land and capital (the plough) to scratch out an
existance, and he owns (subject to mortgages and liens) the land and the capital (the motive power for the plough may or may not be 'owned' depending
on the point of view!)

Early economists thought of three agents in production which they classified as labour, land and capital, labour and land being the 'primary' factors
or agents (their supply being determined largely outside the economic system)
and capital the 'intermediate' factor which in all its varied forms was produced
by the economic system.[19] Complexity involved the emergence of a co-
ordinator of these basic agents called the entrepreneur. Appraisal theory
designates the function of this fourth agent 'co-ordination.' The entrepreneur
is a decision maker in the face of uncertainties and he receives his rewards in
accordance with the degree of success of such decisions. His rewards are

thought of as profits, but profits can and do accrue to any of the three classical agents as implicit wages, rent or interest for self-used labour, land or capital; there need be no fourth factor. Profit does not arise at all in perfect competition.

In the accepted appraisal theory, four agents in production, Labour, Co-ordination, Capital and Land combine together to produce a parcel of 'real estate' which will be used by the owners and/or occupiers as 'real property.' The theory also teaches that the four agents must be paid in the order in which they are listed above. Any revenue left over after paying labour, co-ordination and capital goes to land. This is the doctrine of Surplus Productivity, and it implies that land is always residual.[20]

The principle of balance

Everything in life must be in balance; until recent years such balance was ordered and maintained by nature, but man has done much to upset this, particularly in his use of land and we can see the results in the actions of winds and rains, in the disastrous floods which are becoming part of our way of life and most particularly in the patterns of our urban landscape. From the point of view of the appraiser, the principle of balance affirms that value is created and maintained in accordance with the balance attained in the number and location of the various essential uses of real estate.

The principle also relates to the combination of the agents in production to produce a final product (i.e. a usable piece of real property). If a building is too large for its site, too much capital, labour and co-ordination have been invested in relation to the available amount of land. If it is not large enough, then there is too big an investment in land, relative to that in the other factors. In an imperfect market it is largely fortuitous if a developer happens to hit upon an exact balance of factors, and this is not essential as long as it comes fairly close thereto. The best that the appraiser can do is to analyse each problem on its merits. If it appears that an under-improvement of a site exists, he can suggest ways to remedy the problem (examples would be the installation of an elevator, a modern store front or boiler). He should estimate value on a 'before and after' basis to show what the net return is and would be. If, on the other hand, a property is over-improved, there is no easy solution (short of demolition) and the appraiser can generally only evaluate the condition as it exists.

Diminishing returns[21]

This concept occupied much of the thinking of the classical economists and derived from the belief of Thomas Malthus that population growth would exceed the ability of the world to supply enough food. Modern technology and chemistry have largely dispelled this idea from developed countries, but it is still an important (and practical) part of appraisal theory in that under the principle of balance, the over-improvement of any individual piece of land leads to diminishing returns. And once developed every such property remains improved (at some cost to the community) for a very long time.

The principle affirms that the addition of larger and larger amounts of one or more variable agents in production to one or more fixed agents may at first result in greater and greater returns (say revenue) up to a certain point, but that eventually such returns will decline not only absolutely but also in a relative sense. Generally land is the agent in fixed supply and land economics is really the study of allocating limited supplies of economically scarce land among various competing uses. If a developer adds uneconomically large doses of labour, capital and co-ordination, to a fixed amount of land, diminishing returns will set in eventually. We can visualize a building being erected to such an excess density relative to the size of its lot that an uneconomically large amount of space must be allotted to elevators and other vertical installations, leaving inadequate space available to rent. On fairly small sites a twelve-storey building has only about six times as much rentable space as a single-storey structure, even though there is twelve times as much gross floor area.

The principle of contribution

This states that the optimum value of a parcel of real property is created and maintained when each of the agents in production makes a balanced contribution to the property as an economic whole. If any agent has been used in an insufficient quantity or quality, relative to the other agents, it takes on the characteristics of a fixed factor and diminishing returns will set in too soon; we have an under-improvement. Conversely if too large a quantity or too good a quality of an agent has been used relative to the others, we have an over-improvement which also implies the too early onset of diminishing returns. Consideration of contribution is vital in questions of renovation;[22] the appraiser should estimate the net revenue obtainable with varying additions to or deletions from the different agents in production, and relate the present worth of these revenues to the anticipated costs of the changes in composition of the agents.

As noted, the principles of balance and of substitution relate to the principle of contribution. The chief function of the entrepreneur or co-ordinator is to combine the three basic agents in production into the form of an economic whole. In so doing he substitutes the competing factors one for the other in accordance with their relative prices and efficiencies. For instance, if a developer wishes to excavate for a building, he can choose between using many men with wheelbarrows and shovels or a few trucks and a power shovel; which he will choose depends in large measure on the alternative costs with which he will be faced and upon the society in which he lives. (In China he would use man power, in Canada generally he would use power equipment.)

Other principles

There are a number of concepts of relatively secondary importance with which the appraiser should be familiar, for instance:

the principle of anticipation affirms that as value is created by future benefits to be derived from a property, the appraiser should anticipate the quantity, quality, and duration of such future benefits;

the principle of integration affirms that under the principles of change and conformity, integration of real properties gives resistance against further change;

the principle of disintegration states that the introduction of inharmonious uses into an integrated neighbourhood or community will tend to a decline in value.

REFERENCES

1 / For a detailed analysis, see Chapter 15.

2 / Jean Lacroix v. The Queen, 1954 Ex. C.R. 69 – air-space cannot be owned (subject to condominium legislation). Roberts and Bagwell v. R, 1957 S.C.R., 28: Court felt that a 35′ building-height limitation could cause substantial damage to potential commercial or industrial use in the vicinage of Malton Airport, but not a 150′ limitation.

3 / Diagrammatically the bundle of rights concept can be summarized: (rights are above the line and limitations below)

Rights	Fee simple	Mortgage equity	1st mtge 2nd mtge equity	Leasehold leased fee	Joint tenancy	Tenancy in common

Limitations	Assessment and taxation	Private restrictions
	Eminent domain	Easements
	Escheat	Lease conditions
	Zoning and building codes	Prescriptive rights

4 / A.I.C. Text, Chapter 2.

5 / Woods Manufacturing Co. Limited v. The King, 1951 S.C.R. 504. Alfred Marshall defines 'consumer surplus.' 'The excess of price which he would be willing to pay rather than go without the thing, over that which he actually does pay ... may be called consumer surplus. *Principles of Economics,* 8th Ed., p. 103.

6 / Adam Smith, *Wealth of Nations,* Modern Library Edition, p. 28. It should be noted that 'utility' to the economist is merely a term used to measure a consumer's welfare or satisfaction as he sees it.

7 / Windebank v. C.P.R. (1916) 10 W.W.R. 773; Cardinal v. R. (1961) Ex. C.R., 160.

8 / *Appraisal Terminology and Handbook,* A.I.R.E.A., A.I.C. Text, p. 3.

9 / Appraisal practice evaluates property as though free of mortgages – this implies 'normal' financing; if a vendor takes back a mortgage similar to a conventional one, he has simply made a voluntary investment. Canadian courts have ruled that 'value' must be based on financing 'normal' to any particular type of property; see Chapter 7, Reference 9, Chapter 14 re Ellwood.

10 / In appraisal theory such sales are discounted; this is probably not valid for 'value to the owner,' re Samuel, Son & Co.

11 / Samuel, Son & Co. v. Toronto (1962), O.R., 453 (1963), S.C.R., 175.

12 / Steel v. Metropolitan Toronto (1956) O.W.N., 511. A.I.M. September, 1961, p. 21 says the expression 'almost worthless' applies to the appraisers failing to consider several essentials for the applicable value concept.

13 / At higher prices than P more will be produced than can be sold, while at lower prices more will be demanded than producers will want to sell; under competitive conditions the market will be tending towards equilibrium at E where it is just cleared. See Ruban C. Bellan, *Principles of Economics and the Canadian Economy*, McGraw Hill, 3rd Ed. 1967.

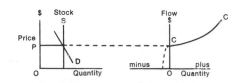

14 / For a detailed analysis, see Chapter 15. S is the completely inelastic stock supply curve of, say, all housing units at a given time while D is the existing demand curve for housing; we assume equilibrium and the price is determined in this stock section of the market. The right hand 'flow' diagram shows how builders will react to this price; CC shows costs of constructing new housing units while the vertical axis shows zero net new construction. At price P we assume equilibrium in the flow side of the market.

15 / *Principles of Economics*, p. 290.

16 / Paul F. Wendt, *Real Estate Appraisal*, Holt 1956, pp. 2, 50.

17 / See Chapter 14. In the Ellwood technique the period of income projection can be much less than the period of economic life.

18 / Village of Euclid v. Ambler (1926) 272 V.A., 359; in the United States a municipality can legally zone. In Canada there has probably never been any doubt that provinces could so empower municipalities, Hablizel v. Metro Toronto (1961) S.C.R., 523; as the only change in use which could have been made was to detached single family dwellings, evidence of the value of commercial properties was irrelevant.

19 / The A.I.R.E.A. Text at p. 143 defines 'capital' as 'money invested in the building.' B.S. Keirstead, *Essay on the Theory of Profit and Income Distribution*, Blackwell, p. 3, defines it as '... the stock of real capital rather than ... capital funds.'

20 / 'Gross Revenue' empties from the bottom while all other receptacles empty from the top and must be filled before the agent in the next one gets any of the revenue flow. A.I.C. Text, p. 23 says that 'co-ordination' means utilities, taxes supplies etc.; this does not include the entrepreneur at all. George Schmutz, *The Appraisal Process*, 1953 ed., p. 50, shows 'profit' in the same receptacle as 'land' which is correct if the entrepreneur also owns the land; but he must deduct implicit land rent before he knows if there is

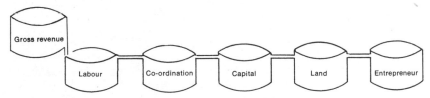

profit or not. Texts of both the A.I.R.E.A. and A.I.C. have ignored this hint from Schmutz.

In deciding on whether or not to develop a certain site with a certain building the entrepreneur (developer) doubtless deducts his anticipated profit very early in his analysis; probably it is the first deduction he thinks of. But once he has completed the project he becomes the final recipient.

The Principle of Surplus Productivity in accepted appraisal theory takes us only to the 'land' receptacle and this shows that land is always residual, which, of course, is the Ricardian long-run conclusion; as noted, this ignores Schmutz's recognition of the existence of the entrepreneur. In fact once a project is completed, the entrepreneur is the only agent which will always receive the 'surplus product,' if there is any left after paying the other agents; in economic theory this is the 'short-run' as contractual obligations have been made by the entrepreneur and must be met before he receives any surplus as profit.

The order in which the various agents share in the gross revenue is not fixed in the short-run but depends on the terms of contracts, bargaining power and social and institutional factors. Only in the 'long-run' is land residual, i.e. in the 'planning' period before contracts for the purchase or hire of the other agents have been entered into by the entrepreneur. The 'short-run' of a real property development may be 60 or more years in duration whereas the 'long-run' period during which the project is planned, approved and built rarely exceeds one or two years. So the strange conclusion emerges that the 'long-run' is shorter than the 'short-run!' Bellan explains the terms and also the role of the entrepreneur and clearly in the real property market the 'short-run' is generally the vital concept as shown in the above stock-flow analysis.

21 / The principle is confused in A.I.R.E.A. Text, p. 34, A.I.C. Text, p. 24, with the very different one of *decreasing returns to scale,* which assumes that *all* agents are increased proportionately; this is clearly a 'long-run' concept. Diminishing returns requires that at least one agent be fixed, which means that it is a 'short-run' concept. Obviously in the real property market the problem is generally one of diminishing returns as we are dealing with at least one fixed agent, a site of a given size and density potential. It is interesting to note that while the above referred to texts describe the principle erroneously, the examples given do not illustrate the principle described but rather that of diminishing returns. See also Chapter 16.

22 / See Chapter 5.

4

General, area and neighbourhood analysis

I ECONOMIC TRENDS[1]

*The importance of international matters
to the Canadian appraiser*

Economic trends affect business and therefore real property use and value. The United States has a large population and diverse economic base, so most important trends, at least until recently, have had an internal origin; this is not true in Canada. Our country has long been an exporter of staples (such as fish, wheat, minerals and forest products) which are sold on world markets at prices determined outside the Canadian economic system; the proportion of our population engaged in primary production is steadily declining, but a large absolute number of workers is still so employed.[2] These sectors use a large part of our land and natural resources and even minor changes in the international markets for basic Canadian exports can have a major effect on our economy. Canada is the fourth or fifth largest trading nation in the world and trades importantly with the United States: hence factors which are considered as 'national' in American texts may be 'international' and hence uncontrollable in Canada.

Other international trends having far greater effects upon the Canadian than on the American economy are immigration, the exchange rate on our dollar, and our high level of interest rates which attracts external capital. The United States has for years severely restricted immigration and its dollar and gold are the basic international exchange standards.[3] Canada is a net importer of capital, partly because her relatively high interest rates attract foreign investment funds. Many other matters of international occurrence and cause have considerable effects on the Canadian economy but little on the American because of its self-sufficient characteristics.

National trends

From the above, it seems that many factors affecting prosperity, land use and property values are beyond direct Canadian control; our economy is less self-sustaining than is that of the United States. The American appraiser could (at least until recently) take international events (short of major wars) as 'given' and concentrate on national, regional and local trends. To the Canadian appraiser there is not nearly as clear-cut a division between national and international factors.

Population

The most important single influence on our various periods of economic prosperity has been a heavy increase in population, although this has slowed in recent years. Since 1956 Canada's population has grown by roughly 350,000 persons per year: such an increase requires about 35,000 acres of land to be taken out of extensive uses annually and redeveloped for other purposes.[4] This means that every time a community grows by 1,000 people it must use another 100 acres of land for urban purposes.

Much of the population increase is due to the high rate of household formation which followed the start of the war and the depression of the 1930s. This continued during the 1950s and 1960s, accentuated in the earlier period by popularity of the relatively large household; the number of households having five or more individual members has declined from 37% of the total number of households in 1951 to 27% in 1971. It is interesting to note that non-familial households of all sizes represent 20% of the total number in 1971 as compared to 13.5% in 1951. C.H.S. 1970, see Table 119. There has also been immigration, averaging about 100,000 a year; immigrants in contrast to the 'diaper set' of natural population increase, include many of working age having effective demands; also they import substantial sums of capital.

Agriculture and government

The Canadian Government participates in the agricultural sector through price supports and subsidies and marketing boards. Counterparts of these exist in the United States but that nation consumes a far larger proportion of its farm products than does Canada and so the effect is perhaps not so noticeable.

Purchasing power

Income
Labour income has been increasing fairly steadily since the war; in 1959 the rate of such increases was 7.8% and in 1967, 6.0% in terms of current dollars; in real terms these increases represented 5% and 3.1% respectively. Also, transfer payments by governments to individuals who did not give productive effort in return rose to a total of $8.2 billion in 1967, which was over 10% of total national income. Small business income and corporate profits have shown declines as a percentage of national income in recent years. Savings increased to a total of nearly $12 billion in 1967 from $5.9 billion in 1959 and the Gross

National Product increased to $78 billion in current dollars in 1969 up 9.3% from 1968 ($61 billion in constant (1961) dollars, up 4.8%). But in the first quarter of 1971 it increased only 0.06% in real, seasonally adjusted terms, which represents a decline on a per-capita basis.

Canada has a major unemployment problem with well over 5% of our work force not being permanently employed. Some of these people form the hard core of 'unemployables' which exists in any society, some are frictionally unemployed in that they live in areas where there are no jobs, or are trained for specific types of work. Unemployment has a direct effect on personal income and hence property values.

Taxes

Income tax reduces the gross income of individuals and business to what is known as disposable income. A multitude of goods and services constantly competes for disposable income: many are necessities ... many are luxuries and many are 'status symbols.'[5] Some sort of shelter must be used by every individual and family but if a new car every year is valued more highly than a new house every five years, there will be an effect on property values.

Lower income groups spend most of their income whereas the higher income earners and corporations tend to save larger proportions.[6] Investment in real property implies the existence of some savings, so the appraiser must recognize this distinction between the various types of income earners. In an area where the income level is relatively low, we would expect to find a predominance of rented accommodation, probably interspersed with a considerable variety of competing land uses. In contrast, where income levels are relatively high we will find owner-occupied accommodation of a reasonably homogeneous type.

The above major economic trends do not exist in a vacuum; their interrelationships result in economic phenomena. Therefore, the appraiser must think of individual statistics as forming part of a dynamic whole which is the background for the shifting real property values which he must analyse and estimate.

Cycles of business and other activity

Economic fluctuations are so much part of our modern way of life that we may think they have always been in evidence; but prior to the Industrial Revolution, say 200 years ago, up and down swings in business were quite different from those which have occurred since. Before the 15th century nations were largely self-sufficient, with economies based on agriculture and barter, and with little circulating money; changes in economic activity resulted chiefly from crop failures, wars or natural phenomena. Fluctuations were irregular in timing and did not result from the workings of the economic system itself, which was inherently stable.

As nations began to trade with each other they became less self-sufficient: also gold and silver, discovered in the New World, somewhat alleviated the shortage of money in European countries. Business activity increased but economics were still stable per se.

As international trade developed and technology advanced, nations could buy and sell in a much wider market. This meant that business men must base decisions on production and shipment of goods on their anticipations as to costs and prices which would prevail perhaps a year or more in the future. It also meant that national and international banking systems had to develop and that complexities replaced the previous economic simplifications. The business fluctuation as we know it emerged; its cause appears to be inherent in the system itself.[7]

The real estate market correlates to some degree with the construction industry and a study of the cycles therein may prove to be rewarding. The following have been the trends in construction since 1950:

Residential construction starts rose steadily from mid 1951 to the end of 1956, and then dropped in the recession of 1956-57; government mortgage money pushed them up again in 1958 but they then declined again until the next up trend in the mid 1960s. Further growth occurred in 1968-70.

Engineering construction has recently shown remarkable stability; its value represented between 40% and 41% of total construction in each year from 1964 to 1968, the last year for which data are available.

Industrial building construction follows the general trend of the economy; it declined from a total of $798 million in 1966 to $583 million in 1969 as excess capacity and unemployment gradually increased.

The cycle for real property does not identically pattern the building construction cycle. Construction contracts are based on the costs of employing the individual agents in production whereas the real estate market deals in properties in which these agents have been combined. The individual agents are bid for in a far more competitive market than that for the individual parcel of real property; a builder must bid for labour against many alternative employers whereas a buyer of real property generally faces only a few competitors. Also labour is mobile and relatively adaptable to different types of work; real property is fixed both in utility and location. Changes in prices of individual factors of production may eventually be reflected in real property prices; but there is no reason why these two changes should coincide closely in either timing or magnitude as they occur in very different markets. The stock-flow analysis of Chapter 15 makes this clear.

That both the real estate and building cycles pattern their movements to general business conditions is to be expected since total construction contracts can amount to 20% of Canada's G.N.P. A heavy demand for the various agents means these are employed and spend money for goods and services; also expenditures on construction have a strong domestic multiplier effect; if building activity is quiet, workers and capital equipment are unemployed, they do not buy goods and services and business activity declines.

The nature of real property makes it appear probable that it may be an important cause of economic fluctuations: improved properties are meant to last a long time and during any given period some buildings will wear out. If the construction industry could be relied on to replace buildings as they fall into disuse and also to supply the appropriate quantity of new space to look after the normal growth of the economy, there would be little fluctuation in it. Such adjustment is, however, unattainable at the present stage of our economic planning: market forces do not work instantaneously and this is particularly true of construction, as once a building is started it must either be completed or abandoned: there are rarely any intermediate use-stages. Changes in demand are not transmitted quickly to the construction industry as many builders are small and ill-informed: but once an upward shift in demand is so transmitted, the new construction floods the market and there is a painful period of excess space in both old and new structures as the over-supply is gradually eliminated. It is partly because of this that the criterion of market value may not fairly measure the concept of value to the owner;[8] typically the market is for much of the cycle a buyer's market because of the peculiarities of the construction cycle.

Price level movements

Four different types of price level movements are distinguishable:

Secular movements of very long term character covering as much as 100 years prior to a reversal. A shorter version is the Kondratieff 50-year cycle. Some observers think the building cycle of about 20-25 years duration causes the major 50 year cycles.

Business fluctuations seem to have a period of from 8 to 10 years in Britain and 3½-4 years in Canada and the United States.

Seasonal movements are particularly important in Canada as its climate and topography limit or extend economic activity in many industries and in many parts of the country: the spring and fall pressure of work on farms, the summer activity of road building, the winter resurgence of the logging industry, the seasonal character of the fishing and building industries are commonplace characteristics of the Canadian way of life.

Accidental movements are, unlike the above, irregular in timing and cannot be plotted in graph form. They result from wars, epidemics, disasters, etc., and tend to modify or accentuate the more or less regular cycles.

Measuring price level movements

Statisticians use index numbers developed with averaging and aggregating procedures for measuring the size of price level movements. The Consumer Price ('cost of living') Index is based on the prices of a 'basket' of goods typically bought by Canadian families in the middle-income range. The 'basket' is under continuing revision to reflect changing tastes; late in 1961, brooms, laundry soaps, overalls, and 28 other items were removed and replaced by frozen foods, airplane tickets, powdered milk, restaurant meals and several other things.

Another index which should reflect economic activity in a given community or region is that based on current local wage rates, also published by Statistics, Canada; but wages are 'sticky' on the downside so this index shows upward movements of economic activity better than it does downward ones.

The index which the appraiser uses most often in his work is a construction price index; it is used in the cost approach to adjust cost estimates to a desired date; this is discussed in Chapter 9. Still another index can be developed for use in the market data approach based on sales and resales of properties. This will be mentioned again in Chapter 7.

Changing value of the dollar
(inflation and deflation)

Canada ranks high among countries of the world in the stability of its currency and yet the value of our dollar has declined steadily. The index, based on 1949 = 100 used to deflate the G.N.P. in current dollars was 162.2 in 1961, 193.6 in 1964 and 226.6 in 1967. Any decline in the value of money is reflected in rising prices in other markets; this creeping increase in prices has characterized the past two decades, and the appraiser must realize that while it causes property values to change, such change is only indirectly related to market forces. Increases in the value of money would have the opposite effect on prices.

II   COMMUNITY ANALYSIS

The community is a place in which to work, live and relax and it must also contain the means of transport between these basic functions. As noted in the last chapter, these functions tend to separate themselves by 'natural zoning' subject to the level of transportation technology. Hence we find work areas separated somewhat from residential and relaxation areas; but the degree of such separation depends upon the ability of transportation facilities to move people. In many cities it is not uncommon to find factories located in the midst of a residential neighbourhood with corner stores scattered throughout the area; such proximity was necessary under earlier levels of transportation technology. But, by modern standards, it is 'economically obsolescent' and value depressing. One of the four major community functions, recreation, is missing: if present in the form of open spaces (both private and public), such neighbourhoods would maintain their value.[9]

The relative importance of the above functions is changing. Sixty years ago workers walked to work in a few minutes and worked ten hours a day; now they drive or use public transportation for, say, an hour, and work perhaps seven or eight hours. They have many extra hours a week for relaxation; speedy, efficient transportation is increasingly important to the individual and the community as the work week shortens and the recreation week lengthens.

The appraiser's prime concern is the effect of trends and cycles on communities. He must understand why the community came into existence; if the reasons for its existence still continue, the general status quo will probably also continue and property uses and values will be fairly stable. On the contrary, if new forces are at work dramatic shifts in uses and values will be observed.

A knowledge of community and regional planning helps the appraiser. He should understand the various categories and functions of towns and the theory and practice underlying different street patterns and transportation schemes. The major factors affecting the community can, as in all real estate analysis, be classified under four main categories: physical, social, economic and political. The following are typical headings some or all of which appear in actual appraisals.

General development
This includes a brief historical account and a statement as to the community's physical boundaries, topography, soil conditions, layout and its location in relation to other communities. Also comments on the social, economic and political situation.

Street patterns and traffic
A map is of assistance to show main and secondary streets, the general type of street plan and possible major changes. An important part of traffic are parking facilities, as well as the type and adequacy of public transportation including external services such as railway, air and interurban bus.

Population
The social and cultural backgrounds of residents, their preference for rented or owned accommodation, employment open to them and their annual earnings are important data. This information is in the Dominion Censi and municipal handbooks contain current details. People make values and it is difficult to picture them in tables and statistics: the appraiser must interpret these in narrative form to explain how he feels the people affect real property values.

Zoning and building restrictions
The existence or non-existence of by-laws should be noted with comments as to their adequacy, relevance and problems involved in obtaining amendments.

The question of highest and best use generally relates closely to the legally permitted use.

Utilities and services

Sewerage disposal and water provision are vital to the development of property and its value: the appraiser should comment on the availability and capacity of these services and others such as gas, power, and telephone: he should indicate probable paths of extension of services and their time-staging.

Land use and new construction

Types of land use should be noted as should the shifting or stable character of such, together with comments as to their conformity (compatibility). New construction indicates investor and owner confidence in a community: this the appraiser is always trying to gauge.

Municipal assessment and taxation

All provinces allow their municipalities to raise revenue by taxes on ownership based on an ad valorum ('according to value') assessment of all real property (only New Brunswick and Newfoundland do not demand the use of this form of taxation), and on occupancy based on use of commercial and industrial real property. Municipalities try to maintain a balance between residential and commercial-industrial real property of about 60%-40%. They may zone land for commercial and industrial use and permit residential development to proceed as though commerce and industry had actually been attracted: if these don't locate, the municipality may be in serious financial trouble.

The appraiser must also consider the equity of assessments and tax burdens both on an intra- and inter-municipality basis.

Correlation

The appraiser should in a paragraph or two correlate his ideas as to the desirability of the community for residence and investment and as to value trends.

III NEIGHBOURHOOD ANALYSIS

Many of the factors which make or depress value exist in the neighbourhood rather than in any individual property. 'Economic' (i.e. neighbourhood) obsolescence may contribute more to accrued depreciation than all other items combined. People tire of their properties rather than wear them out; one thing they tire of is the neighbourhood.

The analysis should be broken down into physical, social, economic and political elements and it is a miniature of the city analysis outlined above.

Definition of a neighbourhood

A neighbourhood is composed of individuals and families who group together for common purposes. Out of the 'natural zoning' which emerges in every community spring its various neighbourhoods. We can make out fairly definite commercial, industrial and residential neighbourhoods with probably a series of transitional districts lying between them.

Origin of the neighbourhood

The appraiser should consider the life stage of the neighbourhood historically: the principle of change is, of course, at work and he must decide whether it is in an evolutionary or a revolutionary stage. If the former, the neighbourhood will almost certainly continue; if the latter, a major transition is inevitable and a new neighbourhood (socially, economically, physically and politically) will emerge. Valuing in such an area revolves about a realistic determination of what the highest and best use of any individual property will be during the transition and once it is completed.

Physical boundaries and characteristics

A neighbourhood is distinguished not only by the common characteristics of its residents but also by its physical characteristics and boundaries. Major streets, ravines and parks insulate the areas along and beyond them from incompatible uses. However topography or soil conditions have effects other than merely defining boundaries and protecting a neighbourhood: they may make development difficult or easy and this will directly affect the value of individual properties.

The relative location of the neighbourhood to the community as a whole is particularly important in towns where noisy, odorous or dangerous manufacturing processes are carried out; the prevailing winds dictate the location of residential areas and these in turn dictate that of commercial districts. These combinations of locations and the physical characteristics determine the street pattern and this is the key factor in determining transportation, water and sewer facilities which are of vital importance in creating or destroying value.

Social characteristics

Compatibility of use implies compatibility of people; therefore the appraiser must consider the racial, religious, cultural and social backgrounds of the residents; also the recreational, cultural, educational and religious facilities.

Economic characteristics

The appraiser is interested in such economic indicators as income and employment levels, in the number and proportion of owners and tenants, in the repute of the area with mortgage lenders, in the number of vacant properties and, of course, in the new construction, renovation and general condition in which the residents keep their properties.[11] Shopping facilities are also important.

Political characteristics

A neighbourhood or community which has been planned and zoned in recognition of the combined physical, social and economic factors affecting it will have a relatively high, stable and balanced level of the main value determinants; but if a zoning by-law is imposed without any real study, the value determinants will be out of balance. This is also true if amendments to a carefully planned zoning by-law are made without considering their full effects.

Another important matter is the relative level of municipal assessments in the neighbourhood. Most assessment departments make a serious attempt to equalize assessments between neighbourhoods, but differences do exist as the dynamism of property use and values make it impossible to keep on top of all shifts in these. Even if no inequity exists between neighbourhoods, the absolute level of taxes in some may be an important determinant of land use and value.[12]

REFERENCES

1 / See also Chapter 15.

2 / In 1955, 19.8% of the Canadian population was employed in agriculture and primary production: this had declined to 10.6% by 1967.

3 / The American dollar has been under severe strain in 1970 and 1971.

4 / Based on the allocations of population shown in the 1961 Census, a 100,000 increase in population means that approximately the following urban land development will take place:

Type of use	Land requirement
Single family dwellings	6,000 acres
Multiple family units	1,000 acres
Industrial space	1,000 acres
Commercial and institutional	1,000 acres
Public	1,000 acres
Total annual land requirements	10,000 acres

These forecasts check fairly well against the actual growth of Metropolitan Toronto. Forecasts of future land needs made by the Regina Planning Commission show that about 6,000 acres of new residential land will be needed between 1960 and 1980 to accommodate an increase in population variously estimated at between 60,000 and 115,000.

In 1971, Census figures will show a larger proportion of Canadians living in multi-family dwellings: this may reduce the area required for single family dwellings but many more municipalities now have zoning by-laws with minimum lot sizes and, of course, apartments require more park space.

The Gordon Commission forecasts a population of 26,650,000 by 1980 compared to 17,650,000 in 1959 and 21,377,000 in 1971. About 80% of these will live in urban areas, so many changes in land use must occur.

5 / *The Theory of the Leisure Class,* Thorstein Veblen, Macmillan, New York, 1899.

6 / Too high a propensity to save can spell trouble; when a small proportion of income is spent, sales and then production may decline, causing a fall in employment and hence in income. Of course adequate savings must exist to fill the demand of investors. See Ruben C. Bellan, *Principles of Economics and the Canadian Economy,* McGraw Hill, 3rd Ed., 1967. This is later referred to simply as 'Bellan.'

7 / Commonly called the 'business cycle'; this implies that each 'cycle' is an exact replica of its predecessor, which in fact isn't true. See also R.A. Gordon, *Business Fluctuations,* Harper, 2nd Ed., 1961. It seems that with the help of 'creeping inflation' modern fiscal and monetary policies may be able to eliminate major downswings; there has been no significant depression in Canada or the United States since World War II.

8 / Assume there are 1000 units (S_1) of centrally located housing units of which 200 are expropriated, leaving 800 (S_2). Figure 1 shows how the use of *past* sales data implies that the value (P_1) of any individual property is unchanged. Figure 2 shows the situation as it actually exists in the eyes of an owner who must relocate in one of the new stock of 800 units. The price he must pay rises to P_2. The situation is only serious when the expropriation causes a major reduction in the supply of some given type of property for which there is no close substitute.

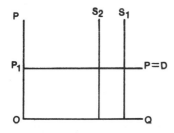
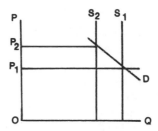

9 / Some planners feel that many of Toronto's high-density residential districts could become slums owing to a shortage of park lands.

10 / The Canadian Tax Foundation, Toronto, November 1959 et seq., *Local Finance.* Two approaches to the problem of municipal revenue requirements seem promising:
    first, the modified single tax concept commonly associated with the names of:
        Henry George, *Progress and Poverty,* Appleton 1882.
        John Stuart Mill, *Principles of Political Economy,* 5th Ed., Appleton 1895.
        John C. Lincoln, *Ground Rent* NOT *Taxes,* Exposition Press 1957.
In Canada, the School of Economic Science, Toronto, actively pursues the concept.
    secondly, the abortive Alberta idea that the assessment of industries be removed from municipal rolls and pooled for provincial distribution of tax receipts to both municipality where industry is located and to those in which employees live.

Exemptions from municipal taxation granted to owners, and sometimes occupiers of publicly used property and that used for educational, health and eleemosynary purposes, may cause undue hardships to tax-paying owners unless higher levels of government provide full grants in lieu of taxes.

11 / Assessment and taxation laws and practices frequently work to penalize owners who maintain their properties to a higher degree than their neighbours; one of the benefits claimed for site-value taxation is that this problem would be eliminated.

12 / Equalization between municipalities is of course vital if equity in Provincial grants is to be obtained.

5

Materials and equipment

I BUILDING MATERIALS

General

Canada is a very large country and since its population is concentrated in
pockets, considerable regional difference in culture and tastes has evolved,
which are accentuated by the patterns of settlement outlined in the Introduction. It saw little or no steady surge of settlement, but rather new communities grew spasmodically and under the guiding influence of investors, older
towns and governments: perhaps an exception could be noted in the settlement of the Prairie provinces in the first decade of the twentieth century.

Both Canada and the United States have widely varied physical characteristics and natural resources but two important distinctions exist between the
countries. Climatic extremes are much more pronounced in the States and the
large areas of semi-tropical country have resulted in a more varied pattern of
life. Secondly, 100 years of American isolationism, together with a rapid
growth in population, resulted in the settlement of a much larger proportion
of the physical area of the country than in Canada.

The United States can develop far more varied building materials and equipment than can Canada. Much of our railway trackage runs through sparsely
populated areas. Shipping building supplies is expensive and in the absence of
intermediate markets, either local materials or those which are universally acceptable and available such as lumber tend to be used; compare this situation
with the United States with its many towns and cities, serving as intermediate
market points between the source of supply of a material and its major market
area.

Frame construction is the rule in Northwestern Ontario and the prairies as it
provides warmth against the severe winters of the region and lumber can be
shipped cheaper than brick, stone or concrete products in relation to the wall
or floor area covered;[1] the market for masonry products, apart from the major

cities has been small and the intermediate markets cannot absorb the freight costs. British Columbia too with its vast forests has relied on lumber as a building material; in fact lumber is an important material everywhere in Canada, particularly for framing. Of course, in the post-war years the impressive contemporary buildings being erected in our western cities include all the modern structural materials.

In Southern Ontario, Quebec and the Maritimes, brick, stone, concrete and steel are the major building materials; lumber is also much used where by-laws permit. The first mentioned materials are manufactured where the concentration of towns makes this attractive from the market viewpoint. In some areas local stone is in high favour, for instance in the Maritimes sandstone and granites are quarried at several points and Kingston is noted for its limestone.

A building can be analysed in terms of its basic structural sections and the various 'trades' which combine to erect it. Starting at the bottom and working up the following are the main headings:[2]

Excavation

Not much need be said about this providing it is adequate in size and depth. It makes no difference to the value of the property whether it was dug by hand or with a powershovel.

Foundation and basement walls and floor

Footings should be about 4½ feet beneath the surface, to avoid frost penetration. The footing is a concrete or masonry base under the foundation; it is wider than the latter and must sit on soil which has not previously been excavated or filled. An inadequate footing will cause uneven settling of the building and cracks in walls and flooring.

Most foundations are poured concrete, concrete blocks or native stone; wood posts may be used in temporary structures. In some areas, where the earth's underlying rock crust is near the surface the foundation can be built directly on it; under such conditions the installation of municipal services is expensive.

Canada, owing to wanton waste of its forest and soil resources, is faced with periodic floods and the wet basement is a pressing problem in many communities; it is aggravated by the fact that roofs, drives, roads, sidewalks and other solid surfaces prevent the slow seepage of rain water into the soil as nature intended. Also in many subdivisions the nonporous subsoil has been brought to the surface during grading operations; this impedes natural drainage. Many foundations and basement walls must be water proofed and under-tiling must be installed around the footings; such work can best be done during the original construction.

Larger buildings require reinforced concrete footings and as in such structures the weight of the framing, floors, partitions and roofing may be borne, not by the walls as in houses and small buildings, but by columns, beams and trusses, individual footings for each column or pilaster may be built. Piles may have to be driven on reclaimed or uncompacted land; such piles often consist of B.C. spruce logs driven to bed-rock, sawed off below the water table and then capped with concrete. Steel beams or tapered steel cones filled with concrete are also used for piles.

Basement floors are generally poured concrete laid on an appropriate fill of sand, gravel or crushed stone. One or more drains should be installed in the floor which should slope toward the drain. The latter will run to either a municipal sewer or a private ditch or cesspool.

The building frame

Lumber or plywood is much used for framing because of its wide availability. It is found not only in frame structures but also in poured concrete, brick or stone veneer construction. The main components of the frame are defined in the glossary.[2] In frame, steel, concrete or solid masonry buildings the walls may bear the weight of the floors and roofs and must be designed to support the beams or joists of the various floors and the roof rafters or beams.

As long as the walls must bear the weight, there are physical limits to height, but with steel columns and beams, unlimited heights are possible (Frank Lloyd Wright planned a building one mile high!). Of course the law of diminishing returns may render very high buildings impractical economically; building by-laws may render them impossible politically; human behaviour patterns may make them unacceptable socially; but physically they can be built.

Retail, office and industrial buildings, apartments, and hotels are commonly constructed with a steel frame, the individual members of which may be encased in concrete to minimize twisting in case of fire; concrete covering also eliminates frequent painting which is essential with steel to prevent rust.

In a single-storey building which does not have to carry heavy loads, the frame just holds up the roof. If a structure is multi-storey and accommodates manufacturing processes or large numbers of people, floors must have adequate load bearing capacities and this requires strong framing. Until the development of structural steel, such framing consisted of heavy timbers or iron and produced the mill-type loft building which predominates in the industrial sections of Canadian cities.

Reinforced concrete is probably the best form of framing over the life of a building:[3] concrete is poured into forms through which run steel rods so that it and the rods complement and reinforce each other. However, it is very rigid functionally as any one will recognize who has tried to drill a hole in such a floor or wall to move a light plug or telephone. A steel or poured concrete framed structure is fluid and adaptable and sections of a wall or floor can be removed with little difficulty, unless pipes or wires are within it.

An industrial building using cranes must not only have a strong frame but also must be so designed that the appropriate types of cranes can be installed. Jib cranes can be suspended from individual columns and a jib crane operation does not imply extra wide bays. With overhead travelling cranes bay spaces must be of sufficient width to make the cranes economically feasible. To the layman heavy crane systems may look alike, but be quite different functionally; for instance, under-slung crane trackage permits the switching of cranes into every bay in the building; the overriding system where the tracks run above the beams confines each crane to its own bay.

Floors

The conventional flooring for single family dwellings is lumber, hardwood being used generally in urban dwellings and in rural homes where it is available. Of course many urban homes have soft-wood flooring, particularly if some covering such as tile, linoleum or broadloom is to be laid. A well built structure should have a soft-wood sub-floor running diagonally across the joists with the floor proper laid at right angles to these; this gives great rigidity and minimizes the chances of shifts occurring or squeaks developing.

Concrete and plywood have come into fairly common use with improvements in heating equipment and floor coverings. The former is generally used with radiant heating while the latter makes an ideal, quickly applied sub-floor or a finishing material.

A double 1″ wood floor on 2″ x 10″ joists at 16″ centres has a load-bearing capacity of 70 pounds per square foot which is adequate for residential and general commercial purposes. By increasing the size of the joists, reducing the space between them and by using thicker lumber this capacity can be increased almost indefinitely, but at excessive cost. Concrete floors are generally used instead; these can be made of any desired thickness and strength and are generally poured integrally with the supporting beams and columns; when finished with a metal-bound compound they give wearing qualities almost equal to those of steel itself.

In the industrial building, the bearing capacity of each floor is important; certain processes need very strong floors or municipal building by-laws may require minimum limits.

Roofs

Flat roofs are used in nearly all industrial, commercial, office and retail buildings; they require adequate drainage to a system of gutters and down pipes and proper bonds between the roofing material and the walls and chimneys. The roof decking may be either soft wood, plywood or concrete over which lies the roof covering, which in Canada is usually tar and gravel, with perhaps tar paper as a first layer.

In single family, duplex and triplex construction and in many institutional buildings, the pitched roof is generally used. Such roofs are of various types and styles as defined in the glossary.[2] Common coverings are cedar or other wood shingles for most dwellings, while churches and some houses use slate or tile. Composition shingles are becoming common as they provide a roof covering suitable to all areas of the country and are attractively coloured and tinted.[4]

In Canada insulation is almost an essential (except in the coastal areas of British Columbia and some readers will say in the Niagara Peninsula and south-western Ontario). There is a swing between the annual maximum and minimum temperatures of as much as 140 degrees farenheit and we must not only keep the heat in in winter but keep it out in summer. The point of greatest vulnerability is the roof and so many structures are insulated, either on top of the attic floor or in the roof itself.

The interior and exterior walls

Residential, apartment and commercial buildings use plaster on lath or building board for interior walls. A smooth building board can be put directly on the studs or strapping; this is quicker than plastering and is not subject to cracking. Some such materials are in a finished state and no decorating is required; dry-wall materials are particularly useful for renovating.

Kitchens, washrooms, cafeterias, and the laboratories of industrial plants may use plastic, ceramic or glazed tile on the walls. These materials are durable, attractive and easy to keep clean.

Exterior walls may be brick, block, stone, poured or preformed concrete, aluminium or the 'space-age' coating of stainless steel and glass.

Trim

The baseboard, wall board, door and window framing and similar items in residences are generally oak, maple, birch and pine; they are either varnished, stained or painted. In other types of building metal trim is common.

Millwork

This term includes doors, window-sash, cupboards, window-sills, shelves and other items produced at a mill. In most residential properties they are lumber or plywood. Office, apartment, industrial, commercial and retail buildings also use wooden doors and windows but metal ones are more popular owing to their fire resisting qualities and low maintenance costs. A recent development is the aluminum glazed and screened combination, which is attractive and weather proof and, being built from a Canadian-made product, will doubtless become increasingly popular.

Hardware

This term refers to hinges, door knobs, locks and the like. It supports and fastens the mill work and must be in keeping with it if the principle of balance is to be fulfilled.

Stairs

The size and type of construction of staircases varies with the intensity of use. In a single family dwelling, the staircase is generally of frame construction and should be at least 3 feet wide with 10″ treads and not over an 8″ riser.

In apartments and office buildings, stairs will be wider and are usually built of steel and/or concrete, perhaps surfaced with linoleum or other material; the front of each step should be abrasive to reduce slipping.

II BUILDING EQUIPMENT[5]

General

Most of the cost of older buildings is in the structure, whereas in newer ones up to 35% of the total cost is in equipment. Buildings are becoming shells within which equipment functions, with extreme examples being elevator-type parking garages or industrial plants where the main functions of columns and beams is to act as a framework for the crane system.

Equipment must normally be replaced at least once during the life of the actual building and if the latter is of an open plan, its economic and physical lives can roughly coincide if modern mechanical and other facilities are periodically reinstalled, to take advantage of advances in technology.

Heating and air changing systems

Furnaces and boilers

Heating systems warm air either directly or by radiators. The open fire-place is the basic installation but in modern homes is more for prestige than for heating. In houses, warm-air central heating is the commonest type, with hot water radiation next in line.[6] The warm-air system has a fire pot inside a metal furnace from which hot air pipes run from the top and to which cold air ducts return to the bottom. Firing is by oil, coal, gas, wood and occasionally sawdust. With no circulating fan it is called a 'gravity' system (although convection currents not gravity really circulate the air), with a fan it is a forced-air system (often miscalled 'air-conditioning'). A hot-air system can be efficient only if the capacity of the cold air return pipes equals that of the hot air outlets.

The hot-air system is relatively cheap to install and will warm a house quickly, which is important in the spring and fall: also a humidifier and/or air conditioner can be added to some systems. The major problem is that the circulation of air may force dirt and odours through the building; filters will minimize this.

The hot water heating system has a fire box inside a boiler with pipes running to radiators, and an open or closed expansion tank; with a sealed tank and system, steam is created and smaller radiators can be used. Most residential hot water heating is of the 'gravity' type (a misnomer again) with no circulating pump; efficiency can be improved and operating costs lowered by installing such a pump and in large homes or if basement rooms are to be heated a pump is essential.

In a radiant heating system, piping is in the floor, walls and/or partitions so that the surface of these is heated; a pump forces the air or water through the pipes.

Low pressure steam heat is used in apartment, office, store and industrial buildings. A high pressure system, also used for manufacturing operations, can have the pressure reduced for the actual heating.

Registers, radiators and air-changing ducts

The relative position of hot and cold air registers, and air changing apertures is important. Individual ducts should serve each room as this reduces sounds and odours, but in some homes and apartments adjoining rooms and suites are served by a single duct. In many houses the cold air register is at the foot of the stairs to the second floor. This is a compromise between installing two registers, one upstairs and one down.

Hot water and steam systems use open pipes, radiators, convectors and unit heaters to distribute heat to the building. These warm the surrounding air by radiation and it is circulated by convection currents. The cast iron radiator relies more on radiation than convection and so is massive. On the other hand the modern baseboard units rely largely on convection and have small bulk but large finned surfaces. Open pipes around the walls of industrial buildings have little bulk or surface and are adequate only in conjunction with a manufacturing operation which itself generates heat.

Individual unit heaters operate either from a central system or by built-in heating devices. They range from the small space heater to expensive hanging units and provide flexibility. An extension of the unit heater system is the community central heating plant such as that in Winnipeg and downtown Toronto; some European cities fuel these by the incineration of refuse.

Controls and fuels

Modern technology has developed efficient control systems and these should be installed in buildings to ensure comfort and to reduce heating costs. The efficiency of a thermostat depends to some extent upon the fuel used. Canada possesses oil and natural gas, both of which are efficient fuels needing little work and being particularly susceptible to automatic regulation of flow; as distribution across the country is improved, these fuels will probably become the predominant ones of the nation.[6]

Coal is an important fuel but the labour required makes it less attractive than oil and gas for residential, apartment and commercial buildings; modern stoker and ash removal equipment makes it popular in industrial buildings. In cities near mines or served by water transportation, the cost of coal per BTU is lower than that of other fuels. If, an engineer must, due to the capacity of the system, be hired anyhow, coal is a cheap fuel.

Other fuels which may find local acceptance are wood, peat and sawdust, particularly if the fuel is a by-product of manufacturing such as sawdust is in a lumber mill.

Domestic hot water

In urban areas the flat rate hydro or gas heater are common. Tanks are generally of 30 to 40 gallon capacity and should be insulated, as should all heating ducts and pipes and also the furnace or boiler. In industrial, retail and office buildings the main boiler may be used as the sole or auxiliary source of hot water.

Plumbing

Piping

The appraiser must consider the durability and life expectancy of piping relative to that of the building. Iron piping may not last for more than a third of the probable life of the structure itself. The plumbing system is only as good as its conduits and inadequate piping is a value depressant.

Wells and many urban water supplies cause corrosion, due to the presence of minerals; a water softener will minimize the problem and such equipment is, of course, essential in some manufacturing processes.

The private water supply (i.e. from a well, pond or cistern) is particularly important in appraising, not only with regard to the adequacy and quality of the water but also its cost relative to that of municipal water. A well and a septic tank add at least their costs of installation to the value of a property until municipal services are available; once these latter come into operation, the private system is a liability.

Fixtures

In our society appearances are important and fixtures must be faulted if they do not conform to accepted styles; a major contributor to curable functional obsolescence is the out-moded bathroom or kitchen.

Sprinkler systems

These are used in apartment, office, store and industrial buildings, but the writer has seen a 50-year old 6-room semi-detached house which had two sprinkler heads installed near the furnace in the basement! Sprinklers are of either the wet type with water in the pipes at all times, or the dry type in which the water is held out of the pipes by air pressure which is released by heat. Both systems require adequate water pressure and a special tower or pump may be needed.[7]

Ventilation and air conditioning

In single family dwellings, the commonest way of keeping the air fresh is to open windows and doors, supplementing this with an electric fan. A forced air heating system can be used in the summer to circulate cooler basement air throughout the house. This can also be accomplished by opening the attic hatch and the door to the basement at night. An insulated house, if cooled at night, will remain cool during the day if windows and doors remain closed.

Equipment can be installed to change, clean, remove moisture and cool the air. For existing structures window units can be installed supplemented by fans to move the cool air. A central unit may be installed when a building is built, or in older buildings as competition forces them to modernize. With high ceilings ducts can be put in false ceilings to reduce installation costs. The initial cost of air conditioning is high, as are operating costs. Costs of installation in an existing reinforced concrete building, can be twice that done during original construction.

Electrical systems

Electric power holds an important place in our economy and it is available to most properties. The electrical system in a building includes the intake, internal wiring, controls, fixtures and outlets. Most North American public systems are 60 cycle, alternating current, with voltages of 110 and higher. In single family, duplex and triplex dwellings if only two intake wires are visible it indicates the building does not have heavy wiring installed and that rewiring may be necessary, if modern kitchen and other appliances are to be used.

The power passes through a meter and fuse box in which it is broken down into sub-systems. Many older structures have knob and tube wiring consisting of insulated wires fastened to insulators running from the fuse box to the various outlets; modern structures usually have wiring encased in a flexible cable or a rigid pipe.

The principle of change is quite noticeable in the field of electrical fixtures and appliances as these are subject to functional obsolescence. But with good wiring and a flexible system containing adequate, well-placed outlets, it is relatively simple to minimize or eliminate such obsolescence.

Light fixtures in modern dwellings are generally confined to the kitchen, bathroom, halls and front and rear doors: other lighting comes from floor and table lamps. In industrial, office and store structures the tendency is towards fluorescent fixtures.

Elevators and Conveyors

Much usable industrial space exists in centrally located multi-storey buildings and a freight elevator is essential, perhaps supplemented by conveyors. Older elevators were manually operated; newer installations are often automatic and self-levelling. The elevator can serve as a truck-level loading dock if the shaft has an outside door. Good elevator service is essential in all types of multi-storey buildings if occupancy is to be maintained.

Refrigeration

In some older apartment buildings a central refrigeration unit serves the individual suites; such systems should be discounted completely even though in good working order. The individual units cannot be adapted to the requirements of each family, particularly as the whole system must be defrosted at the same time. The modern tenant expects an individual refrigerator with ample freezer space.

III RENOVATION

General

The purpose of renovation is to add value directly or to increase economic life.[8] The three degrees of 'renovation' are:

Rehabilitation: the building is to be made adequate without any changes in plan or style.

Modernization: outmoded equipment and finish are to be replaced with modern counterparts.

Remodelling: the building plan or style is to be changed to minimize or eliminate functional or economic obsolescence.

The above are not air-tight compartments: in most renovations all three will be carried out contemporaneously. The following principles come into play:

> Highest and best use   Contribution
> Balance   Conformity
> Diminishing returns

Rehabilitation

Problems which are remedied by rehabilitation are included in those classified as 'physical deterioration curable.'[9] Rehabilitation implies immediate curing of the deficiencies in question, and its purpose is to permit the building to continue in use, although economic life may also be extended.

Modernization

Modernization attempts to remove 'functional obsolescence curable.' The distinction from rehabilitation is that, if a usable but outmoded kitchen sink is replaced by a new stainless steel, double drain board type, this is modernization; if a worn-out sink is replaced with a new but similar unit, it is rehabilitation.

Modernization is undertaken in a deliberate attempt to extend useful life. Buildings become outmoded before they wear out physically and modernization attempts to make their useful lives as long as their physical lives.

Remodelling

This is undertaken to minimize functional obsolescence incurable and economic obsolescence by making extensive structural changes. The highest and best use say of a theatre can be changed by levelling the floor, installing a second storey and putting in boutiques and small shops.

In all renovations the structure must lend itself to the type of work in question. Also the expected costs of renovations must weigh favourably against the expected future benefits to be derived and such work will almost certainly cost more than if done as part of the erection of a new building. Putting a sprinkler system in an existing reinforced concrete building can cost twice as much as if the installation had been made during the original construction. (A mill or steel framed building being more flexible of plan does not present this particular problem.)

The principles of balance and contribution state that each agent in production and each part of a property must contribute to its utility and revenue productivity; renovation tries to correct any imbalance.

The principle of conformity applies to the renovation programme in two ways. First 'value' is created if compatibility exists between the materials and equipment used. Secondly, the principle relates to the compatibility of the property with its neighbours. Will the cost of the added amenities be amortized over a reasonable future period, in light of possible neighbourhood changes? Whether the capitalized value of the difference between the 'before' and the 'after' net incomes is sufficient to write off such costs and show a competitive return depends largely also on the period of time over which the extra income will be received. This depends partly on what happens in the neighbourhood.

The principle of diminishing returns indicates that, up to a point, renovation will probably result in increasing net revenue, or amenities but that eventually these extra benefits will level off and then decline. Therefore the extent of renovation should be limited to the increasing phase.

REFERENCES

1 / A.W. Currie, *Economic Geography of Canada*, Macmillan 1945, pp. 153-66.
2 / *Dictionary of House Building Terms; Choosing a House Design*, C.M.H.C. The evolving concept of System Building as analysed by Peter Barnard Associates is discussed in

Ontario Housing, September 1970, published by the Ontario Housing Corporation. See Chapter 13 for an abbreviated quantity survey.

3 / Clarence Stein, *Toward New Towns for America,* Reinhold, 2nd Ed., 1957.

4 / Such roofing is a 'natural' for Canada with its large deposits of asbestos.

5 / *Selected Readings in Real Estate Appraisal,* A.I.R.E.A., p. 472, 'Building Equipment Systems,' John M. Burlake.

6 / The contrast between statistics in the 1951 and 1961 censi is striking:

Type of heating (in 1000s of units)

Steam or hot water		Hot air		Stove		Other	
1951	1961	1951	1961	1951	1961	1951	1961
529	830	1,053	2,242	1,724	1,324	48	158

Coal and coke		Wood		Oil		Gas	
1951	1961	1951	1961	1951	1961	1951	1961
1,470	481	951	540	775	2,565	163	858

Electricity		Sawdust		Other	
1951	1961	1951	1961	1951	1961
8	30	36	15	7	14

Note: in the 1961 Census oil is shown under 'liquid fuel.'

7 / The owner of a lumber yard in Ontario installed an 8-lane, 25-meter swimming pool as his sprinkler system reservoir! Fees for its use pay operating costs and maintenance, while savings in insurance premiums will amortize the capital cost over about 10 years.

8 / As value measures the present worth of future benefits, increasing economic life automatically increases value. It should be noted that 'economic life' must be given two distinct meanings. In single family, owner-occupied dwellings, economic life is the future period over which the property will yield net benefits or amenities. In revenue producing properties, economic life is the future period over which an investor should recapture his investment.

9 / The confusion noted in reference 8 page 84 of the first edition of this book has been clarified in the 5th edition of the A.I.R.E.A. Text, 1967. See also Chapter 9 hereof.

6

Property analysis

The appraiser is concerned with the physical, social, economic and political characteristics of a property, many of the value-adding attributes of which are in its environment not in its own confines; he must see how its basic characteristics relate to those of its neighbourhood. While we are concerned with the utility and value of a composite property made up of land and buildings there are institutional, political and economic reasons for analysing it under its component parts.

I ANALYSIS OF THE SITE

Physical characteristics

We must consider whether a site's physical characteristics lend themselves to social and economic use. Man adapts physical matter to his needs and this costs money but adds value only if it increases utility and desirability. Have the site improvements been socially and economically advantageous; have they made it possible to develop the site to its highest and best use? If so, then the optimum level of value can be derived.

Location
The relative and absolute location of each site with regard to the community, neighbourhood and other individual properties is important.

Dimensions, shape and area
A site may not be symmetrical; one side may be longer than its counterpart. Minor irregularities in shape generally have little effect on utility, but substantial ones may, and a third linear dimension, namely width (or depth) becomes important. Frontage is generally more important in creating value than either width, depth or area, providing that these are not less than some acceptable minimum; with frontage, even a shallow, small lot may be useful for certain

purposes. Frontage, width, depth or area in excess of an acceptable minimum may not add proportionally to value. Irregularities in shape may raise construction costs or make it impossible to provide adequate loading, storage and parking facilities; hence they may decrease utility and value.

Topography and soil conditions

Filling, levelling or installing a culvert may be required to make a site usable. Also, the bearing qualities of the soil may be inadequate for the contemplated development unless spread footings or pilings are used. Costs of remedying site deficiencies and the value created thereby must be weighed against the value of competitive sites which do not require such work.

Man-made site improvements

Land has traditionally been thought of as being God-given and indestructible,[1] but in fact very little of that being used by mankind remains in its natural state. The appraiser must consider such improvements as roads, water mains, telephone, gas and electric lines, sewers, under-tiling, grading, gravelling and paving, trees, shrubs, and lawns. Public utilities add to the value of land, but this is true of private water and sewerage systems only until public facilities become available.

Paving or gravelling and landscaping, normally add to the enjoyment or utility of a property and hence to its value; but if not in keeping with the requirements of the typical user they constitute under- or over-improvements and may even detract from such value.

Social characteristics

Man's use of land is based on the physical, economic and political characteristics of the property. Social considerations are implied in the institutional relations which dictate acceptable types and degrees of land use.

Economic characteristics

The property as an economic entity is dependent on its location with respect to the uses to which it can be put and also on its physical characteristics and on political considerations.

Political characteristics

As noted, the utility of land may be directly or indirectly limited by government. In analysing a property the appraiser must also consider ways in which government adds to or detracts from such utility by making available or withholding transportation facilities and utilities.

Correlation

The appraiser should complete his analysis with a correlation of his interpretation of how various site characteristics affect its value.

II   ANALYSIS OF THE BUILDINGS

General

In analysing buildings and other improvements the appraiser considers their utility and value-adding attributes, not their cost. The design of shelter has always reflected the physical, social, economic and political factors shaping the culture of the area and period. Primitive buildings provided shelter against the elements and enemies; modern buildings add to these basic requirements, a differentiation in function between various spaces and areas.

   Throughout history architecture has modified bare shelter to satisfy man's functional needs. A move from the cave led to compact urban growth in temperate climates; medieval and later period design structures were laid out for defence and social status; modern notions are based on function. But modern design is not different in concept from what was acceptable in any earlier period: 'contemporary' design means that modern techniques and materials are blended into a building which satisfies contemporary physical, social, economic and political standards. Superficial architectural details which do not add to utility probably do not add to value; but we must never forget the importance of status symbols; 'gingerbread' maybe a sine qua non of social status and so will add value to a building.

   Contemporary architecture tries to produce space for optimum use and to relate indoor and outdoor space; physically, socially, economically and politically this is now practicable. For instance the trend in factories is to one storey, production-line structures which blend into the storage, loading, parking and access facilities of the property and cause minimum damage to other types of property. Also their siting and construction can be controlled by proper zoning and building restrictions.

1 Residential buildings

Single family dwellings

The professional appraiser evaluates relatively few single family dwellings unless these have been expropriated, and even then a full appraisal may not be warranted;[2] hence we will not consider such properties in detail.

   Modern family life differs greatly from that of the era which produced the 'period' design of dwelling, and architecture has developed to serve this. The development has been evolutionary not revolutionary and its physical exemplification should be the result of sensible adaptations of existing forms and material rather than a mere attempt to achieve a 'new look.' A dwelling is meant to serve an owner's functional requirements and this depends not on outward appearances but on the interior plan and on how the house relates to the site: modern living revolves around the integration of house and site.

The analysis starts with the materials and techniques used in construction. There should not be too wide a range of such materials and these and the style should suit the site. Canada differs from many other countries in her climate and yet how many times do we see a 'California' bungalow or Spanish hacienda on a snow covered 50' lot!

In most older cities, many houses have been built on lots 12' to 20' wide. This was acceptable when the telephone was non-existent and public transportation was horse drawn; the dislike for spending more than an hour going to or from work is not a product of the motor age! Factories, shops and work-places were within walking distance of many homes. Communities were compressed in size by using narrow lots, row-houses and walk-up apartments, and it is interesting to note the growing re-interest in the town house, maisonette, row-house and apartment in the central city. But the original layout provided little or no open spaces to which the residents could turn for relaxation and this basic function of the city was lacking.

The demands of our growing population on our land resources are accentuated by the move to the suburbs with bungalows on 50' to 60' lots. This is a repetition of the older pattern with wider and lower buildings but relatively little public open space. Modern transportation lets workers travel farther to and from work, but does not make the trip any shorter in time.

Functionally, a house has four major areas: sleeping, eating and relaxing, working and communication between these. It should be possible to enter each of the first three areas without going into the others: this implies that each room has at least one doorway to a hall and also that with the trend towards using the outdoors as an extension of the dwelling, access thereto should be reasonably direct.

Each of the four areas must be large enough to properly perform its function; for instance, single bedrooms should contain at least 100 square feet of floor area with double rooms at least about 50% larger; each bedroom should have self-contained cupboard space (preferably in a dividing wall to form a noise buffer) adequate for the age and requirements of the visualized occupant; the bathroom should be located close to the bedrooms. The living room (or living-dining room) should contain at least 200 square feet and have access by a hall-way to both the kitchen and the front door.

The basement occupies an important place in modern living; (it used to be the 'cellar' which means a place to store things; 'basement' means the floor next below the principal floor). It should be high enough for tall people to stand in and this also permits natural light to enter; access to the outdoors should be possible without the need to go through the kitchen or other rooms.

The garage area is very important; most families have at least one automobile and lack of parking in the older areas of cities is a major problem and acts as a value depressant.

The principle of balance must be kept in mind: do the agents in production mutually contribute to produce maximum value? If so, reproduction cost and value will coincide; if not, then cost probably exceeds value. If a house is too good in relation to its lot, its value may be pulled down by its relatively less valuable neighbours. The converse is probably not true and the worst house on a street may command a relative premium in value. The land-building ratio for single family dwellings should be from about 1 to 3 to 1 to 5. If in a particular property it is only 1 to 2, the house may be an under-improvement of the site. But in a popular neighbourhood many families may want to buy the property which will be priced somewhat lower than its more expensive neighbours so its price may be bid up. As the reproduction cost does not change, such 'bidding up' really means that the site value is increased, which results in a still lower land-building ratio.

A house which cost 10 times the value of the lot and includes an elevator and a built-in pipe organ would be beyond the desires of typical purchasers. The principle of change tells us that the initial balance of the agents in production, which resulted in cost coinciding with value in the eyes of the owner, may be disrupted on a resale and that value will be substantially less than cost.

Multi-family dwellings and condominia[3]

Canadians (with the exception of those in Montreal) were primarily single-family home owners or occupants at the end of World War II. The following census figures (in 1000s) show the trends and the 1971 census will indicate an even greater reversal of tradition (roundings keep totals from correlating).

	1941	1951	1961	1966
Population	11,500	13,623	18,201	19,972
Occupied dwellings	2,576	3,338	4,547	5,172
Single attached and detached	2,043	2,457	3,383	3,636
Apartments and flats	533	881	1,151	1,516

The main reasons for the change are the high cost of urban land and the recognition that since cities cannot expand indefinitely, building density must increase. Communities also look upon the apartment building as an important source of tax revenue which may represent 50 to 100 times that from the single family dwellings which previously occupied the site.[4]

Apartments must functionally fulfill their role as the provider of living accommodations to specific classes of tenants, an important segment of which is made up of people who have not sufficient savings to make a down payment on a house. Such families may have several children and are unable to pay the going rent for an apartment, so they occupy inadequate rental accommodations in run-down areas of our cities. Publicly subsidized and limited dividend developments are attempts to provide living space for these unfortunate people.

Other classes which occupy apartments are the young and elderly couples which either have not yet had any children or whose families have grown up, and set up their own establishments. Other categories are the unmarried business man or woman and the childless couple.

With such diverse needs to be satisfied no single analysis of the multi-family dwelling is possible. Such buildings range from the duplex located in a single family dwelling neighbourhood through four, six and eight-plexes to the apartment complex of hundreds of suites.

Apartment accommodation is limited both in space and utility. In Canada, construction has consisted largely of mixed bachelor, one and two bedroom suites. In the subsidized or limited dividend developments on the one hand and in luxury buildings on the other, larger suites are found.

Apartments have a place in suburban areas but their true role is fulfilled in the central city: people move to the suburbs to get space; this is not found in apartments. On the other hand in the central city people do not expect private open space, hence apartment life suits them.[5] This illustrates the major consideration in apartment analysis: is it optimally located relative to the demand for the accommodation provided? If so, it will have few vacancies and cost will coincide with value. If not, cost will exceed the value of the property and incentives in the form of free rental will have to be given, while tenants may make unreasonable demands for service and decorating; management problems will arise which will be reflected in lower net income and in a higher investment risk.

The appraiser must also consider whether the building contains sufficient suites for professional management. If not, the owner must manage it himself and few owners can manage more than six suites; it requires at least twenty suites to make it economical to use professional managers. Buildings between these limits may be either inadequately managed or professional management may be uneconomically expensive.

With regard to the suite size, a lot of accommodation can be obtained in a relatively small well-planned area; many bachelor suites contain no more than 400 square feet. But the principle of competition operates quickly and it is unwise to reduce suite size unduly just to meet a current but temporary demand. The author feels that average suites should contain about 700 square feet (including a proportionate allowance for walls and all public space); then bachelor units will contain say 500 square feet, one bedroom suites 700 square feet and two bedroom 850 square feet. Small units are more acceptable in central areas, while large ones are demanded in the suburbs.

It is poor policy to skimp on wiring, fixtures, plumbing, stove and refrigerators; or on the size and adequacy of cupboards and closets. A good elevator installation is an essential in any building of more than three storeys in height: modern Canadians are not fond of walking, particularly up and down stairs.[6]

The laundry equipment is important and must be of good quality and ruggedly built. Refuse disposal, boilers and heating (including domestic hot water) systems must be efficient in both performance and cost. The intercommunication and door-opening system connecting each suite to the front lobby and the mail boxes are also important, as are landscaping, drives and off-street parking.

Now the appraiser is concerned, not with the individual items of equipment or the frame of the building as such, but rather with the composite whole. The principle of balance in its second meaning says that property value depends upon the relative use made of the agents in production. But the principle of change implies that an acceptable balance of agents may become unacceptable over time. The central television antenna presents problems in buildings when cable is desired but not provided, while older elevators may have to be replaced by automatic installations. But it might be poor policy to over-invest in automatic installations and reduce unduly the co-ordinating ability of human management, except perhaps in small buildings when professional management is not retained; on the other hand, reliance on too much labour-using equipment can create just as bad an effect. The tendency is to use automatic equipment as far as possible, for while this entails high initial costs, it reduces reliance on labour. Wage rates will almost certainly increase while work-hours decline, which while good for the general economy could play havoc with the net revenue of an apartment designed without considering the principles of change and balance.

Another aspect of balance is that between the various types of suites; a building with, say, bachelor, one bedroom and two bedroom suites, will probably maintain better occupancy than one with only a single type.

2 Commercial buildings

There are many types of commercial buildings of which we will discuss two major categories, office buildings and retail stores.

Office buildings

Office structures can be classified as being either those occupied by a single company (or perhaps a parent company and its subsidiaries) or as buildings for multi-tenant occupancy.

The owner-occupied (or owner-tenanted on a lease-back) building may provide amenities in excess of normal tenant requirements; government buildings and those of life insurance and other national or world-wide concerns are examples. Value to the actual user based on the cost approach may substantially exceed market value estimates under the other two approaches.

Physically the analysis revolves around the type of construction, the siting of the building on the lot and the relationship of the lot to other properties. Also the building must be laid out for efficiency and the calibre of equipment must be in keeping with the type of occupancy expected: head office buildings may have manually operated elevators rather than automatics, if it is felt that the personal touch offsets continuing wage bills. One of the requirements in office buildings is air conditioning: this can be either from a central system or by individual units; both methods have merits and demerits which the appraiser must weigh in relation to the effects on occupancy and net rental.

Socially, an office building provides space for business relationships and it cannot be successful unless it is laid out to facilitate these. Inadequate elevator service or improperly located washrooms are two examples of deficiencies which will plague a building with constant human problems.

Economically, a building should fulfill its function at the minimum of cost over the many years of its physical life. It can look after changing tenant requirements if it has a fluid floor plan, the exterior walls, columns, beams, flooring, elevator shafts, plumbing, other utilities and stair wells being the only fixed installations; each floor can be used as large or small individual spaces by erecting partitions: ceiling and floor conduits make telephone and electric cables relatively flexible. Space requirements change over time; 80 square feet of office space per employee used to be acceptable, whereas now 120 square feet is better; even larger requirements may be the rule when currently new buildings attain maturity.

The shape of a building and the ratio of rentable space to total area is also important; this latter 'efficiency ratio' should be 80% to 85%. An efficient building is about half as deep again as it is wide so that an optimum sized office structure is about 70' – 80' wide by 100' – 120' deep; this also permits natural light to enter all parts.

Retail stores
There has been a marked change in the style, size and layout of retail buildings; stores now cluster in shopping centres in contrast to the older shoe-string development along main streets. This trend is due to the automobile, but contributing has been the development of materials which make the concept of openness both attractive and economically feasible. Many pre-war stores are brick and frame on 15' to 20' lots forming part of a row of identical buildings, each owned or occupied by an individual merchant. Since the war use has been made of steel framing for wider spans and more openness, generally with off-street parking and loading space.

The function of a store is to provide display and sales space to serve customers, who are of many types, each with different service requirements. In shopping centres, department stores and retail outlets, the comfort of the customer is important, so the heating and air conditioning systems must be efficient and subject to fairly fine thermostatic control. Fluorescent or indirect lighting is also necessary in most stores and convenient parking facilities are essential.

As much retail buying is done on impulse, adequate display space is important, but the proportions of such space to total area varies with the type of merchandise and the clientele served. Supermarkets consist largely of self-service display and aisle space. Specialty shops use sales staff to supplement merchandise displays and they must have space for counters and cases with adequate electric outlets to serve them; relatively more staff rest-room facilities must also be provided than in a display-oriented operation.

3 Industrial buildings

Congestion in the central city and the efficiency of single-storey production lines attracts many industries to the suburbs. There will always be a demand for centrally located stores, apartments, and office buildings, but that for similarly sited industrial buildings is weak, except, say, for a newspaper.

In a newish factory or warehouse the chief considerations are openness of space and bay sites, ceiling height, loading and transportation facilities, and parking. Most such structures have been built under rigid zoning regulations covering the siting of the building on the lot and the loading and parking space. The following minimum standards are normally acceptable:

> Single storey – steel framing
> Bay sizes 20' x 20' (minimum)
> Ceiling heights 14' to 16'
> Truck level loading
> Land to building ratio – 1 to 6
> Parking to floor space ratio – at least 1 to 3
> Fluorescent lighting
> Office space – 10% of building area
> Heating – individual units from low pressure steam boilers

Older buildings must compete with the above and are penalized for functional obsolescence for major deviations. Multi-storey buildings in smaller communities may sell on a square foot basis for about 10% of the price of new one-storey buildings on adequate sites, and even in major cities such buildings may bring only about 30% of the price of such a new building.

4 Mixed purpose commercial buildings

If a building is used for combined office, manufacturing, warehousing, display, sales or other purposes, the appraiser can estimate the value of each part under its own highest and best use, but such a building may not be acceptable to purchasers on the market. For instance, if a building contains offices, warehousing, processing, sales and repair spaces with a motion picture theatre for merchandise display films, its market value must reflect the cost of eliminating the sloping floor in the theatre and installing a second storey therein.

5 Special purpose buildings

The highest and best use of a property for typical purchasers rather than its actual use is the guiding principle in market appraisals. One exception is expropriation as special value may accrue to an owner's unique use; another is if an assessment or other statute states that the valuation must be based on actual use. Types of special purpose buildings include

Parking garages

Older ramp garages can only accommodate perhaps two-thirds the number of modern cars relative to their designed capacity owing to too narrow ramps or bays. The analysis is based on income and the most acceptable unit of measurement is 'per-car.' Elevator garages are more mechanical installations than buildings.

Theatres

The principle of change is well illustrated by television rendering many theatres economically obsolescent. An appraiser may be retained to propose an alternative concept of highest and best use with two considerations being of major importance. First, a theatre is generally well located in relation to the neighbourhood or community and so its site offers redevelopment possibilities. Secondly, theatres are open in plan with good ceiling heights; churches, bowling lanes and boat-building could use these features if the slope of the main floor is levelled out; also a second storey could be installed and a small shopping and office mall could be created. Once the best market use is determined, the principles of substitution and balance take over.

Hotels and motels

The tendency towards decentralization of manufacturing and the organization of vocations and professions into unions and associations means that business people are constantly on the move. Many travellers prefer the informality and ease of access of the motel; but this may be offset by the need for a central location for conferences.

One of the most important features of a modern hotel or motel is its conference accommodation and catering facilities so the appraiser must pay attention to these. However, a true hotel or motel sinks or swims with its relative room rentals and hence the rate of occupancy is a very important criterion of its value.

In most provinces, hotels are the chief recipients of licences to sell beer, wine and spirits. Room rentals and the dining room yield some revenue, but the licence really creates the value of many of these premises. The unit of value is the 'gallon' or the 'bottle' into which all other types of revenue is converted for comparative purposes.

The motel is evolving in a highly competitive field. A modern traveller has great mobility and can choose his accommodation within a wide geographic area. Hotels do not generally require as much land as motels and also land values are lower and land availability higher in the periphery of towns, where these latter tend to locate. Motel accommodation can be constructed in a few months, particularly if part of a chain, whereas these factors for a major hotel may take years. But motor traffic patterns are volatile and the principles of change, competition and substitution dictate that what is acceptable now may not be next year and that the strategic location of 1971 may be the backwater of 1981. The central city on the other hand is relatively permanent, although its uses are in transition, and motor-hotels frequently locate there.

A good restaurant within the motel or located nearby is an asset and this can be enhanced by providing room service and by having conference rooms available. Other features are air conditioning, room telephone service (and an ice-making machine!); the swimming pool too is an attraction despite the relatively short season in our country. Another convenience is a nearby service station.

Other 'drive-in' operations include restaurants, dairy stores, cleaners, car-washes. The investment in buildings is relatively small while that in planning, land and equipment is substantial. They are frequently franchised and must handle flows of customers through the facilities and back onto the highway and the chief criteria of efficiency are ease of ingress and egress, and adequacy of parking space. The inherent worth of any franchise complicates the appraisal.

Service stations

The principle of substitution (i.e. the value of substitute stations) is of major importance. Estimates of value of potential service station sites based on sales of nearby properties for, say, commercial use, are generally much lower than the prices the oil companies actually pay. These companies option but do not purchase the site until a permit has been granted by the appropriate municipality and/or the Provincial department of highways; such permits have monopoly value as their number and location is related to the requirements of residents and travellers. The evolution of self-service stations is indicative.

The analysis is not of the improvements (these are standardized) but rather of the pulling-power of the location and of the ability of the site to handle the business obtained. Oil companies can pay a certain price for a property of usable size, so an estimate of value based on, say, square foot unit prices of other service station sites of different sizes may be of little help; if an adequate site of 20,000 sq. ft. sold for $50,000, then one of 70,000 square feet may be worth little if any more. Similarly in central city areas a station may have only 5,000 square feet of land but be worth $100,000.

Another problem in service station appraisals concerns road widenings and corner daylight cuts by local or provincial governments; these may be accompanied by restrictions on access which reduce the effective area of a station by far more than the amount of land expropriated. Ten feet taken from one frontage of a corner station, plus limitations on access imposed, may involve acquiring up to 40' of land on the far side of the property, if the same utility is to be maintained.

The salaried appraisers and negotiators of the oil companies carry out studies of projected gallonage sales; however, the professional appraiser generally evaluates potential sites, not on the basis of gallonage but rather from comparable sales. He should develop a comprehensive collection of such sales for speedy reference as there is generally urgency in this type of appraisal.

Professional buildings

Private hospitals, medical or dental clinics, and other professional structures may have to be appraised for financing, sale, expropriation, assessment appeal, partition of a partnership or otherwise. Comparable sales data are scarce, so reliance is often placed on the cost and income approaches.

These buildings may contain unique partitioning, plumbing, electrical, air, gas and other installations, which will be included in the cost approach. Estimates of value based on income may or may not include such installations depending upon whether the rentals used include them or not; dentists and doctors renting space in office buildings normally pay for them separately, so rentals paid in the market would not reflect this. If the professional building is to become a general office building, both the depreciation and revenue schedules must recognize that such special installations and partitioning may add nothing to value under this changed use.

Both the rent obtainable and the functional obsolescence which has accrued depend on the efficiency ratio of the particular site and building. Dentists, some physicians, chiropractors, and osteopaths have heavy investments in equipment and conduct their practices in their offices and require a higher space efficiency than say a psychoanalyst (whose couch fits any wall!). A dentist may have up to 40% of his office area in such non-revenue-producing space as reception rooms, office, laboratories and storage, while some doctors use as much as 60% of their suites for such purposes.

REFERENCES

1 / This is a key concept in Ricardo's concept of economic rent which has not been recognized in appraisal theory. See Chapter 16.

2 / The expropriating body will have appraisals made by its staff or fee appraisers. The owner can usually rely on their ability and integrity.

3 / Habitat, Vol. XII, Numbers 4-5, 1969, contains an interesting analysis of the condominium.

4 / In the as yet unreported case of Minto Construction Limited v. the Township of Nepean, the practice of assessing a multi-family dwelling at a higher percentage of value

than single family dwellings was held to be invalid. This principle had actually been established by the Ontario Municipal Board in a case in which the author's firm was engaged about 10 years earlier.

5 / But note the installation of apartment swimming pools to meet tenant demands.

6 / But see Reference 3, Chapter 5. In the Phipps Garden Apartments in New York, four-storey walk-up buildings have been more economical and just as attractive to tenants as six-storey elevator buildings.

7

The market data approach

I GENERAL

In many appraisals this is the only relevant approach and in others it contributes importantly to the validity of the other two approaches.[1] Market data are also important in assessment, mortgage and insurance appraisals. Even in appraisals of properties which do not typically sell on the market, the value of the site may have to be estimated and capitalization rates or gross and net income multipliers computed; these are best done by market comparison; estimates of accrued depreciation can also be developed from such comparison.

The market approach has the blessing of the courts and as these courts reflect public opinion, it is presumably the type of approach which the average person wants and understands. Also, the application of market data to specific appraisal problems has less subjective bias than have the other two approaches, in which the estimation of accrued depreciation and the selection of capitalization rates may be fairly subjective matters.

In the market data approach the appraiser puts himself in the position of a typical buyer in comparing the subject and other similar properties which together (through the intervention of buyers and sellers) make up the market. The applicability of the approach depends upon the frequency and type of market transactions.

The basic principle is that of substitution: equal market prices will be established for real properties which provide equal advantages either for use or for earning income. In perfectly competitive markets this is the overriding principle. In the real estate market the principle has modified application since properties are not identical and since there is no single market place knowledge of prices is imperfect and delayed. This means that adjustments must be made; these are the heart of the approach.

Certain limitations exist to the applicability of the approach:

Price may not coincide with value

Real property is often bought and sold for other than economic reasons, particularly in the market for single family dwellings. The value judgments of individual buyers and sellers make up the price structure of this segment of the market.

In the industrial-commercial sector of the market, owners of properties may 'sell' them to an investor with a lease-back. Such 'sales' may not represent value.[2]

No two properties are exactly similar

Even two seemingly identical new houses on adjoining lots are not exactly the same on the day construction is finished, and will grow more different as time and use take their toll. Account can be taken of some differences; for instance, if one house has a porch or an oil burner while another is similar but lacks these features, a dollar allowance can be made. However, it is difficult to measure the difference in market value of two similar houses, one of which has slightly more inherent charm. The market data approach unlike the cost or the income approach deals in generalities not exactitudes.

There may be no 'market' for a given property

Special purpose properties or those with unique features may change hands so infrequently as to deny the existence of a 'market.' Churches, schools, special purpose commercial or industrial properties (such as boat building plants, transportation systems, distilleries, etc.) and luxury or uniquely constructed homes rarely sell on the open market; if there are no sales, there can be no market data and this would preclude the use of the approach.

II   SOURCES OF MARKET DATA

The sources of Market Data are of three broad types; official records, public information and private records.

Official records

Registry, and land titles offices[3]

Grants, mortgages, leases, etc., containing particulars of transactions are registered in the appropriate office. Many of these instruments mention only a nominal consideration, but some provinces impose a land-transfer tax and the affidavit covering this will show the true consideration. The actual instrument should always be inspected and information on price and description, as summarized in the abstract book, should not be relied on alone. If the true price or rental is not obtained from some official source, the appraiser must remember the 'hearsay' rule, as in court he may be unable to give evidence of such price or rental.

Municipal records

Most assessment records include the registered (or concession) lot and plan number, the dimensions and the names of owners and tenants of the subject and comparable properties. This information should be used only after comparing it with that contained in the relevant deeds and leases.

Public information

Newspaper articles

Public opinion, trends, installation of sewer and water mains, potential major developments, etc. are all discussed in the daily papers. A scrapbook containing such information is invaluable to the appraiser, although, of course, it must be carefully screened before it is used in an appraisal.

Classified and other newspaper advertisements

Most properties listed for sale or rent appear in either the classified or display ads; these should be filed and supplemented by information from the parties or agent.

Sales reporting services

In many cities such services provide appraisers and realtors with information; these data are fairly accurate but complete reliance should not be placed upon it and at least the most relevant transactions must be checked at the registry office.

Private records

Every appraiser accumulates data from word of mouth, newspaper ads, or searches in public offices and must organize it efficiently. A card system of individual properties is recommended with cross-indexing by both location and type of property.

Information obtained in conversation with realtors, owners, and tenants must be carefully sifted to separate rumour from fact, and even this latter may be inadmissible evidence in court under the hearsay rule.

III MECHANICS OF THE MARKET DATA APPROACH

The basic idea of the approach is to translate data from known sales of properties into an estimate of the value of the subject. By breaking each comparable transaction into component parts using a properly designed worksheet the chances of committing a gross error are minimized; a simple worksheet can be set up as follows: (columns 5 to 9 would have headings describing variables such as market conditions, physical condition, terms of financing, etc.)

Property address	Sale[4] date	Sale price	Price per front foot	Adjust	Total adjustment	Adjusted price per front foot
1	2	3	4	5 to 9	10	11

The address of each comparable is written in one line in column 1 with the relevant information being put in columns 2 to 4. In columns 5 to 9 adjustments are entered to reflect the appraiser's opinion of the dollar or percentage[5] differences between some relevant variable in each comparable and the subject property. Column 10 shows the total of these adjustments to be added to, subtracted from, multiplied by or divided into the price of the comparables; the resultant figure is then placed in column 11. The same procedure is followed for each comparable and then all the adjusted unit prices are correlated to indicate the unit value of the subject property. Adjustments for minor differences can generally be ignored.

Analysis of and adjustment of variables

Adjustments will be upwards when a variable favours the subject property and downward when it favours the comparable; the subject is always the 100% base.

Location

The relative merits of different neighbourhoods constitute an important variable. If the subject property is in a better neighbourhood than the comparable the adjustment will be upwards and vice versa. If all comparables and the subject properties are in the same neighbourhood, the only locational adjustments will be for proximity to schools, transportation, noise, etc.

Physical factors

This can be broken down into subheadings such as construction, size of lot, decorating, number of rooms, amenities, physical condition, etc., but in many transactions physical differences may not be important to purchasers. For instance, the average purchaser of a 6-room home will pay a certain amount for such a house of optimum size, and little or nothing more for a slightly larger house. Similarly if a house is well decorated it may not sell for much more than one which is rather dingy, as purchasers generally prefer to redecorate to suit their tastes and furnishings. The typical purchaser stresses utility, location and financing more than he does physical factors, subject of course to the assumption that the structure is basically sound.

Utility

The functional utility of a property is very important. Inadequacy of cupboards or loading space, awkward floor plan, insufficient bathroom accommodation, too narrow or non-existent driveways and many other matters must be carefully considered by an appraiser who will make upward or downward adjustments to reflect his ideas of the relative difference of such items between the subject and each comparable property.

An important phase of 'utility' concerns the availability of municipal services, particularly water and sewerage. These are the keys to development and their presence or absence affects values greatly. Their installation, or even the registration of a plan of subdivision (if this is a legal prerequisite to development) can result in threefold or greater increases in land prices.

Asking price or offers to purchase

In an active market many sales occur so listing prices are given little weight by the appraiser.[6] In considering an asking price the adjustment would be downward, as the ultimate sale is almost invariably lower than the asking price. Conversely for prices offered by a possible purchaser, the adjustment will be upwards.

Special factors

This is a 'catch-all' for variables not falling under the other headings. In general such adjustments cover the myriad of personal matters in the minds of the parties, and if a sufficient number of comparable sales is used these special factors tend to cancel out; they need not be adjusted for.

The key points in the market data approach are:

A reasonable number of sales should be considered

A gross error in adjusting for a variable will be minimized by using several comparable sales; if just one is used any error is carried directly into the adjusted price but, if, say, four are included, the final error would be cut by four.

There is no rule as to how many comparables to use;[7] the more we use the smaller are the chances of gross error; also 'special factors' which are so important (particularly in the purchase of the single family dwelling) tend to average out.

Prices paid by public bodies having the power of expropriation must be carefully considered as they may or may not represent market value.[8]

There are many prices but only one value[9]

More than economic reasons may enter into the purchase and sale of real property. Some of these fall in the category of 'special factors' and perhaps cannot be analysed, but the following can:

Market conditions

The sale price of a property during a recession cannot be directly related to its value in a buoyant economic period. Also a sale of a single family property in May of a given year may be at a higher price than one made the day before Christmas, although the 'value' of the property may not have varied. If 'adding' percentages, the 'market' adjustment must be made first to obtain a current base price, so that the other adjustments will be applied to the market-adjusted and not the original price.

Changing value of the dollar

An important reason for general increases in prices in recent years has been the decreasing value of the dollar; as the value of money falls, prices rise.

Terms of financing

An appraiser estimates the value of a property as though it were free and clear of mortgage, but this implies normal financing for the class of property in question. If in a neighbourhood, mortgaged indebtedness generally runs to 80% of total price, such financing must be related to each transaction and on the comparative worksheet a plus or minus adjustment should be entered to reflect the easier or harder financing on the subject property.

In expropriation the criterion is 'normal' financing terms for the type of property in question.[10] In appraisals of 'fair' market value the prices of comparable properties may justifiably be reduced to reflect the discounted value of second and subsequent mortgages. See Chapter 2, Reference 3.

Depreciation as such is not considered

In the cost approach, accrued depreciation is deducted from reproduction cost to obtain an estimate of value, and in the income approach, recapture of capital is allowed for in the capitalization rate. In the market data approach purchasers have, in paying a certain price for comparable properties, considered the depreciating factors; hence no direct allowance for depreciation need be made by the appraiser in relating the comparable sales to the subject. (See also Chapter 9.)

IV   UNITS OF COMPARISON (See Table)

To compare things we reduce them to their money equivalents (i.e. prices). We relate a dozen eggs to three pounds of apples by comparing not only our individual likings and the nutritional benefits but also their prices; so also we can compare a gallon of gasoline, a taxi-ride, a magazine or an electric light bulb.

Eggs and apples can be analysed in terms of their caloric, protein and mineral content as well as their money equivalent. Also in comparing their money value we use accepted units of measurement; eggs are generally sold at retail by the dozen and apples by either the pound or the basket and these units are subdivided into grades and sizes. If we know the number of calories, proteins, minerals and so forth in each size of egg and apple, we could set up comparative worksheets and decide how much to spend on each of these items and how many to buy. Eggs and apples are divisible and a shopper can in theory buy one, two or any number of either.

Real property does not lend itself to such divisibility. Most types of improved properties cannot be divided at all, and limitations on the division of even vacant land are fairly rigid. This is inherent in the immovable nature of real property; it must be used where it is and then for only a limited number of purposes. How different from the apple which can be eaten in the orchard, the store, on the street or in the home and can be made into pies, cider, or apple butter. The indivisibility of real property also traces to our social customs concerning the use of land and to the way in which these customs have developed in their economic and political contexts.

And yet purchasers, sellers and users of real property *do* divide this: there is a very real division on the market between a 5-room and a 7-room house; between a bachelor and a two bedroom apartment and between a 5,000 and a 50,000 square foot factory. Such divisions constitute logical units for comparing individual properties as they are those which are used by parties in the market. It would in most cases be inappropriate to compare two houses solely on the basis of the number of windows contained. But hard and fast rules are impossible to lay down in the dynamic real estate market.[11]

Purchasers of real property pay for utility and in selecting his units the appraiser should consider what contributes most to utility in each type of property: some units which may be suitable for one type (or for the same type under different uses) will be inappropriate for others in that they do not measure utility. For instance, two 6-room houses, one on a 30-foot lot and the other on a 31-foot lot, should generally be compared, say, on a per room rather than a front foot-of-lot basis; the extra foot probably adds little or no extra utility.

The amount which a purchaser or tenant will pay per unit of property varies inversely with the number of units, once a certain minimum point is passed. If he can obtain a 7-room house at $2,500 per room and if this is all the space he wants, he will not pay much more in total price for an 8-room house: (and under the principles of balance and of diminishing returns, he probably would not buy, say, a 15-room house at any price).

Also just as it costs less proportionately to build an 8-room house than it does to build two 4-room dwellings, so also does the unit value of a property decrease as its size passes a certain point. For instance, a farm of 100 acres will be worth more per acre than an identical farm of 200 acres, as the value of the buildings is spread over only half the amount of land. Comparison is easier if confined to properties of like size and utility; it is difficult to compare a 50' lot to a 10 acre parcel.

Use of assessment – sale price ratios

In many jurisdictions the assessed value must (among other things) consider the 'actual' use to which a property is put. On the other hand, estimates of market value and value to the owner are based upon 'highest and best' use; obviously the concepts are completely different.

Assessment appraisals must also be aimed at equity between properties. This might indicate that in every municipality the ratio of assessed to market value should correlate closely and this is generally true at the time the assessments are made. But the principle of change tells us that such equivalence will get out of kilter as time passes. In most provinces the ratio of assessed to market value varies from a low of about 10% to a high of 100%, even more within and between municipalities.[12]

The ratio of assessed to market values should be used largely as a rule of thumb for preliminary estimates, although they may, of course, be included in the report to illustrate the level of probable values under such a technique or to corroborate the estimates arrived at by other approaches. Such ratios are useful in 'bulk' appraisals: for instance, we may be able to estimate the probable cost of acquiring a certain area for, say, a redevelopment project by applying an average multiplier to the total assessed value of all the properties required.

Assessment – sale price ratios are helpful in assessment appeals. Assessors, particularly in larger communities, cannot possibly reflect all changes in the market value of properties instantaneously; hence an analysis based on the ratio of the assessed to the market value of comparable properties may disclose inequities. See Chapter 6, Reference 4.

Value-trends

If certain properties have sold and resold (perhaps a number of times) over a period of years, and if no renovation was carried out in the interim, the trend of prices may indicate shifting levels of value, subject to changes in the value of money.

Gross income multipliers

The value of a revenue producing property can be estimated by multiplying gross revenue by an appropriate factor: therefore 'gross revenue' is a unit of comparability. Such a computation is crude but useful as it is easier to get information on gross rent than to find out the operating expenses. Many leases are registered against title, and also most tenants will tell an appraiser the amount of rent they pay as will real estate brokers with whom properties are listed. Gross income multipliers are derived by dividing the annual rental of comparable properties (monthly in the case of single family dwellings) into their sale price. If a series of price-rent relationships is obtained, a correlated multiplier can be developed and applied to the gross rental earned by the property being appraised.

Dr Ratcliff in his article 'Don't Underrate the Gross Income Multiplier,' A.I.M., Winter 1969-70, describes an analysis of 385 Vancouver residential income-property sales. The arithmetic mean of the gross income multipliers predicted the probable selling price almost as accurately as did regression analysis. He concludes '... that a sample of 10 well-selected comparables would produce a G.I.M. of acceptable reliability for predictive purposes.'

It should be noted that the arithmetic mean should generally be used to represent an array of data. A.I.C. Text, p. 253 says that the median should be used as the mean distorts the conclusion; in the example given the array of values ranges from $1000 to $6000, so clearly these cannot be comparables. In the table of adjusted sale prices on p. 251 the median is $18,000 while the mean is $18,050, so the difference is not significant. The median cannot be further manipulated arithmetically to develop a regression analysis while the mean can; hence this latter average should be used in the first place.

REFERENCES

1 / Paul F. Wendt, *Real Estate Appraisal,* Holt 1956. The other approaches revolve about the market one; if this was refined, the others would rarely be required.

2 / An AAA owner could in theory 'sell' a property for almost any amount with a commensurate leaseback rental.

3 / There are two registration systems in Canada. The older is the Registry and the newer the Land Titles or Torrens system; in the text the term 'registry office' is used generically. Under the Registry system, abstract books summarize all instruments affecting individual properties; these are in geographic pattern so that lot 2 comes after lot 1 and before lot 3, etc. in any concession or plan. The appraiser can readily search any area or neighbourhood for sales or rentals. Under some Land Titles systems each property is given a 'parcel' number in chronological order of registration, unrelated to location, so a search is expensive both in search fees and time. Prescriptive rights cannot arise under Torrens.

4 / Initially the only available date is that of registration, but later evidence may show that a binding contractual agreement had been reached earlier; this prior date is then appropriate.

5 / Percentage adjustments may be added and subtracted or multiplied and divided; this latter being described as factoring; different answers may result.

Confusion arises due to inconsistency in the assumption as to whether the subject or the comparable is the 100% base. A.I.C. Text, p. 250, illustrates two variables: subject – 10% better than comparable – divide by .90; subject – 10% better than comparable – multiply by 1.10. If price to be adjusted is $10,000, $10,000 ÷ .90 = $11,111, $10,000 x 1.10 = $11,000.

The discrepancy is in not consistently making the subject property the base. If the subject is the 100% base, the comparable would be rated at 90.91% as 100% is 10% greater than 90.91%; $10,000 ÷ .9091 = $11,000.

See Jay S. Berger, 'Resolving Confusion in Percentage Adjustments,' *The Appraisal Journal,* April 1971. See also Chapter 13, Reference 7.

Another misconception (A.I.C. Text, p. 249) is that in factoring, any adjustment for 'market' must be made first but not in adding or subtraction percentages. The opposite is, in fact, the case. If we adjust upward 10% for market and 10% for some other adjustment based on the current market:

$$\$10,000 \times 1.10 \times 1.10 = \$12,100$$
$$\$10,000 + 10\% + 10\% = \$12,000$$
$$(10,000 + 10\%) = \$11,000; \$11,000 + 10\% = \$12,100$$

6 / An owner in considering what he would pay for the property rather than fail to obtain it would certainly look at asking prices and prices paid by neighbouring owners for property needed to expand their operations.

7 / Clients and courts are impressed with the number of sales used by an appraiser, but rarely are more than a few true comparables found.

8 / Gagetown Lumber v. R. (1957) S.C.R., 44.

9 / In economic theory, price and value are synonymous.

10 / Re Pultke & Pultke (1957) O.W.N., 318.

11 / At one time the number of windows was a key unit of comparison as taxes were based on it.

12 / The ratio between site and building assessment may bear little relationship to the actual relative values. See Chapter 8. The revised Ontario statute calls for assessment at market value and does not require separate site and building assessments.

In two multi-municipality analyses for the Ontario Committee on Taxation 1967, the author and his partner Gerald Young found very wide discrepancies which could only be clearly established through regression analysis, which requires that the arithmetic mean be used. The Committee's Report, Vol. II, p. 250, cites a range of from 13% to 168% in the City of Toronto.

Type of property	Area or linear units	Use and other units
Vacant land	acre, hectare, square foot, front foot, rod, chain, meter	the suite (apartment sites) the space (parking lots) sq. ft. of rentable space (office bldg.) assessment ratio
Single family	sq. ft. of floor, sq. ft. of site, fr. ft. of building, fr. ft. of site	the room the whole property monthly gross rent assessment ratio
Duplexes to 6-plexes	as in single family dwellings	the suite annual gross revenue
Apartment houses and condominia	sq. ft. of building area	the suite annual gross revenue
Retail stores	sq. ft. sales space, fr. ft. show window, sq. ft. building fr. ft. building	the cash register annual gross revenue
Industrial	sq. ft. of building area	the loading door annual gross revenue
Farms	acre, hectare including all buildings	stumpage, cords (wood lots) the tree (orchards) the yard of gravel the animal (dairy, beef, poultry) the can (etc.) of milk the bushel (etc.) of crop
Hotels & motels		the room or unit annual gross revenue gallonage
Office buildings	sq. ft. of rentable area	annual gross revenue
Theatres		per seat, per car annual gross revenue
Parking garages	sq. ft. of building area	effective car space annual gross revenue
Service stations	sq. ft. or fr. ft. of site	the 'bay,' the gallon

8

Valuation of the site

I GENERAL

The site must be evaluated separately from the building for a number of reasons. Some assessment acts require this, as do income tax regulations and accounting practice; fire insurance too is confined to the buildings. Also in the appraisal process, the cost approach and the income approach in general require that separate estimates of land or building value be made.

II METHODS OF SITE VALUATION

There are four basic methods of evaluating a site:

> 1 Market data comparison
> 2 Land-building ratio
> 3 Projected development
> 4 Land residual technique

We can dispose of the first and last of these rather quickly, the first because the market data approach has already been discussed and the last because we have not yet forged the necessary tools to weld the income earned by a property into an estimate of its value.

1 Market data comparison

The basic principles of the market data approach apply: the appraiser considers sales, listings, offerings for comparable sites; the sources of data are identical as are the conditions of analysis.

All that differs are the units of comparison and their adjustment in accordance with the physical, social, economic and political limitations on the potential development of the site. See the sample report in Chapter 13 for examples.

2 Land-building ratio[1]

The agents in production must under the principle of balance be so combined that in any given type of improved real property an acceptable ratio exists between land value and building value representing the contribution of all the other agents. To find correct ratios for different types of properties, we must know the value of vacant sites on which similar types of development have been carried out and also the value of the developed properties. If, say, one type of single family site cost builders $5,000 and these latter sold the finished houses for $25,000 (and if these two prices represented value), then 20% of the total value is land and 80% is buildings. The appraiser could use this ratio to estimate the value of similarly improved sites when he knows the total value of the properties.

The ratio varies with land use; in Canada a single family site is generally from 15% to 25% of total property value (in recent years in some urban areas, 35%); in apartment and office buildings about 10% to 20%. No fixed ratio appears in industrial, store or service station projects.

The ratio must be developed from the market, not from municipal assessment figures. These may reflect present, not highest and best, use, and also the basis of land assessment may differ from that for buildings. For instance, in Ontario until 1970 land was assessed at 'actual' value and buildings at the amount they add to this; the ratio of land and building assessment may bear little relationship to such ratio under market value conditions. See Chapter 6, Reference 4.

3 Projected development

This really applies the cost approach to vacant land: it is primarily used in expropriations when the property in question was reasonably ripe for development. The procedure is to lay out a hypothetical subdivision or other development. The total gross sale price of all the lots is estimated and from this the costs of development are deducted; the balance will be the value of the property to the owner, including his profits. The amount of profit based on similar developments which have actually been completed and sold is then deducted.[2] The remaining figure is then deferred so that it will represent the present worth of the property. If the land is ripe for development and all necessary municipal and other approvals have been obtained, the only delay in the owner actually getting the net price of the developed property will be the time taken to install the services and roads and sell the lots; this may take only a few months. However if no actual plan of subdivision has ever been prepared, then the delay may be several years. In any event some deferment will be necessary.[3]

The approach has the limitations of any cost approach; few appraisers can draw subdivision plans and compute service and other costs. A.I.C. Text, Chapter 9, explains the problems very well.

4 Land residual technique

In our discussion on the agents of production it was noted that in appraisal theory land is always residual in that the other agents are paid their shares of gross revenue before land receives anything. If we can estimate the gross revenue and deduct amounts payable to labour, co-ordination and capital the remaining revenue will be what the land and the entrepreneur earn. This is the theory of the land residual technique, but we must leave it until our tool kit is complete enough to handle income capitalization.

III DEPTH, WIDTH AND CORNER INCREMENTS

Increases in frontage and/or area generally increase the front foot, square foot and total site value up to the point of optimum size; then the law of diminishing returns tells us that further increases in size will not increase value proportionally. As the depth increases past the optimum, the front foot value of a site increases but not proportionally, while the square foot value declines and vice versa.

The appraisal question is whether the physical increase raises, and the physical decrease lowers, the utility of the site proportionately. Chapter 12 illustrates a site analysis in which the efficiency of a proposed office building could be increased greatly by adding the neighbouring 43' x 90' to the site; this extra land has special value. But, if the zoning required the adjoining land to be used for landscaped space (and assuming that the original site was large enough to accommodate an optimally sized building) the additional land might have only nominal value to the owner of the main parcel. Also if under the zoning, a single family dwelling lot must have a frontage of 50 feet and an area of 6,000 sq. ft., a 55' lot containing 7,000 sq. fr. will not sell for a proportionately higher price.

Appraisers have developed various tables of adjustment factors to reflect the difference in value between sites of varying depths. Such mathematical adjustments tend to mislead by their very appearance of refinement; when a depth table shows that, if a lot 100' deep is worth $100 per front foot, one 125' deep will be worth $108.50, such a precise adjustment to an estimate of value, which is by necessity not in itself precise, is pointless. Of course, in assessment appraisals where equity is an important consideration, and to a lesser degree in mortgage appraisals, such tables have a valid place.

It is, however, often necessary to distribute the value of a site in accordance with its depth. If roads are widened or put through anew, this generally requires partial expropriations of properties. Valuations are made on the basis of 'before' and 'after' estimates and the question is whether, after the expropriation, the depth of the property is adequate for highest and best development. If it is, then any frontage expropriated is perhaps equivalent to the same depth off the rear of the property:[4] but if the remaining depth is inadequate, the land lost must be considered as being more valuable than merely rear land. If the zoning prohibits development on site-remainders after a partial expropriation, then the 'value after' may be zero. See Chapter 3, Reference 2.

When the overall value of a site must be divided in accordance with the distance of its various parts from the street the 4-3-2-1 rule can be applied:

> 40% total value lies in the front 25% of site depth
> 30% total value lies in the second 25% of site depth
> 20% total value lies in the third 25% of site depth
> 10% of total value lies in the rear 25% of site depth

The percentages must be applied to total value, not to either the front foot or square foot values.[5]

The refined depth tables discussed above have been developed from the 4-3-2-1 rule, but while this latter may appear to be rough and ready, it is in practice more useful than its refined derivatives; complex depth tables not only give the mistaken appearance of unverified accuracy, but are also difficult to explain to clients and courts: any error attributable to the use of the cruder computations is probably minor in the final analysis.

The shape of a property has considerable influence on its utility: in general a lot with greater relative frontage can be more economically developed than a narrower one of the same area. But each property must be considered on its merits and a deep, narrow lot may for some purposes be preferred to a square lot with an equivalent amount of usable area; if the productive processes of a manufacturer requires a depth of 500' and a width of only 60' he will prefer to pay for no more frontage than necessary to get the needed depth.

Corner influence

Property users (such as service stations), who can reduce their land requirements or obtain greater visual prominence or access by having a street along one side, benefit greatly from a corner location. On the other hand a single family dwelling on a corner may be subject both to heavier traffic and higher municipal taxes. Corner influence tables have been developed to indicate the added value attributable to a corner location, but as with depth tables they should be used with discretion and their basic underlying premises should be understood.

IV   SITE IMPROVEMENTS

To Ricardo 'land' consisted of the 'original and indestructible powers of the soil.'[6] Much of the economically valuable area of Canada is not 'land' in this sense but rather land plus improvements such as undertiling, ditches, sewers, water mains, roads, lanes, lawns, manured or fertilized fields, orchards, planned wood-lots and forests and so on. In appraisal practice we distinguish between site improvements and building improvements and a full explanation of the differences between these could be lengthy and complicated; we can rely largely on intuition and common sense. Obviously there is a difference in principle between a rosebush and a garage; or between tiling under a farm field and that around the footing of a house to keep the basement dry: the former is a 'site' and the latter a 'building' improvement.

Once a 'site' improvement has been made it contributes to and forms part of the value of the site. But such site improvements as, say, lawns and flower beds rarely add the amount of their original costs to the value of a property, except to the person or family who installed them. An analogous situation prevails with regard to private water and sewerage facilities: as has been noted, these probably add the amount of their costs to the value of a property as long as they are maintained and not replaceable by equivalent municipal services: if neglected or if public water supplies and sewerage facilities become available, the private system loses all value and may even become a liability.

REFERENCES

1 / A.I.C. Text, p. 84, 'The Abstraction Method'; A.I.R.E.A. Text, 5th Ed., p. 125, 'Land Value by Distribution, Abstraction or Allocation.'

2 / While the A.I.C. text does not recognize the entrepreneur in discussing the agents in production, it does so in subdivision development as 'profit' is correctly deducted before arriving at land value. As noted in Reference 20, Chapter 3 hereof, in the 'long-run' of the planning period, profit can be accounted for at any stage and land is residual. But if the subdivision is actually developed we have, the 'short-run' and the entrepreneur is residual. Deducting profit before arriving at land value contradicts the principle of surplus productivity which on p. 85 of A.I.C. Text is called 'the basic principle of real estate.' The conflict is due to failing to distinguish the 'long-run' from the 'short-run.'

3 / A 'before' and 'after' analysis of a partial expropriation is summarized on p. 95.

4 / Gibbons v. Middlesex (1956), O.W.N., 147.

5 / Assume a site 100' x 100' valued at $10,000 ($1.00 per square foot; each 25' of depth contains 2500 square feet)

		Adjusted square foot value	Adjusted overall value
Front 25'	− 40% of value	$0.40 per sq. ft.	$4000 − $1.60 per sq. ft.
Second 25'	− 30% of value	.30 per sq. ft.	$3000 − $1.20 per sq. ft.
Third 25'	− 20% of value	.20 per sq. ft.	$2000 − $0.80 per sq. ft.
Rear 25'	− 10% of value	.10 per sq. ft.	$1000 − $0.40 per sq. ft.
	100%		$10000

6 / As noted in Chapter 6, Reference 1, this definition of land is a vital simplifying assumption in Ricardo's concept of rent; his model sees land as so defined, suitable only for growing 'corn' with no alternative uses. A concept of economic rent based on such a limiting assumption has no validity in the real property market; yet as pointed out in Chapters 12 and 16, the definition of the accepted appraisal theory seems to be so based.

Summarized 'before' and 'after' analysis (see reference 3)

		'Before'		'After'
Estimated gross sale price		$1,226,000		$1,030,000
Less developmental expenses	'Before'		'After'	
Service costs	$252,000		$209,000	
Engineering fees and levies	84,000		73,000	
Total engineering costs	336,000		282,000	
Performance bond	4,000		3,000	
Management, overhead & sales	122,000		102,000	
Legal survey & taxes	15,000		12,000	
Total deductions		$ 477,000		$ 399,000
Net value upon subdivision		749,000		631,000
Present worth (defer 1 year –				
12% factor 0.8929		669,000		563,000
Less estimated raw land value		495,000		
Estimated potential profit		174,000		
Less estimated profit ('after' computation is based on % of profit to present worth shown in 'before' computation)		26%		$ 146,000
Estimated value after expropriation				417,000
Estimated value 'before' expropriation		495,000		
Estimated value 'after' expropriation		417,000		
Estimated value of part taken and injurious affection to remainder		78,000		

9

The cost approach

I GENERAL

The theory of the cost approach is that by subtracting the amount of accrued depreciation existing in the buildings from their current reproduction cost and then adding the value of the site, an estimate of market value will be obtained. This recognizes that supply is affected by cost while demand is affected by depreciation; we have already noted that demand dominates the current market. This is analysed in detail in Chapter 15 where the stock-flow exposition shows why cost has little effect on price in the real property market.

The cost approach is very important in appraisals whose purpose is to estimate assessed value, insurable value or value for mortgage purposes.[1] But the approach has practical, legal and theoretical weaknesses.

From the practical point of view few real estate appraisers are qualified to estimate costs, and the real estate market does not indicate amounts attributable to each of the types of accrued depreciation.

Legally, the depreciated cost of a building, plus the current value of its site, has been held not to be a good indicator of market value unless the property is of a type uniquely suited to the needs of the owner.[2] In this latter case the value to the owner is probably closely approximated by the land value plus the current reproduction cost of the building less physical deterioration but with little or no allowance for functional or economic obsolescence, since the building is uniquely suited to the needs of the owner.

Theoretically, the cost approach has been criticized on the grounds that '... there is no logical reason for expecting that the three approaches to value will yield identical or nearly identical value estimates.'[3]

The cost approach rests on the principle of substitution which is fully applicable only under perfect competition, and as far as costs are concerned only when the subject of the valuation is new. Then the sum of the payments to individual agents in production can equal or approximate the value of a finished building. The real property market is far from perfect and a building is new momentarily; over most of their lives, buildings are 'old' to a lesser or greater degree.

In light of these limitations and others imposed by the courts,[4] the cost approach, if used at all, is generally based on some relatively straightforward method such as square-foot building costs minus accrued depreciation measured by an overall age-life percentage of such cost; in correlating the three approaches in a market value appraisal generally little or no weight is given to the cost estimate. And yet, every appraiser must be proficient in the approach, which in some appraisals is the only possible and in others an important secondary one; in still others it may complete the analysis of a property by indicating its insurable value at current construction cost levels.

The approach also guards against gross error in the other two approaches, as the current reproduction cost of a building plus the current value of the site must set the upper limit of value. But while current *cost* sets this limit, the estimated value by the cost approach does not do so per se, as it includes a deduction for accrued depreciation.

In a well-leased new property the estimated value by the income approach may exceed that based on cost, since the site has taken on added value as a result of beneficial development; if the 'new' site value is used, the estimate by the cost approach will equal or approximate that of the income approach.

The apparent ease and objectivity of the cost approach is misleading; it seems so simple to apply unit costs and percentages from appropriate tables to a building. The approach may be an objective, accurate and easily supported method of estimating value in the hands of the experienced practitioner but not when the neophyte is involved. Yet the appraiser must be able to estimate costs and depreciation if only to be able to recognize the limitations of the approach and know when it is applicable and when it is not.

Published tenders on public works show great differences between bids. Some differences are due to the anticipation of disposing of an already owned site on favourable terms, or using cheaper or more expensive materials. Others arise from mathematical mistakes. But the major cause of discrepancies can generally be traced to two things:

First, as has already been pointed out, the market for the individual agents in production is much broader than is that for a finished parcel of real property. Prices and qualities of the agents can be ascertained far more accurately than can their total price combined into a building, and prices of the agents can vary considerably over the period of construction of a building, but the contractor's tender once made must be adhered to.

Secondly, a contractor with equipment and work crews on a job which will be completed at the date a new job is slated to start can submit a lower tender than a competitor whose equipment and men are going to be fully engaged on another job. Also if the contractor has his equipment located in the vicinity of the new job, he will be more attracted to it than would a competitor located many miles away.

If cost estimates computed by contractors show considerable variance, it is inevitable that such estimates when made by relatively untrained appraisers will show even more: and if the cost estimate is inaccurate the whole cost approach is suspect.

II   BUILDING COST ESTIMATES

A distinction should be drawn between:

Reproduction cost

Refers to the current cost of reproducing the structure as much like its existing form, plan and style as possible, using similar materials and equipment.

Replacement cost

Refers to the current cost of replacing the structure with a modern one having the same utility. Replacement cost automatically eliminates functional obsolescence as the existing building is replaced by one having its same utility but none of its disutility. But the real problem is that the appraiser has not, in fact, evaluated the subject property.

Cost versus value

Even in a new building, cost and value will rarely be exactly equal because of the long period of gestation of most buildings and the short time it takes the principle of change to operate: but for all practical purposes, if a new building improves a site to its highest and best use, cost will equal value at the moment construction is completed.

But a building begins wearing out functionally and perhaps locationally as soon as the architect starts the plans and it begins wearing out physically as soon as construction is commenced. A well-conceived, well-built structure will have a long life, but the forces of change sooner or later cause physical, functional and economic (i.e. locational) depreciation; by deducting its dollar amount from the current cost the appraiser tries to bring the depreciated cost into rough equivalence with value.

Methods of estimating costs

Several methods are available, but only two are useful, unless the appraiser has some special background in construction or in costing. Of the following four methods the average appraiser must generally rely on the comparative or index methods.

Quantity survey

When building tenders are called for, the general contractor obtains subcontractors' quotations for the costs of the various trades, each based on estimates of the direct costs of materials and labour and the indirect costs of overhead and profit. The general contractor totals the subcontractors' quotations, adds in estimated costs of specific trades which he may carry out on his own and an allowance for overhead and profit. This final total plus any allowance for contingencies is the amount of the tender. This quantity survey cost estimate must cover all the items which would be included in the subtenders and main tender.[5] Few appraisers can estimate costs in such detail and even if so qualified, since cost estimates are of little use in many appraisals, it would be hard to justify spending substantial time on this part of the appraisal. The appraiser's proper function may not be that of estimating costs but rather of advising on depreciation.

Unit-in-place[5]

In this shortcut to quantity survey the component parts and surfaces such as walls, floors, etc. of a building are analysed to ascertain their costs.[6] By multiplying the unit cost by the total surface area in question, an estimate of the cost of each type of surface area is obtained. The same can be done for all component parts and trades. For instance, the cost of painting or papering interior walls can be broken down into a square foot unit which will be applicable to the total surface area so covered; so also the cost of all doors and windows installed and the cost of the bathroom, kitchen and heating system, all fully installed can be computed. The total of all the costs of component parts and surfaces is the reproduction cost by the unit-in-place method. Few appraisers are competent to make unit-in-place estimates.

Index adjustment methods

The original cost of a building or an estimate thereof based on quantity survey or unit-in-place methods can be made current by applying an adjustment factor. This will be as accurate as a current quantity survey estimate providing both the original estimate and the adjustment factor are accurate. The appraiser can do nothing about the accuracy of the cost estimate but he should know the basis on which his adjustment factor was developed. Such factors are provided by recognized costing services and are index numbers which get out of date if construction techniques change. If, for instance, the index assumes that labour cost makes up 50% of a certain trade, and in the meantime this class of labour has been largely replaced by mechanical equipment, the results will be inaccurate. Such a major mistake could not long continue, but technology is in a constant state of transition and no index can reflect cost changes with accuracy for long unless it is under continuing review and revision.

With the problems facing the appraiser in making his own estimates, the adjustment factor is possibly his best cost tool: it is not time consuming and is usable by an appraiser who can obtain original or intermediate construction cost estimates of the subject building.

Comparative method

An appropriate unit obtained either from a costing service or from known costs of similar buildings can be applied to the subject building. The most common units are the 'square foot of floor area' or the 'cubic foot of building contents'; 'per suite' etc., as in the table in Chapter 7. This is the only procedure normally open to the average appraiser.

The comparative method requires that the number of the 'units' in the building be computed; and if the units are such general ones as 'per suite' they must be reduced to an average unit. The more commonly used square foot and cubic foot units have greater applicability and are easier to come by. The accuracy with which an appraiser can convert such costs into an estimate of reproduction cost depends upon his knowing how the master costs were divided into the units in question (i.e. say on a gross rather than a net area basis) and also upon how readily he can adjust for extra or deficient items not included in the base.

An increasingly larger proportion of costs, is each year, represented by equipment. The appraiser must be able to reflect in his cost estimates the presence or absence of such equipment. Most standard unit costs assume an average quantity and quality of equipment for the particular type of structure and such costs must be adjusted to reflect the presence say of an automatic elevator when the basic data assume an operator-controlled one. Unit costs provided by recognized cost services permit of extensive variations of this nature.

Another important consideration is the shape of the subject building and the length of its outside walls in relation to those used in computing the unit costs. The more jogs there are in the walls, the greater the costs; also as exterior walls are expensive, the relatively longer these are the higher the overall cost. For any given perimeter the largest area can be contained in a circular building, and the closer the shape of an actual building is to a circle, the lower the perimeter cost per square foot of floor space. For practical purposes a building which is square yields the largest area for its perimeter. A building measuring 100′ by 100′ contains 10,000 sq. ft. in its 400′ of perimeter; contrast this with a building measuring 400′ by 25′ which also contains 10,000 sq. ft. but in a perimeter of 850′

To convert the area of a structure into cubic contents, we multiply area by height, which is the distance from the bottom of the basement floor to half way up in the pitch of the roof; with a flat roof the height will merely include the ceiling joists plus the thickness of the roof decking and covering. A cube shaped building will yield the greatest volume relative to floor and wall area.

Unit costs are higher for small structures than for large ones of the same shape and quality. For instance, if the unit cost of a 10,000 sq. ft. industrial building is $8.15, that for a similar 5000 sq. ft. building could be $10.50 and for 15,000 square feet, $7.30. Such basic equipment as a heating system and a bathroom are included in even the smallest structure but can serve a much larger area; up to a point their cost per square or cubic foot of building can be reduced by increasing the building's size. But remember our old friends the law of diminishing returns and the principal of balance; after this point, the efficiency of the equipment will start to decline and its capacity should be enlarged even though this will increase initial unit costs.

Indirect costs and profits

The above discussion is largely in terms of direct costs although most of the available unit cost figures will include the overhead and profit of the subcontractors which are direct costs to the general contractor. But some components of total cost may not be included in unit costs obtained from a manual; the general contractor's overhead and profit and the architect's fee may be omitted. Unit costs derived from actual costs of completed buildings will, however, include such items. This again illustrates the need for the appraiser to know what is and what is not included in his basic unit costs.

Fees of land surveyors, lawyers and accountants or consultants cannot be reflected in standard unit costs nor can municipal taxes, insurance and interest paid during the construction period; they must be computed and included in the overall cost estimate. Other important indirect costs arise between the completion of construction and the occupation of the building. If insurable value is being estimated or if a cost base is used for assessment or value to the owner purposes, all indirect costs are included. But in a market value appraisal, some of these costs add nothing to value and the accrued depreciation schedule must include off-setting entries.

Owner-built improvements

Estimating the cost of these buildings should logically offer no special problems, but in practice it does. If the owner of a new factory acted as his own general contractor and also had his employees do quite a bit of the work, his actual cost might be $70,000, compared to, say, $130,000 which a similar building erected by a general contractor would cost. A municipal assessor would consider this latter figure, and if the property was expropriated the owner would want to claim that the building was worth its competitive cost. The appraiser would so consider it, providing the building is, in fact, an acceptable improvement constructed in an acceptable manner. If it is not, because, say, the owner used scrap lumber and sawdust for insulation, these deficiencies should be allowed for either in the cost estimates or in the accrued depreciation schedule.

III   DEPRECIATION

General

Buildings start to wear out physically, functionally and economically, perhaps
from the date they are planned and certainly from the date of construction.
This wearing out process is called depreciation and it goes on over the life of
the structure although not at a constant rate. In the cost approach we are concerned with the 'accrued' depreciation which has actually taken place up to the
date of appraisal. When the income approach is discussed our concern will be
the future period over which a building can produce net revenue. This can be
thought of as being the period of 'future' depreciation, but really it is that
during which an investor must recapture that part of his investment which is
represented by the wasting assets (i.e. the building and improvements).

In the market data approach, depreciation does not enter directly. It has been
allowed for by vendors and purchasers in their individual transactions. Of course,
the appraiser's adjustments will reflect differences in the condition and utility
of the various properties, but this is an indirect recognition of depreciation
whereas the cost and the income approaches allow for it directly.

Accrued depreciation

Value is created by the forces of supply and demand, but like the weather
everyone talks about this while few appear to appreciate the complexities involved. For our present purposes we repeat that cost affects value only by affecting supply.[7] When we estimate value on the basis of cost estimates we are
only looking at one side of the matter. Remember Alfred Marshall's example
of the scissors; a cost estimate is one blade of the scissors, called 'supply.' A
second blade called 'demand' must be hinged to the first and this blade the
appraiser forges and sharpens through his estimates of accrued depreciation.

If the reader remembers that accrued depreciation represents the demand
side of the value equation, he will not fall into the definitional trap which has
ensnared unwary theorists who define the term as being 'a loss in value from
any cause.'[8] Instead he will recognize that the dollar amount of accrued depreciation is the difference between the reproduction cost and the actual value of
buildings as of the same date. Only if cost and value coincide can accrued depreciation exactly equal the 'loss in value'; this can only be when a new building
improves the site to its highest and best use.

Apart from the above confusion as to definition, the concept of depreciation
may mean different things depending upon the purpose of the appraisal and
also it may mean different things to other specialists. The physical-value appraiser in insurance valuations is governed by the legal principles that limit the
liability of insurers in the event of the total or partial destruction of a building:
in general this is determined by the reproduction cost of a building less its physi-

cal deterioration providing this does not exceed market value. In contrast, a market value appraisal will recognize that the major component of depreciation is generally not physical, but rather functional or economic.

The accountant is concerned inter alia with showing a financial picture of an enterprise to serve as a basis of periodic comparisons and for other purposes; he therefore uses original cost which will not change over future accounting periods. Against this cost he sets up annual dollar allowances which over the expected life of the asset will total such cost. This use of a historical unchanging cost is very different from the appraisal practice of using constantly changing current costs. Both approaches are valid for their purposes; the accountant is not concerned with value,[9] while this is the main interest of the appraiser.

Types of depreciation

Appraisal theory recognizes three main types of depreciation, namely physical deterioration, functional obsolescence and economic obsolescence:

Physical deterioration

This results from wear and tear due to time and the elements. The principle of substitution states that buyers do not typically pay as much for an old structure as they do for a new one even if the utility and location of the two buildings are identical. Physical deterioration can be broken down into three subclasses namely:

Rehabilitation: deterioration which can and must be cured now.
Physical deterioration curable
Physical deterioration incurable

Functional obsolescence

This second component of accrued depreciation is caused by changes in tastes and demands: the principle of substitution states that buyers do not typically pay as much for an outmoded, poorly planned building as they do for one which is well laid out even though physically and locationally the two are identical. The principles of change and balance guarantee that functional obsolescence will generally be an important part of total accrued depreciation.

Functional obsolescence can be divided into three types, just as was the 'physical' classification above:

Rehabilitation (This term is generally confined to 'physical' renovation.)
Functional obsolescence curable
Functional obsolescence incurable

Economic (locational) obsolescence

The third component of accrued depreciation is caused by external (i.e. neighbourhood) factors which influence the utility and value of a property. As

the causative factors are located outside the property itself, economic obsolescence is nearly always incurable, relative to an individual property.[10]

The very nature of economic obsolescence indicates that it relates to the
whole property and not to the building alone and as accrued depreciation is a
deduction from building cost an adjustment must be made to remove that proportion of the obsolescence which is related to the value of the site. The computation is simple; we multiply the estimated total amount of economic
obsolescence by the proportion of the total value of the property which the
building represents. If the land-building ratio is 1-4 (i.e. 20% and 80%) and the
total economic obsolescence is estimated to be $25,000, the deduction from
building cost would be 80% of $25,000 or $20,000. The remaining $5,000 is
ignored as it is not a deduction from building cost.

Methods of measuring depreciation

Many techniques have been developed to indicate dollar amounts to allow for
depreciation; the most important for real estate appraisal are:

Cost to cure is the measure to apply to rehabilitation and physical deterioration curable or functional obsolescence curable.

Age-life methods: a percentage of the estimated reproduction cost of the
building is deducted for each year of its age: this method is commonly used by
accountants. The system is rigid and fails to recognize the fluctuating effects
of the principle of change. The major contributor to depreciation is obsolescence and this does not accrue gradually but piles up in waves as new techniques evolve which sharply diminish the usefulness of existing structures.

However, in appraisal practice, the use of age-life percentages is common:
the method is simple and is accepted by taxation authorities (with the percentages being applied to the declining undepreciated balance)[11] and so is favoured
by clients, counsel and courts. Also in light of the limited relevance of the cost
approach in many appraisals, the use of a simple, direct and quick method of
estimating depreciation has much merit despite the obvious deficiencies. The
concept of 'effective age' introduces flexibility into the procedure, as effective
age may be less than the actual age of buildings because of better physical condition or greater utility than the typical building of actual age would possess:
flexibility can also be obtained by using a gradually increasing percentage as
the building gets older.

Observed condition estimates are based on the fact that various parts and
functions of a building wear out at very different rates. If the estimate is confined to the physical structure, what is known as an 'engineering' depreciation
schedule is developed; if extended to also include the utility of the improved
property the resulting schedule is said to be developed by the 'break-down'
method.

In appraisals where the cost approach is of over-riding importance, its validity depends on the estimates of accrued depreciation. The break-down method measures such depreciation with greater accuracy than can age-life percentage tables, but is complex and difficult to justify to a client or a court. Functional obsolescence incurable and economic obsolescence are measured by the loss in rental attributable to the deficiency in question; unless such rental loss can be measured objectively in the market, the validity of the approach will be in question. It is next to impossible to find rentals of similar properties which reflect only functional or only economic obsolescence.

The break-down method occupies a strong position in appraisal theory and if sufficient time is spent in developing the depreciation schedule, it is an important member of the appraiser's kit of tools. This is not solely because of the uses to which the method can be put, but perhaps just as important is the fact that a full understanding of the problems of measuring accrued depreciation will bring into clear focus the limitations of the cost approach in Canadian appraisal practice.

Market measures of depreciation rely on a strict interpretation of the definition of accrued depreciation as being the difference between the reproduction cost and the value of a building as of the same date.

The procedure is to estimate the reproduction costs of each comparable building used in the market data approach and subtract from these costs the portion of the actual sale price which is attributable to the building alone. This indicates how much each purchaser actually depreciated the comparable property and it can be expressed as a percentage of the reproduction cost of the comparable and then reduced to an annual percentage. The annual percentages from each comparable can then be correlated to give a market-based age-life percentage which is applied to the estimated reproduction cost and age of the subject building. The method is simple and is derived from actual market data, but it has not to date found acceptance in appraisal theory. The reasons given do not appear to the writer to be valid and, if as much time and thought were put into the development of the technique as has gone into the refinements of the break-down method, a more satisfactory way of measuring depreciation would result.[12]

Accrued depreciation and the income approach

The income approach is concerned with future not past depreciation. But if expenditures on rehabilitation must be made immediately and net income is estimated on the assumption that these expenditures have been made, then they should be deducted from the estimated gross value by the income approach.

REFERENCES

1 / Mortgage (and in the final analysis, insurance) appraisals are of course based on market value and so the other two approaches are also used, but the cost approach is of considerable importance.

2 / Sisters of Charity v. The King (1924) Ex C.R. 79, Samuel, Son & Co. v. Toronto (1962) O.R., 453 (1963) S.C.R., 175.

3 / Paul Wendt, *Real Estate Appraisal,* Holt 1956. See also Laura M. Kingsbury, *The Economics of Housing,* Kings Crown Press 1946.

4 / Peterkin v. H.E.P.C. of Ontario 1958 O.W.N., 225. Real estate appraisers held incompetent to give cost estimates.

5 / The appraisal report in Chapter 13 shows the unit-in-place tabulation taken from a quantity survey. It also shows the actual cost approach of the property in question.

6 / Build-up or unit cost in place for external wall

	Cost per sq. ft. of surface
4" face brick, mortar and pointing	$2.45
Insulating	.40
8" block back-up, mortar	1.10
Vapour barrier	.03
Strapping	.15
Wall board	.90
Painting	.12
Total Cost per sq. ft.	$5.15

7 / In most markets the supply curve slopes upwards to the right (see Chapter 3, Reference 13) and is based on marginal costs; hence cost affects price only through supply. As shown in the stock-flow analysis of Chapter 15, supply does not enter into price determination in the real property market and so neither does cost at least until such time as new buildings can be erected and put on the market.

8 / A.I.C. Text, p. 152.

9 / Old accountants never die, they just lose their balances!

10 / An example of possibly-cured economic obsolescence is the remodelling of one house on a short street as a result of which all the other owners follow suit. Collier Street in central Toronto is just one example.

11 / This results in smaller and smaller sums being deducted for depreciation as the structure gets older; such a pattern conflicts with common sense and experience.

12 / A.I.R.E.A. Text, 5th ed., p. 206. The criticisms are of two kinds: first, that the measure of accrued depreciation relies on market data and this may not be truly comparable. To carry this argument to its logical conclusion would mean that the market data approach is not applicable let alone the risk, capitalization and overall rates which are developed from it for use in the income approach.

Secondly that 'while the approach usually produces the approximate answer, it lacks refinement.' Presumably it is better to be precisely wrong than roughly right!

Surely it is the fact that it is based on the interplay of market forces which guarantees that the method will avoid the subjective bias which could creep into a break-down schedule. The same text at p. 328 treats the gross income multiplier as part of the market data approach (which, of course, it is), despite the fact that these use data from the income approach; also at p. 275 the selection of capitalization rates (for use in the income approach) by using market data is described. In a dynamic, complex market such as that for real estate, there is bound to be an interplay of cost, market and income data.

10

The income approach[1]
Gross rental and operating expenses

I GENERAL

The value of real property is closely related to the amount which a purchaser would pay in a lump sum for the right to receive all the future income or advantages the property will yield. But because it requires the use of mathematics (of which most of us are afraid) and also because accepted theory has overcomplicated its straightforward concepts the income approach is hard to understand.

While value and future income are closely related, there are several major impediments to the use of the approach:

first, in most single family dwellings, people buy amenities, not income;

secondly, even for rental properties expense figures may be unobtainable;

thirdly, the appropriate capitalization rate is hard to find and yet a minor change in it can produce variations, in the value estimate.

The gross income multiplier is one method of converting rental into an estimate of value.[2] In the income approach we consider not only the gross rent but also the period over which it will be received and the operating expenses incurred.

Financial statements can be grouped into two general classes as far as real property is concerned. First, if the property is actually rented, the statement will show details of rental and expense. These figures can be used directly by the appraiser in his income approach although they may have to be reconstructed, as will be explained later.

In the case of 'related' owners and tenants (whether by personal or business relationship) the amount of rent being paid under a lease may not reflect the true market rent at all. Such internal arrangements have as their basis the accounting for all revenue and expense whether actual or implied and within fairly wide limits the amounts set out in them are subject to the discretion of the parties and their accountants. When we further remember the imperfections of the real estate market it will be obvious that rents and expenses shown in statements covering non-arms-length leases may differ substantially from those which would normally be attributable to the property in question.

The second type of financial statement covers the actual business operation of an owner-occupier of real property; these cannot be used by the appraiser directly. To ascertain how much of the net profit of the business operations is attributable to the real property, the owner's accountant must separate business revenue and expenses from that which is representative of the real property. Or in the alternative, the appraiser can estimate how much a third party would pay an owner for the right to receive the net business revenue shown in the statements; some of this would be equivalent to rent for the real property. The problem revolves about our earlier analysis of the agents in production.

The business statements of an owner-occupier can help the appraiser to see if the owner has any special value in the property. In partnerships and sole proprietorships the financial statements will not show any salary for the principals: these receive the net profit after paying for supplies, merchandise and business expenses. This net profit is the amount the proprietor or partners have earned and if it does not exceed the wages they could have earned working for someone else, probably no special value to the owner exists. Many small store owners spend long hours and earn a net profit of $3000–$5000. If they could get alternative work at, say, $100 a week for 40–50 hours' work, their real property clearly contributes nothing in excess of its market value to the owner's revenue. The analysis could, of course, be applied to the statements of a corporate owner.

II GROSS REVENUE

This is the total amount of money a property can earn per rental period (usually a month or a year). If a lease exists, it will state the gross rent (unless it is a 'net' lease) and the tenant is legally bound to pay this amount. But the rent may at times exceed that which the property would then command on the market and the tenant may press the owner to reduce the amount of the rental. In the past decade or so a more common situation would be the tenant negotiating a new lease at a higher rent before the old one expired, to gain some concessions from the owner. The former situation describes 'excess' and the latter 'deficient' rental.

Effective gross revenue

The rental actually received may differ from the rental called for in the lease, owing either to the receipt of extra revenue or to vacancies. Extra revenue might be earned from a sign located on the roof or wall, from washing and drying machines, parking space, pay telephones, from the sale of steam or water and from many other sources; such revenue would form part of 'gross.' Vacancies may be due to many reasons but their effect is always to reduce income. Actual revenue received (or expected to be received) less an allowance for vacancies and/or uncollected rent is called the 'effective gross revenue.'

In the owner's income statements for a period of representative years, actual revenue received and effective gross revenue will be identical. But if a building is new or has been converted to a new use, the appraiser must estimate the amount of gross rentals and deduct for possible vacancies and/or rental losses. Also if no statements are available or if the statements are for non-representative years (say if economic conditions have changed noticeably), the amount of revenue shown may not represent the amounts which will probably be received in future years. Another situation when a discrepancy between expected future and actual revenue could arise is when an existing lease runs for only a short period relative to the probable life of the building.

Quantity of rentals

The owner of rented property must report such income in his income tax returns and from him or his accountant the appraiser should obtain these revenue and expense figures, particularly in expropriations as special value to the owner often depends on them. The most reliable financial statements are those acceptable to the tax authorities.

Quality of rentals

An owner of real property either occupies it or rents it to a third party and in this latter case he is concerned not only with the amount of rent and the length of the lease, but also with the calibre of the tenant. This tenant 'covenants' to pay rent and also to do (or not to do) quite a few other things:[3] whether the covenant is good, bad or indifferent, depends on the personal and financial characteristics of each tenant. There are advantages to having nationally known and respected tenants as compared to, say, Harry's Hash House. The rent will be paid by the former on the day it is due whereas rentals from the latter may be on a most irregular basis. The appraiser distinguishes between such extremes under the general concept of quality.

Another facet of 'quality' arises under percentage leases requiring a fixed rental plus a specified percentage of gross sales either in total or on the excess over a stated minimum. The quality of the fixed rental can be considered by the same criteria as those used in ordinary leases; the percentage portion will vary with the tenant's business and so is of lower quality than the fixed rental.

Durability of rentals

Durability refers to how long a property will produce the rental income of which the present worth is to be estimated. This depends on two things:

first, the remaining economic life of the property,
second, the length of the actual or anticipated rental contract.

In the income approach we define economic life as being the period over which a typical prudent investor would be willing to leave part or all of his initial investment tied up in the property in question.[4]

The second problem concerns the period of time over which a specific tenancy runs or may be expected to run. This depends on the calibre of the tenant, as most good tenants, in planning their needs for space, also plan a programme of growth. To be sure that they can remain in the premises for a fairly long period they generally enter into long leases, perhaps with renewal options. Such leases are of high quality, not only because of the tenant's covenant but also because of its immortality: nearly all such tenants are limited companies and such companies, unlike individuals (except old soldiers!), never die.[5]

The actual length of any given tenancy rarely coincides with the period specified in a lease because of renewals, either under options, in the original contract or under separate agreements. The appraiser can be more confident of his estimates of rental if he is considering either a specified lease-period or this period extended under contractual or optional renewals; for instance, an industrial building erected specifically for a tenant and leased at a rental of $27,500 a year for 21 years, with options to renew for two further 10 year periods at $17,500 and $12,500 respectively per year. If the rent originally yielded a fair return on construction costs plus land value and the renewal rentals are so reasonable by current and anticipated future comparison that the tenant will almost certainly remain in occupancy, the present and future rentals are predetermined for 41 years.

Analysis of gross rentals

The appraiser is concerned with the rental a property will earn over its future economic life and so he must analyse the actual leases in relation to the terms and conditions of other leases for similar properties. The most important clauses are those governing the payment of rent and of expenses, but others may affect the amount of the present worth of the rentals under the lease. For instance, if a lease requires the lessee to demolish the existing improvements at its conclusion, the present worth of future benefits to the lessor are greater than under an identical lease which said nothing about demolition costs, as typically an improvement belongs to the lessor at the end of a lease and he would have to pay for its demolition. The appraiser may require legal advice as to any specific clause so he can consider its effect on the present worth of the rental income.

Clauses which have a considerable influence on value include:

a The amount and terms of payment of the rent
b Provisions for renewal
c Covenants of lessor and lessee re payment of operating expenses
d Covenants concerning construction, alterations and eventual removal of improvements
e Provision with regard to subletting or assigning
f Cancellation or changes in the lease due to fire or expropriation.

Comparative rental units

The appraiser must relate the amount of gross rent to that prevailing in the real estate market. He will, following the procedures of the market and cost approaches, reduce rental to a unit basis. The same units are used in all three approaches and so it is common to consider single family dwellings on a per-room-per-month and apartments on a per-unit (or per-room) per-month basis.

The unit for retail stores is rent-per-front-foot per year. In shopping centres and larger retail outlets, the net rentable or sales area is used.

The industrial space unit is the gross or net square foot and that for office space the net square foot.

Vacant land is subject to local custom: the front foot, square foot, acre, etc. are most commonly used.

In a mixed-use building each rental is reduced to a unit fitting the specific use.

III ALLOWANCES AND EXPENSES

Having estimated the gross revenue a property can earn, the appraiser then considers the expenses which must be incurred to rent the property at the estimated gross. Some expenses will inevitably arise while others may never have to be paid in cash but an owner or purchaser would be imprudent if he did not consider them. Most operating statements are for income tax purposes, and generally include all items which can legally be deducted and omit those which cannot: the appraiser must use his knowledge and experience to reconstruct the statements.

Another problem is the way in which capital (as opposed to operating) expenses are treated: an owner or investor treats mortgage interest (and often principal) as an operating expense. But the mortgage is part of the overall capital value, so the appraiser looks on interest as a capital expense. Accounting statements record all cash payments made in a given period, and also depreciation or capital cost allowances; the appraiser puts them on an accrual basis so that each expense and allowance is related to the future period over which it will benefit the property; depreciation is not deducted but rather is allowed for in the capitalization process, through the recapture rate.

Deductions from gross revenue fall under four main headings:

    a Allowances for contingencies and for owner-performed services
    b Fixed expenses
    c Running expenses
    d Allowances[6] for repairs and replacements

Allowances

An owner's operating statement may omit any allowance for vacancies (and credit losses) or for management services. The appraiser as already noted treats the first of these as a preliminary deduction from gross revenue, the residue being effective gross revenue. The magnitude of the vacancy and credit loss allowances are estimated by analysing the local real estate market for the particular type of property.

The allowance for management is treated as an operating expense and an amount equal to what a professional property manager would charge should be included. Such allowance probably need not be made in relatively small rental properties such as neighbourhood stores with apartments above, or duplexes, triplexes or even sixplexes, particularly when the owner occupies part of the space.

Operating expenses and standards[7]

Fixed expenses
These are recurring items which do not vary much from year to year.

Municipal taxes and insurance premiums
These are simple to check. An insurance broker can provide the amounts of premiums per $100 of insurable value. These vary with construction and use and as between tariff and non-tariff companies.

Municipal taxes can be estimated accurately at least for the current year. As explained in Chapter 4, municipalities in Canada have the power to levy a mill-rate tax on assessed property values; multiplying assessed value by mill rate shows the annual tax.

The real problem with regard to both insurance premiums and taxes is not their actual but their future amounts. The income approach estimates the present worth of the future net revenue which will be earned by a given property; this will vary with changes in either gross revenue or operating expenses and the appraiser must consider the probable trend of each expense item.

Insurance premiums may be too high if the coverage is excessive in light of building value, since as pointed out earlier, unless a 'replacement rider' is attached to the policy, the liability of an insurer is, in law, limited to the value of the building. But we must realize that 'value is a word of many meanings' before advising an owner to reduce his coverage. An estimate of market value reflects the economic and functional obsolescence of the improvements as well as their physical deterioration, whereas the insurable value may only consider the latter. Building costs have risen rapidly in recent years and insurance policies should reflect this. There are many kinds of insurance; premiums for all applicable ones for the particular property must be considered by the appraiser.

The future trend of municipal taxes is more predictable, they will probably increase. While analysing the taxes, the appraiser may find the assessment of the subject property is out of line with those of comparable properties. If the assessment is too high, a successful appeal means lower taxes for future years; if too low, then future increases in taxes are probable. This illustrates an anomaly; as the value of the property increases, so does its assessment, but this latter increase results in higher taxes, lower net revenue and hence in lower value.

Contracts for services
Many building owners retain independent managerial, janitorial and waste disposal services for the property, as well as elevator, air conditioning and heating system maintenance contracts at an annual fee; depending upon how comprehensive these latter service coverages are, replacement allowances may have to be set up.

Running expenses
These include.

Heat, power and water
Such costs are best obtained from actual operating statements covering a period of years. Power and water charges won't change much from year to year if the property is used for the same purposes, but heating costs can vary in accordance with the severity of the winter. The appraiser must consider average temperatures for his locality, and how temperatures in the relevant years compare to such averages. Average heating costs should be reduced to a unit basis (say per square foot).

Air conditioning
Climatic conditions vary greatly in Canada and even within major metropolitan areas (the extreme temperatures in Metropolitan Toronto ranged one May day in 1971 from 56° at the harbour to 80° at Malton!). Average cost standards must be applied with care in any given locality or building. Also the cost of power and water used cannot generally be separated from general consumption. The principles of replacement allowances apply, but as technological and aesthetic advances in air conditioning have been rapid, such allowances should be generous. The use of window or other units owned or at least operated by a tenant may make it unnecessary to include any item in an owner's statement.

Administration and payroll
Most buildings require at least a one man staff. In an owner-occupied property, such staff may be employed in the production end of the business and be responsible for the building, as a side-line; the appraiser should include payroll cost, except in very small buildings.

Provincial, municipal and trade union regulations may require certain minimum staff and wages and maximum hours of work; details of these and of actual wage rates and hours should be obtained to estimate such costs. Cleaning is a major item in office and some other buildings. Automatic elevators are largely replacing operators, chiefly in response to high wage rates in urban areas. A large multi-tenanted building may also have an accounting and administrative staff.

Supplies and miscellaneous
Costs of cleaning and other materials, light bulbs, small items of hardware, panes of glass and so on, are based on actual expenses over several years.

ALLOWANCES FOR REPAIRS AND REPLACEMENTS

These are of two main types:
For parts of the building: this includes allowances for the cost of decorating, exterior and structural maintenance, and eventually replacing the roof, floor coverings, and hardware.

For items of equipment which wear out faster than does the structure itself such as allowances for replacing the elevators, boiler and heating equipment, light and plumbing fixtures, stoves, refrigerators, air conditioning, and store fronts. Such replacements may be needed due to obsolescence as well as physical wearing out, and so allowances may be set up for rehabilitation, remodelling and modernization.

NET REVENUE

The income approach, converts net revenue into capital value. Deducting the total operating expenses and allowances from effective gross revenue gives an estimate of net revenue which is then capitalized into an estimate of value.

REFERENCES

1 / Chapters 10, 11 and 12 cover the whole of the income approach; they could be read through quickly together and then re-read more slowly to clarify the general principles involved. Chapter 13 includes the complete approach.

2 / Richard U. Ratcliff, 'Don't Underrate the Gross Income Multiplier,' A.I.M., Winter 1969-70.

3 / Recent revisions to the Ontario Landlord and Tenants Act, R.S.O., 1960 Ch. 206 as amended by S.O., 1968-69, Ch. 58 (now R.S.O. 1970, Ch. 236) have made the covenants and obligations of residential tenants much less onerous. This may have effects on the value of such rental properties if owners have to absorb losses and expenses previously recoverable from a tenant.

4 / See Chapter 5, Reference 8, and Chapter 14.

5 / Old appraisers never die either; they just lose value!

6 / These are described as 'reserves' in other books. This is misleading as 'reserve' implies that a fund is actually set up: in fact, all that is generally done is to make a bookkeeping allowance.

7 / Every appraiser should develop unit standards to measure expense items: the same units are used as in sales and rental comparisons. See *Office Building Exchange Report: National Association of Building Owners and Managers,* Chicago.

11

The income approach (continued)
Capitalization rates

I THE THEORY OF INTEREST[1]

Interest is thought of as being the price paid for the use of money, just as rent
is paid for the use of land and wages are paid for the use of labour. But the
analogy cannot be carried too far; supply and demand theory states that as a
price rises, the supply is increased and vice versa. The supply of savings does
not necessarily react this way. Few individuals save more just because the rate
of interest on savings accounts rises from 4% to 4.5%. Also with a higher rate
of interest, less savings are required to produce the same revenue.

In advanced countries, the Central Bank controls the cash assets of the banking system. The government is also a major demander in the money markets in
which basic interest rates are set and so neither the supply of, or the demand
for, money nor the rate of interest are fully market determined. Some basic
interest rates in Canada are either fixed by legislation or are under a ceiling;
this was true of the 6% ceiling on bank loans until 1967; and the N.H.A. mortgage rate is fixed relative to the yield on Government Bonds. Other mortgage
rates relate to N.H.A. rates.

If interest isn't strictly a 'price,' then what is it? It has been considered as
being the 'real' cost of abstinence or saving. Also it has been said to be the
value of the marginal product arising from the use of capital. Still another explanation is that interest is based on time-preference; this is significant when
value is estimated by discounting future income. Another idea is that interest
arises due to the uncertainties inherent in a dynamic economy.

Perhaps it is unimportant how we classify interest: it does exist ... it is in a
sense a price ... it is in a sense a payment for the abstinence of saving ... and it
also recognizes in a sense that present worth is greater than future worth ...
and, of course, the variance in interest rates in relation to the certainty or uncertainty of an investment is obvious. The important thing is that the appraiser
should recognize that the role of the interest rate is not crystal clear. The limits
within which interest rates settle are determined by profit rates and uncertain-

ties while the specific rates within these limits are to a considerable degree determined institutionally.

Interest and rates

Appraisal literature distinguishes between 'interest' as being fixed by contract agreement and a 'risk rate,' as being an estimate of what the interest would be under given conditions of risk and desirability of income. The distinction is probably worth making but it should not be allowed to becloud the matter. For all practical purposes the appraiser can consider a 'risk' rate and an 'interest' rate as both reflecting the degrees of risk and desirability of income inherent in a given property or other investment.

Preference of investors

A further consideration is that the liquidity preferences of various classes of investors varies.[2] Financial institutions require capital and income certainty; pension holders, widows, etc. require income certainty; speculators are less concerned with either of these. The pattern of the rate of interest will therefore depend on the distribution of wealth relative to the supply of different kinds of assets.

II INVESTMENTS

Quality of an investment

The less desirable the income stream, the higher the rate to use in capitalization. But what do we mean by an income being 'desirable?' The components of an investment can be considered under the following major headings:

1 Safety and certainty of the investment and its income
2 Marketability of the asset
3 Denomination in which the asset is traded
4 Value of the asset as collateral
5 Duration for which the investor must invest
6 Freedom from trouble in reinvesting the income and eventually the capital
7 Possibilities of capital appreciation, to hedge against future inflation

The following types of assets are illustrative:

Treasury bills in duration of 91 and 182 days (with occasional issues of 273 and 364 days), and in amounts of from $1000 to $1,000,000 (but mostly $100,000 and $1,000,000), provide safety of capital and yield, acceptable short term duration and acceptable denomination. From January 1967 to April 1971 the average yield on 91-day bills ranged from 3.0% to nearly 8.0%.

Government bonds do not depend on profit earning ability and so provide certainty of income. Their denomination is acceptable to all investors and duration of the investment is varied. Certainty of capital is only high if held to maturity (except for Canada Savings Bonds) as prices fluctuate considerably. The average yield from January 1967 to April 1971 has ranged from 5.5% to 8.33%.

Corporate bonds have the same general attributes as government bonds but with varying degrees of certainty of capital and income. The average yield from January 1967 to April 1971 has ranged from 6.6% to 9.8%.

Preferred and common stock: These are not investments in the same sense as are bonds and treasury bills but rather represent ownership. The owner takes greater risks and should get larger returns than the lender, but much of this comes from anticipated capital appreciation. From January 1967 to April 1971 the average yield has ranged from 3.8% to 4.6%.

Real property equities: The best such are probably as good as the average common or preferred stock but the average equity investment is not. Safety of the investment and certainty of yield vary between properties; marketability, denomination and freedom from care are fair while value as collateral and duration are generally good. The possibilities of capital appreciation or depreciation affect the yield desired by equity holders.

Mortgages: These are debt[3] and partake of the characteristics of bonds, but their security and covenant varies as between properties and mortgagors; yields in 1970 often exceeded 10% and government subsidies are common in residential mortgages.

Recapture of an investment

An investor wants to get income but he also wants his capital back in due course, so if the asset will waste away, part of the annual income must be allocated to cover its wearing out. This can be called 'future depreciation,' but is really a periodic recapture of capital. Real property combines land which is assumed not to wear out and buildings which do;[4] the investor must receive a return on his total investment and also recapture the building part of it.

In appraising real property we are concerned with its future life, and recapture of capital is based on the future period over which an investor is assumed to be willing to have his investment outstanding. This is generally shorter than the expected physical life of the building in question and so an age-life percentage used to estimate physical depreciation in the cost approach may be much lower than the recapture rate used in the income approach, which is obtained by dividing 100 by the desired recapture period.

We must think of two types of rates or returns, namely a return *on* capital and a return *of* capital. The return *on* capital is variously described as being a 'risk' rate, a 'land' rate an 'interest' rate or a 'proper interest rate.' The return *of* capital is described as being a 'recapture' rate, a 'safe' rate or a rate for 'future' depreciation. The sum of these two rates is described as being a 'capitalization' rate, a 'building' rate, a 'combined' rate or an 'overall' rate.

We will call the two basic rates the 'risk' and the 'recapture' rates, while their sum will be called the 'capitalization rate.'[5] The risk applies to the whole of an investment whereas the recapture rate is added to it, whenever we are dealing with wasting assets such as buildings. We will also discuss overall rates.

III   METHODS OF SELECTING RISK RATES

Appraisal texts show four methods of finding risk rates.

> Summation process
> Band of investment
> Comparative – (real estate market)
> Competitive – (other investments)

The author uses the last three of these in combination with each other. The summation process is highly theoretical and impossible of application.

Summation process

Starting with the current rate on risk-free securities,[6] the appraiser adds full or fractional rates to reflect the various ways in which the investment in question is inferior to the risk-free security, and arrives at an appropriate risk rate for the particular investment.
   The following example is self-explanatory:

Safe rate	6.00
Burden of management	0.50
Non-liquidity	0.50
Risk	3.00
Indicated 'risk' rate	10.00
(A.I.C. Text, p. 200)	

Band of investment

This type of summation method (and of the competitive method to be discussed a little later) applies rates on real estate mortgages and equities. The appraiser considers the maximum proportions of value which could be obtained on a property by way of first, second, third, etc. mortgages and the rates on each. The remainder of value, the equity, is also related to its risk, liquidity and so forth to ascertain an appropriate risk rate for equities, in this type of property. We work in percentages, not in values, prices or mortgage amounts.

70% of value in 1st mortgage at 9.5% – .70 x .095	6.65%
20% of value in 2nd mortgage at 10% – .20 x .10	2.00%
10% of value in equity at 12% – .10 x .12	1.20%
100% Indicated 'risk' rate	9.85%

Percentages of value and rates must relate to the particular market: we cannot develop a risk rate for an old apartment building using mortgage and equity data from the sale of a new, limited-dividend apartment or a factory.

The chief function of the band of investment method in the Residual Techniques is to guard against gross error in rates developed by the comparative or competitive methods; but it plays a central role in the mortgage-equity method of capitalization, as shown in Chapter 14.

The comparative method

The only really relevant risk rates for the appraiser are those prevailing in the real estate market for properties similar to the subject. Using the same sales, as in the market data approach, he can develop a risk rate for the income approach.[7]

Property	Sale price	Net revenue	Overall rate[8]
1	$215,000	$23,650	11.0%
2	175,000	16,205	10.8%
3	225,000	24,975	11.1%
4	220,000	24,640	11.2%

Transactions on the market are taking place at an 'overall' rate of about 11%, which implies a net income multiplier of about 9.1 (i.e. 100 ÷ 11).[9]

Common practice uses the 'overall' rate as the 'capitalization' rate, but really it should be refined; this 11% rate reflects recapture of capital represented by both improvements and land: in appraisal theory this latter requires no recapture.

If the subject property and the comparables have remaining lives of about 40 years, the recapture rate is 2.5%. If the land-building ratios are about 1 to 7 (say, 11% to 89%), then 89% of the investment is represented by improvements. The 'true' recapture rate is therefore .89 x .025 = .022 = 2.2%

We now make the following computations:

'Overall' rate found	11.0%
Less 'true' recapture rate (89% x 2.5%)	2.2%
Indicated 'true' risk rate	8.8%
Add actual recapture rate	2.5%
Indicated capitalization rate	11.3%

The higher the recapture rate and/or the relative land value, the more important the adjustment.

Competitive approach (See C.H.S. 1970, Table 75)

This method of selecting rates helps explain why, in light of the yields obtainable on relatively liquid investments, a certain rate developed from the real estate market (by the Band of Investment or Comparative methods) is reasonable or unreasonable. The competitive approach relates the degree of desirability of an investment in a particular property to that of other investments. It involves a comparison of relative yields obtainable and in an appraisal can consist of narrative to the effect that yields on bonds, stocks and mortgages range from 5% to 10% and that to attract investment to the subject property a risk rate of, say, 8.8% would be necessary.[10]

Investors method (See also Chapter 14)

The appraiser should understand the investor's approach as risk and recapture rates must reflect the market. Also in the band of investment method the return on equity is the key to the approach.

An investor is generally concerned with how much he has left out of gross revenue after making all cash payments. He therefore may not include allowances for maintenance, repairs, replacements or management. Nor may he recapture the capital invested in the wasting assets. Rather he includes both mortgage principal and interest payments as deductions from net revenue to find his cash flow. Cash flow as a percentage of his equity investment will represent the yield on equity in the Band of Investment shown above.

A property with an estimated future life of 40 years shows net income before depreciation or mortgage payments of $23,500. It can be bought for $220,000 with $55,000 in cash and a 9.5%, 25-year amortizing mortgage for $165,000; investors require 12% on their equity investments. Site value is estimated to be $25,000.

Investor's approach

Mortgage amortization $165,000 for 25 years at 9.5% – annual charges	$17,048
Interest on equity $55,000 at 12%	6,600
Total	23,648

The investor gets 12% on his equity

Appraiser's approach

Net rental	$23,525
Recapture of investment in building, $195,000 x 2.5%	4,875
Net income after recapture	18,650

The appraiser's risk rate is 8.44% on $220,000.

REFERENCES

1 / Interest theory is also discussed in Chapters 15 and 16.

2 / The most liquid of all assets is money. A long-term, low interest mortgage is non-liquid.

A.I.C. and A.I.R.E.A. texts ignore liquidity preference aspects of interest theory, closing the door on theoretical advances of the 20th century and reinforcing the Classical biases of the accepted appraisal theory; however in discussions of the practical aspects of appraising, liquidity is prominent. See also Chapter 15, Reference 7.

3 / The distinction between debt and equity is important in law. Bonds, debentures and mortgages are forms of debt; contractual obligations have been entered into by the debtor to adhere to certain covenants; failure to carry them out permits the creditor to sue the debtor or even take over the asset securing the debt.

An equity represents ownership and includes no contractual obligation, say, for the payment of dividends. The equity holder pays losses and receives gains including possible capital gains.

4 / Maurice Seldin, 'Does Land Depreciate,' Appraisal Journal, July 1961, 345.

5 / The risk rate is designated 'R' herein, the recapture rate, 'r' and the capitalization rate 'R + r.' In Chapter 14, overall rates are designated R_0. A 'rate' is always earned in arrears, a 'discount' in advance.

6 / A.I.C. Text, p. 200 uses Federal Government Bonds as representing the safe rate. As shown later, this is incorrect. The appropriate security for the safe rate would be 91-day Treasury Bills.

7 / See Chapter 2, Reference 6.

8 / The overall rate discussed in detail in Chapter 14 is the percentage net income bears to sale price. It can be applied directly to net revenue to obtain value.

9 / The net income multiplier is sometimes translated into 'years purchase.' Refined multipliers have been organized in present worth tables which will be discussed in Chapters 12 and 14.

10 / It is explained in Chapter 12, Reference 12, why an overall rate of 11.3% and/or a risk rate of 8.8% may be quite compatible with a 12% requirement on equities and a 9.5% rate on first mortgages.

12

The income approach (concluded)
Methods of capitalization and the residual techniques

I CAPITALIZATION

General

There are two alternative ways to convert an income stream into capital value; the income can be divided by a percentage 'rate' or it can be multiplied by a factor as is inherent in the annuity methods of processing income.[1]

The basic capitalization equation if no recapture of capital is involved is:

$$\text{Value} = \frac{\text{Income}}{\text{Rate}} \text{ or } V = \frac{I}{R} \text{ where R is the risk rate,}$$

and if recapture at rate 'r' is involved, some appraisers use $V = \frac{I}{R + r}$, but this provides no recapture, just capitalization at a higher rate.

The formula can be rewritten $\frac{I}{V} = R$, or $V \times R = I$. These permit one to find the rate of return a property yields when its net income and value are known, or to find the income, knowing the value and the rate.

When capitalizing income we know its amount and we wish to find the capital value; the other thing we must know is the rate, and as this is the denominator, the higher it is, the lower will be the capital value and vice versa.

Methods of capitalization

There are four basic methods of converting net income into capital value: These in descending order of the size of the resultant value are:

Process	Relative size of value estimate
1 Straight capitalization in perpetuity	highest
2 Inwood compound interest premise	next highest
3 Sinking fund premises	
a Hoskold compound interest premise)	next highest
b Straight capitalization + sinking fund)	
4 Straight capitalization + straight line depreciation[2]	lowest

Appraisal theory says these are used under specific conditions as follows:

1 Straight capitalization in perpetuity

This should only be used to capitalize a net income stream which is unchanging in amount, perpetual in duration, and which flows from non-depreciating property such as a ground lease where the lessor has no interest in any building. Only the risk rate is used as no recapture is involved. The formula is $V = \frac{1}{R}$. With a 9% risk rate and $5000 net income we get $\frac{\$5000}{.09}$ = say, $55,555 capitalized value.

2 Inwood (single rate) premise (Table 1)

This should only be used to compute the present worth of a net income stream which is unchanging (or changing according to a known pattern) in amount over a given period.

The appraiser decides on the appropriate risk rate and time period and from the table gets the factor by which he multiplies the amount of net income. Using the same figures as above the values for 20 years, 100 years and 'in perpetuity' are:

20 years

$5000 x 9.128 = $45,640

100 years

$5000 x 11.109 = $55,545

in perpetuity

$5000 x 11.111 = $55,555

The Inwood computation for finite time periods gives a lower capitalized value than does straight capitalization, as it does not account for the total amount of the capital invested as it does in straight capitalization. If the present worth of the value of the non-wasting property at the end of the lease is added to that of the income, this sum will equal the value derived by straight capitalization; this will be discussed later.

3 Sinking fund premise

a *Hoskold* (double rate) premise (Table II)

This is used with the same type of net income stream as in Inwood, and the mechanics are the same. Using the above risk rate and income, we get:

20 years

$5000 x 7.861 = $39,305

100 years

$5000 x 10.911 = $54,555

in perpetuity

$5000 x 11.111 = $55,555

Like Inwood, Hoskold recaptures the total investment and so we must consider the 'reversionary' property value for finite periods.

b *Straight capitalization plus sinking fund* (Table IV)[3]
This is a combination of methods 1 and 3 and results in the same estimate of present worth as does Hoskold.

The appraiser adds the sinking fund figure for the 'safe' rate and period in question.

	20 years	100 years	in perp.
Risk rate - 9%	0.0900	0.0900	0.0900
Sinking fund 20 years - 3%	0.0372	0.00165	0.0000
Total	0.1272	0.09165	0.0900
Rental of $5000 ÷ 0.1272, etc.	$39,308	$54,555	$55,555

4 Straight capitalization + straight line depreciation

As noted, other texts call this either 'straight line capitalization' or 'straight line.' This latter term is adopted in the present book, because of its brevity and wide acceptance, but it doesn't describe the process.

The method is used in 95% of all appraisals, as it is appropriate to net income streams, from improved (actually or hypothetically) properties, which are not fixed in amount and which may consequently decline as the improvements age. Straight capitalization in perpetuity is used with rent from land, or fully net rent from improved property if the lease is for say 500 years.[4] Inwood and Hoskold can be applied to any type of property subject to the 'reversionary' value.

A further distinction between this 'straight line' method and the others is that in the latter the income stream is treated as flowing from the property as a whole whereas under 'straight line' it is considered as flowing partly from the site and partly from the buildings. This will be explained later.

Using 'straight line,' the appraiser must have estimated the value of the site and the future period for recapture of the investment. If the rental is $5000, the site value $10,000, the recapture period 20 years (and alternatively 100 years) and the risk rate 9%, the following are the computations:

	20 year (5% recapture)	100 year (1% recapture)
Annual net rental	$ 5,000	$ 5,000
Minus rental to land (I = V x R)		
9% x $10,000	900	900
Residual rental attributable to buildings	$ 4,100	$ 4,100
Capitalized at (R + r)	14%	10%
Indicated value of buildings V $= \dfrac{I}{R+r}$	$29,285	$41,000
Add estimated value of site	10,000	10,000
Estimated value of property	$39,285	$51,000

The answer derived by using 'straight line' or 'straight capitalization' represents 'value,' whereas that given by Inwood or Hoskold only represents the present worth of the income stream; to get 'value' we must add the 'reversionary' value.

As noted, the 'straight line' method assumes that the periodic income stream will decline as the buildings wear out: the percentage amount of such decline can be computed from the formula $\frac{R \times r}{R + r}$. In the 20 year example the annual decline in income allowed for is

$$\frac{9\% \times 5\%}{9\% + 5\%} = \frac{45\%}{14\%} = 3.2\%.$$

A property under a good 5-year lease will have no decline for 5 years and then the 'straight line' method would automatically allow for a 16% decline in the renewal rental; if this was not less than 84% of the original rent, the 9% risk rate or more would be earned on the outstanding balance invested.

II   PRESENT WORTH AND DEFERMENT TABLES[5]

Present worth tables

The Inwood and Hoskold methods give the present worth of a rental stream through the use of compound interest tables. As noted, this only represents 'value' when the annuity factor is 'in perpetuity'; for finite time periods the 'reversionary' value of the property must be computed by means of a deferment factor and added to the present worth of the income stream to represent value.

There are three differences between the Inwood and the Hoskold premises:

1 Inwood is a Single Rate and Hoskold a Double Rate Table; these names describe the inherent processes. In Inwood, the annual recaptured amounts must be invested at the risk rate compounded (only a single rate is used, the risk rate). In Hoskold these amounts are invested at a 'safe' rate compounded (two rates, risk and safe are used).

2 Under Inwood the periodic payments are used by the owner; Hoskold assumes they are put in a separate account to accumulate at compound interest.

3 The original investment in Inwood is reduced annually while that in Hoskold is considered as remaining outstanding in its entirety; then on the final day of the investment period the original investment falls to zero and is replaced by an equivalent amount from the sinking fund.

The investor is far more likely to be able to invest the recaptured amounts at a safe rate than at the risk rate compounded. Only by reinvesting in his own business or repaying an interest-bearing debt such as a mortgage might he earn the risk rate and this is the justification for using Inwood;[6] it is impossible to invest small sums at high compound interest, but these can be used in an owner's business or to repay a debt and thus earn the compounded risk rate. Accepted appraisal theory does not, of course, consider the mortgage debt position.

Apart from this the only investors who can earn a high rate of compound interest are corporate investors and governments; for them, Inwood makes sense, but for the average property owner it doesn't; if the recaptured amounts do not earn the compounded risk rate then the investment itself will not earn this rate either and the estimate of value will be excessive. Hoskold is more realistic. Even small sums can earn 3% to 5% compounded, and so estimates of value based on Hoskold are unlikely to be too high. But the accepted theory teaches that Inwood will always be used unless the investor in fact uses (or is planning on using) a sinking fund.[7]

Deferment (i.e. 'Reversionary') Tables (Table III)

Both Inwood and Hoskold automatically provide for the recapture of 100% of the outstanding investment over the period in question (normally taken to be the period of the lease).[8] As this period is generally shorter than the future revenue earning life of the improvements, there will be some value remaining in the property at the end of the lease. This remaining value having been recaptured by Inwood or Hoskold must be put back into the picture if a true estimate of value is to be obtained. A deferment table is used to compute the present value of this so-called 'reversionary' interest. The deferment table works in the opposite direction to 'present worth of income' tables. Annual factors for the latter are always greater than one (for periods of more than one year) while in a deferment table they are less than one.

Other tables

Most appraisal texts discuss other compound interest tables such as Increasing and Decreasing Annuities, The Future Worth of One Dollar, and the Future Worth of One Dollar Per Annum. These are rarely used in practice and are omitted in this book.

Interpolation

We can find an approximate factor for say a 9½% risk rate when our tables show only 9% and 10%, by taking the arithmetic mean of these two latter factors for the period required. Exact factors for any rates or time periods can be found with formulas (see each Table) and, of course, in more comprehensive sets of Tables.

We can also find the exact risk rate at which a property sold or is listed. For example, if a lease interest of $18,000 a year for 20 years sold at $200,000, the relevant factor is $\frac{\$190,000}{\$21,000}$ = 9.0476. The Inwood factor for 9% is 9.129 and for 9.5% is 8.819: hence the difference in factors for ½ or 1% is 0.310. The

factor found is 0.228 greater than that for 9.5%, so the applicable rate is .095 –
$\frac{0.228 \times 0.005}{0.310}$ = 0.091 = 9.1%.

If rental is paid half yearly, we divide the rate by two and then use the appropriate number of half-yearly periods: similarly for quarterly or monthly rentals
we divide the rate by four or by 12 and use the appropriate number of quarterly
or monthly periods. Such tables are also available.[9]

Rental paid in advance

The Inwood and Hoskold tables assume that the rent is paid at the end of the
period; if paid in advance, the factor can be adjusted by taking the factor for
the previous year and adding 1 to it. For instance, if a lease runs for 21 years
with rent paid annually in advance and the appropriate risk rate is 9%,

Inwood 9% factor – 20 years	9.129
Rental payments at start of year add:	1.000
Adjusted factor – 21 years in advance	10.129

III THE RESIDUAL TECHNIQUES

If all property incomes flowed from non-wasting assets like ground leases, only
two methods of capitalization would be used, namely straight capitalization in
perpetuity and the annuity premises using either Inwood or Hoskold. However,
most appraisals relate to properties which combine non-wasting (land) and
wasting (building) assets. Therefore two 'true' residual techniques have been
devised, in which the income attributable to the non-wasting (land) portion of
the property is separated from that attributable to the wasting (building) portion. The 'land' income is processed at the risk rate alone. 'Residual' roughly
means 'left over'; in using a residual technique we capitalize the net income
that's 'left over' after we have deducted the part of the income earned by
either the land (Building Residual) or building (Land Residual).

Actually there are three residual techniques, but the third isn't 'residual' in
the same sense. In the 'land' and the 'building' residuals, the net income stream
is 'split' between land and buildings, with one or other of these parts of the
stream being a left-over residual. In the Property Residual Technique, no such
split is made and the whole income stream is processed as a single sum: no residual income remains as an unprocessed left over.

Other text books state that any of the three residual techniques can be used
with any of the four methods of capitalization, except straight capitalization
in perpetuity.[10] The present author feels that it is impossible to so combine
the techniques and methods of capitalization. It is contended that 'the straight
line' method of capitalization should only be used with either the Land or
Building Residual, while the annuity methods of capitalization should only be
used with the Property Residual Technique. If these contentions can be

accepted, much of the mystery surrounding the income approach disappears; in the two 'true' residual techniques, the basic steps are:

		Land residual	Building residual
1 Net revenue		I_T	I_T
2 Deduct $V_B \times (R + r) =$		I_B $V_L \times R = I_L$	
3 Residual net revenue		I_L	I_B
4 Capitalize $\dfrac{I_L}{R}$	$=$	V_L $\dfrac{I_B}{R+r} = V_B$	
5 Add		V_B	V_L
6 Estimate of value		V_T	V_T

I_T, I_B, I_L — Net income: total, to building, to land

V_T, V_B, V_L — Value: total, of building, of land

Land residual technique

We have seen that, in the accepted theory, land as an agent in production receives the gross revenue not required to pay for the services of labour, co-ordination and capital; land is residual. But in practice, use of the Land Residual Technique is inadvisable for two reasons. First, we must know the value of the buildings and this is impossible to estimate unless similar structures on leased land have sold in the market. The alternative is to use depreciated cost, and this rarely reflects 'value.'

Secondly, the technique is very volatile and minor variations in estimates of gross revenue, expenses or risk rates can produce large variations in the residual income to land. Land value is generally a small part of the total property value, so any errors in the above estimates are magnified in the final result. On the other hand, building value is generally a large proportion of total value so similar errors are minimized in the building residual technique.

The example illustrates the relative volatilities of the two techniques arising from varying the risk rate by 1% either way; assume 50-year recapture.

Land residual

Risk rate	Net revenue	Deduct income attributable to building value of $242,350: I = V \times (R + r)$	Residual income attributable to land $V = \dfrac{I}{R}$	Indicated residual land value
8%	$28,035	@10% (8% + 2%) = $24,235	$3,765 ÷ 8%	$47,000
9%	28,035	@11% (9% + 2%) = 26,658	1,377 ÷ 9%	15,300
10%	28,035	@12% (10% + 2%) = 29,082	ϕ ÷ 12	ϕ

Building residual

Risk rate	Net revenue	Deduct income attributable to land value of $95,900: (I = V x R)	Residual income attributable to building $V = \dfrac{I}{R + r}$	Indicated residual building value
8%	$28,035	@ 8% = $7,673	$20,362 ÷ 10	$203,620
9%	28,035	@ 9% = 8,631	19,404 ÷ 11	176,400
10%	28,035	@10% = 9,590	18,445 ÷ 12	153,700

In changing the rate from 8% to 9% and also from 9% to 10% the variations in 'value' under the Land Residual are much greater proportionately than in the Building Residual.

Under identical assumptions as to revenue, expenses and risk rate, and using fully supportable estimates of value of the building or the land, the estimate of value by the land residual will be identical with that obtained under the building residual technique. But in light of the volatility of the former and lack of such in the latter technique, it is clearly preferable to use the building residual just in case one or more of our assumptions are not fully correct.[11]

An illustration of the land residual technique follows. The problem was whether a new multi-storey office building should be erected on a 60' x 90' site or whether a neighbouring 43' x 90' site should also be acquired. This shows the proper place of the technique in the appraiser's tool kit, namely to estimate the value of a site under a series of hypothetical buildings.

Assumption I	Assumption II
Site – 60' x 90' – 5400 sq. ft.	103' x 90' = 9270 sq. ft.
Estimated building cost – $1,613,000	$2,727,000
Gross building area – 65,000 sq. ft.	118,000 sq. ft.
Efficiency ratio – 79%	83%

Site valuation

Estimated net revenue	$214,500	$391,760
Less income attributable to building cost:		
$1,613,000 x 11% (9% + 2%)	177,400	$2,727,000 x 11% = 299,970
Residual income to land	$ 37,100	$ 91,790
Capitalized at 9% = land value	412,000	928,000
Indicated sq. ft. land value	$ 76	$ 100

The efficiency ratio (rentable to gross area) increased from 79% to 83%, the ratio of expenses to gross revenue remained the same and a 'plottage increment' of $24 per square foot accrued to the site.

Building residual technique

This is the only 'true' residual technique which is of general application, as is clear from the requirement that the 'straight line' method of capitalization must be used with all 'non-annuity type' incomes: most leases of improved properties are short term and the tenants do not have 'annuity' type covenants.

The procedure is just the opposite of that in the land residual. We want to find net income 'residual' to the building and so we deduct from total income sufficient to represent the earnings of the land, by multiplying the site value by the risk rate.

The technique requires a supportable estimate of the value of the site. This is almost always obtainable; sales of vacant land (or of land with worthless buildings on it) are far more common than are sales of buildings (without the land); if there are no such sales other methods of estimating site value have been pointed out.

Using our illustrative apartment building, the following are the computations:[12]

Net revenue	$ 25,452
Less income attributable to land – $25,000 x 8.8%	2,200
Residual income attributable to building	23,252
Capitalized at 11.3% (8.8% + 2.5%) building value	205,769
Add land value	25,000
Estimated value by income approach, say	$231,000

The property residual technique

This is not a 'residual' technique in the same sense that the land and building residuals are. The net income is not divided between land and building so there is no residual income 'left over.' Rather the income is treated as flowing from the property as a whole and is converted into an estimate of its present worth.

However, it is a residual technique in another sense which cannot be fully understood unless one accepts a further contention of the author that the property residual technique can be used only with annuity type incomes. This requires that either Inwood or Hoskold be used to estimate the present worth of the income stream to which the present worth of the reversionary value of the property at the end of the Inwood or Hoskold period is added.

The procedure can be summarized as follows:

1 Estimate net revenue.
2 Compute present worth of this by multiplying by an Inwood or Hoskold factor.
3 Add reversionary value of the property at the end of the Inwood or Hoskold period using a deferment factor (this is the 'residual' value).
4 The resultant sum represents the value of the property.

Assume that a new building on a $20,000 site is under net lease to a municipal government for $10,000 a year for 40 years and that this is also the estimated period of the building's future revenue earning life and also an acceptable 'recapture' period; this means that at the end of the 40-year lease the building will have no reversionary value. The appropriate risk rate is 9%.

Present worth – Inwood – 40 years, 9% – 10.757 x $10,000 $100,757
Deferment – 40 years, 9% – 0.0318 x $20,000 (land value)   <u>636</u>
Indicated value of the property $101,393

IV INTERESTS IN LEASED PROPERTIES

The appraisal of these 'lease' interests is the simplest valuation problem facing
the appraiser. This is due first to the nature of the lessor – lessee relationship
and secondly to the assumptions implicit in the valuation approach.

The lessor (i.e. the 'owner') of real property gives up his right to use it in
return for periodic payments of rental. His remaining rights are:

the right to receive the rent;
the right to get his property back at the end of the lease.

The sum of the money equivalent of these two rights is the value of the
'leased fee' estate or the lessor's interest.

But this may not be the end of the matter. If at the date of the appraisal the
lessor is receiving in rent the same amount that the property would command
if available to rent on the open market, then the value of the lessor's interest
will be equal to the value of the property. However, if the rent being paid is
less than this market rent, then we have a 'lessee's' (i.e. 'leasehold') interest,
the value of which will be the present worth of the difference between the
annual contract and market rents for the remainder of the lease.

Appraisal theory uses two definitions of rent which must be understood:

Contract rent – This is the rental actually called for in the lease; it is fixed
in amount.
Economic rent[13] – This is the amount of rent the property would command
on the market if no lease existed; it will fluctuate with the
market demand for the type of property in question.

The appraisal assumptions are twofold. In the first place, the concept of
lease interests is, under the accepted theory, only applicable if the net rent
received under a lease has the characteristics of an annuity. This implies that
the lease must have a considerable number of years to run and that the covenant of the lessee must be such that there is no question as to his ability to pay
the rent even though he vacates the premises.[14] Secondly, the reversionary
interest of the lessor is based on the current value of the land plus the value of
buildings at the end of the lease; it is computed by means of a deferment table.

The appraiser must consider three variables, namely the current value of land,
the current market rent of the property, assuming it was not under lease, and
the appropriate rate of return to represent the risk in light of the lessee's covenant. Both Inwood and Hoskold have built-in recapture factors so only when

the question of the reversionary interest of the lessor at the end of the lease period arises need we consider future building life; many lease interests do not involve buildings at all, arising rather under ground leases.

Let us look at some simple examples.

Ground leases – fixed rental

Example 1: This is the simplest type of lease-interest problem. Assume a 21-year renewable lease for a parcel of land with the AAA lessee paying a net annual rental of $7000 at the end of each year plus all taxes and other charges. Market conditions indicate that the appropriate risk rate is 7% and that the market value of the site is $100,000.[15]

Present worth of right to receive $7000 per year for 21 years	
Inwood factor, 7%, 10.836 x $7,000	$ 75,852
Present worth of reversion	
Deferment factor: 21 years 7%, 0.2451 x $100,000	24,150
Total value of lessor's interest, say	$100,000

Example 2: Now let us assume that the above ground lease has been in effect for 5 years (i.e. 16 years still to run) and that the market value of the site is now $150,000, so the market rental would be $150,000 x 7% = $10,500. This gives rise to a lessee's interest equal to the present worth of $10,500 - $7,000 = $3,500 for the next 16 years, computed at a higher risk rate than the 7% applicable to the lessor's interest.[16]

The following computations show the estimated value of the two interests:

Lessor's interest ('leased fee')

Present worth of right to receive $7,000 per year for 16 years	
Inwood factor, 7%, 9.447 x $7,000	$ 66,129
Present worth of reversion	
Deferment factor: 16 years 7%, 0.3387 x $150,000	50,805
Total value of lessor's interest	$116,934

Lessee's interest ('leasehold')

Present worth of $3,500 per year for 16 years	
Inwood factor, 9%, 8.313 x $3,500	29,095
Indicated total value of all interests, say	$147,000

The sum of the two interests is about $3,000 less than the $150,000 market value. If the lessee had actually sublet to an AAA subtenant, a 7% risk rate would be used for the lessee's interest and the sum would be $150,000.

Ground lease – graduated rental

Example 3: If the ground lease called for annual rentals (at the end of each year) of $7,000 for the first 7 years, $8,000 for the next 7 years and $9,000 for the final 7 years, and if the current market value of the site was $100,000, the computations are a little more complicated. The lease is for 21 years and the rent varies every 7 years, so to compute the present worth of the right to receive the annual rent we must account for each of the 7-year periods in order, having in mind that the last two such periods do not start immediately, but only after the lapse of 7 and 14 years, respectively.

The procedure can then be tabulated as follows:

Period	Time of its start	Deferment & duration
Initial 7-year period	starts at once	No deferment required, go to end of 7th year
Second 7-year period	starts in 7 years	Defer start 7 years; go to end of 14th year
Third 7-year period	starts in 14 years	Defer start 14 years; go to end of 21st year

We can now translate this into arithmetic terms:

Lessor's interest			P/W of rental
Present worth of right to receive rental			
Initial 7-year period – $7,000 per year for 7 years			
Inwood factor 7% – 7 years 5.389 x $7,000		=	$37,723
Second 7-year period – $8,000 per year for 7 years starting in 7 years			
Inwood factor 14 years 7%	8.745		
Subtract Inwood factor 7 years 7%	5.389		
Inwood factor 7 years deferred 7 years	3.356 x $8,000	=	26,848[17]
Third 7-year period – $9,000 per year for 7 years starting in 14 years			
Inwood factor 21 years 7%	10.835		
Subtract Inwood factor 14 years at 7%	8.745		
Inwood factor 7 years deferred 14 years	2.092 x $9,000	=	18,810
Indicated present worth of right to receive total rental			$83,351
Present worth of reversion			
Deferment factor, 21 years @ 7% – 0.2415 x $100,000		=	24,150
Indicated value of lessor's interest, say			$107,500

All kinds of variations can be introduced into the above pattern. For instance, if the lessee could sublet at an annual rental of $9,500, we can estimate the value of the lessee's interest in the difference between $9,500 and the contract rents of $7,000, $8,000 and $9,000 over the appropriate 7-year periods by combining the computations of examples 2 and 3; as the market level of rental is now $9,500 the implication is that the market value of the property has increased to about $135,000 and this is the figure to use in computing the lessor's reversionary interest.

Improved property

Two additional problems arise when considering lease interests in an improved property; first, the rental payable under the lease may be gross and hence must be reduced to a net figure in the manner described in Chapter 10.

Secondly, the improvements will be gradually depreciating during the term of the lease and the lessor's reversionary interest must reflect this. The most straightforward method of estimating what the value of the improvements will be at the end of the lease is to project the probable amount of depreciation (of all sorts) which will accrue between the date of appraisal and the termination of the lease. In practice, the use of a straight line depreciation projection appears justifiable; it is difficult to isolate factors of functional and economic obsolescence which have occurred over the past life of a building and impossible to forecast these over its future life. Also, deferment factors used to compute the reversion minimize errors in estimating future depreciation; with a 7% risk rate and a 21-year lease the deferment factor is 0.2415, so that any error in estimating depreciation is reduced by the discounting process from 100% to 24%.

There is one further pitfall; in computing the present worth of the lessor's contract rent and of any lessee's interest, it would be 'double-counting' to allow for the future depreciation of the building. Inwood and Hoskold factors include an allowance for recapture which in this case is the same as future depreciation.

Example 4: Assume that an improved property (including the site used in Example 1 and a new building costing $300,000 which improves the site to its highest and best so that cost and value coincide) is under a 21-year lease. The net contract and market rental is $39,000 per year in arrears and the appropriate risk rate is 9%, while the investment is to be recaptured over 40 years. (The example computes only the lessor's interest; estimates of a lessee's interest in an improved property are made in the same way as in ground leases.)

Applying straight line depreciation of 2.5% per year, the building will have a remaining value at the end of the lease of $142,500 to which must be added $100,000 to represent land value.

Lessor's interest

Present worth of right to receive rent:
Inwood factor 9%, 21 years 9.292 x $39,000 $362,388
Present worth of reversion:
Deferment factor 9%, 21 years 0.1637 x $242,500   39,693
Indicated value of lessor's interest, say $402,000

Interests in special types of leases

Revaluation lease

Most leases call for either fixed or graduated rentals and if they contain renewal options, will set out the way in which the amount of the renewal rental is to be determined. A common provision is that if the parties cannot agree on this rental, the matter will be decided by a board consisting of one nominee of each party and a third nominee appointed by the other two. No special problems are involved in estimating the value or the rental under such leases.

Index leases

This is a refinement of the revaluation lease, with periodic changes in the rental being determined in relation to some common index such as cost of living.

Percentage leases

Under these leases the tenant generally pays a fixed minimum rental plus an appropriate percentage of gross sales over a certain level. (Tables of these percentages are available, but must be interpreted in light of local market conditions.)

Two special problems arise in appraising interests under such leases.

First, any lessee's interest will normally be confined to the fixed minimum rental; the percentage, if in keeping with market conditions, will not result in any favourable lessee's position.

Secondly, a projection of the annual amount of percentage rent which may be paid by each tenant must be made in order to compute the lessor's interest. The procedure is to estimate what the gross sales per square foot should be for the tenant in question and then apply the given percentage to the excess of such gross sales revenue above the minimum called for in the lease. The risk rate used to capitalize the percentage portion should be higher than that used to capitalize the fixed minimum part of the rents; while the tenant's covenant applies to both parts of the rental, the minimum is 'guaranteed' while the percentage is not. The following computations were made for a supermarket; it was felt that gross sales would not be high enough to call for payment of any percentage rent for 3 years. (Some figures rounded.)

Example 5:

Present worth of minimum rental

Area occupied	Minimum rent	Unit rent	Term of lease	Risk rate	Inwood factor	Present worth of minimum rental
25,000 sq. ft.	$67,500	$2.70	20 yrs	9%	10.274	$689,000

Present worth of percentage rental

Area occupied	Estimated gross sales per sq. ft.	% of gross sales	Estimated[18] percentage rental	Risk rate	Inwood[19] factor 37 yrs deferred 3 years	Present worth of % rental
25,000 sq. ft.	$200	1.5%	$7,500	15%	4.359	$ 32,700
Present worth of total rent						$721,000

The following tabulates the assumptions of the accepted appraisal theory on the four capitalization methods with an annual net revenue of $5,000. (9% risk)

Method	Income pattern	Outstanding investment				Estimates of value		
		Income treated as a whole or 'split'	Pattern	Interest earned	Recapture	20 years	100 years	In perpetuity
1 Straight capitalization	fixed in amount	whole	fixed	annually	none			$55,555
2 Inwood	fixed in amount	whole	declines regularly in increasing	annually on outstanding balance	increases regularly in increasing amounts: must earn risk rate compounded or will fall short of total invested	$45,640	$55,545	$55,555
						Plus reversion		
3 a Hoskold	fixed in amount	whole	fixed for period then drops to 0	annually on original investment plus safe rate on sinking fund	fixed amounts but growing annually at compound interest at safe rate	$39,305	$54,555	$55,555
						Plus reversion		
b Risk rate + sinking fund	fixed in amount	whole	as in Hoskold	as in Hoskold	as in Hoskold	$39,308	$54,555	$55,555
						Plus reversion		
4 'Straight line'	considerable annual decline	'split' between land & building	declines regularly in equal amounts	annually on outstanding balance	increases regularly in equal amounts: no interest earned on recapture	$39,285	$51,000	

The patterns of outstanding investment, net rental and recapture assumed under the different methods are illustrated in the following diagrams which are not, however, drawn to scale. Horizontal axes show time; vertical axes show level of outstanding investment, net rental and recapture.

Outstanding investment (——————)
Net rental (··············)
Recapture (— — — —)

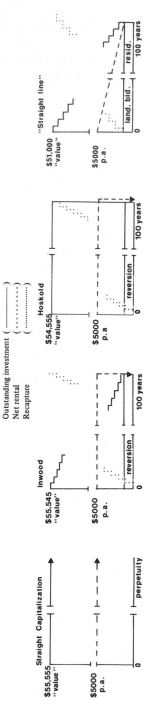

Appraising under evolving financing techniques

Within the context of this book no analysis is possible of the new financing techniques such as mortgagee participation, sale-leaseback, sale-buyback, sale contract (this, of course, is not new by any means, but its application to investment properties is), wrap-around mortgage, joint venture, trust arrangement, etc. The appraiser is cautioned to seek competent outside advice if faced with such assignments unless he is familiar with the problems and required analyses.

REFERENCES

1 / A simple factor is derived by dividing a rate into 100. Using 8% the factor is $\frac{100}{.08}$ = 12.5.

2 / A.I.C. Text, p. 207, calles this method 'Straight Line Capitalization' and this is an accepted term.

3 / Some books call the 'sinking fund' table an 'amortization' table; this is incorrect.

4 / To find the recapture rate, divide the estimated future period of income expectancy into 100. At 500 years it would be .002.

5 / Both 'present worth' and 'deferment tables' show present worth, but Inwood or Hoskold give factors for a 'flow' of income. They show 'The Present Value of $1 per annum.' The Deferment table deals with a 'stock' (i.e. a property) which will not be received until some time in the future. It shows 'The Present Value of $1.'

6 / The description given of Inwood as providing for reinvestment of the periodic payments at the risk rate is not strictly correct and is used to highlight the fact that if the 'safe' rate in Hoskold is the same as the risk rate, the Hoskold factor is the same as Inwood; and as Hoskold provides for reinvestment, in this case at the risk rate, interest must be earned in Inwood or the two factors would not coincide.

But in Inwood, as in amortizing mortgage, the amount of interest on the outstanding capital is declining while the periodic returns of principal are increasing and these returns of principal must be re-invested if interest is to be earned on the total investment. In Hoskold both of these flows are constant in amount but the latter flow earns compound interest.

If Hoskold with, say, a 3% reinvestment rate is used, the appropriate risk rate will be lower than that in Inwood if the same amount is to be paid for an asset producing a given income stream. The tables will show that, say, for a 20-year period the Hoskold 9% factor is 7.861, almost the same as Inwood 11% which is 7.963. One reason Inwood must command a higher rate is the greater burden of management; if an investor is to earn 11% on his total investment, he must regularly reinvest the partial returns of principal.

7 / As shown in Chapter 14, the Ellwood principle is based primarily on Inwood.

8 / The 'period' can be whatever we want it to be for any particular problem.

9 / In Canada most rentals are paid monthly in advance: tables have been published by Harvey P. Jeffers. A.I.C. publishes monthly tables, compounded semi-annually in arrears.

10 / A.I.C. Text, Chapter 17, and A.I.R.E.A. Text, Chapter 19.

11 / The author has *never* had an actual appraisal problem for the use of the Land Residual Technique as the main method of capitalization.

12 / With net revenue of $25,452 the Inwood rate to develop a value of $230,000 with 40 years recapture is about 11% as multiplying $25,452 by the 11% factor of 8.951 will

show. A risk rate lower than that on mortgages is appropriate in the building residual technique as amortized mortgages are based on Inwood-like compounding.

13 / The term 'Economic Rent' shows inconsistent use of terms in appraisal jargon. The meaning for appraisers is as given in the text. But for economists, the term for 200 years describes the difference between the payment made to any agent in production in fixed supply (at least in the short run), and its transfer earnings. A sports star earns say $80,000; his transfer earnings in his best alternative occupation (say shaving with 'cut em' razor blades) would yield him $5000 a year. The difference of $75,000 is his economic rent.

$$\text{Using symbols} \quad \begin{aligned} C &= \text{Contract rent} \\ M &= \text{Market rent if no lease} \\ E &= \text{Economic rent} \end{aligned}$$

To the economist: $E = C - M$; this will be positive if C exceeds M as in the above example and negative if M exceeds C; in either case it is the difference between C and M.

In appraisal theory: $E = M$; so $C = 0$ which means the property is not under lease and yet the concept of economic rent only arises in appraisal theory when there is a lease, as is clear in A.I.C. Text. See also Chapter 4, Reference 10; also Chapter 16. Surely 'economic rent' in the appraisal sense should be called 'market rent.'

14 / Bignall v. Metro Toronto (1957) O.W.N., 408 indicates that a lessee's interest may arise in a 'distinct probability' of lease renewal; Murray v. Metro Toronto (1962) O.W.N., 173 did not follow this since Murray was only a monthly tenant. Section 18(2) of the Ontario Expropriation Act and Section 24(1) of the federal act both provide for consideration of the reasonable prospects of renewal.

15 / The lessor's interest in a ground lease is often estimated by straight capitalization at the risk rate.

16 / The lessee could either sublet and earn $3500 a year or continue to use the site for $3500 less than any one else could ... this $3500 is analogous to 'economic rent' in the true sense of the term. If he sublets, we get a 'sandwich' position: the lessee-in-chief becomes the sub-lessor and so occupies a dual position as both lessor and lessee. The appropriate risk rate for lessees' interests depends on the covenant of the sub-lessee if one exists or if no sublease, on the competitive position of the lessee-in-chief.

17 / An alternative method of deriving the 'deferred' factor is to multiply the present worth factor by the deferment factor

Inwood factor – 7% – 7 years	5.389
Multiplied by 7% deferment factor – 7 years	0.6227
Present worth factor for 7 years deferred 7 years	3.356

18 / The computation is:

Total rental on percentage 25,000 sq. ft. x $200 x 1.5% =		$75,000
Minus minimum fixed rental	=	67,500
Indicated percentage 'overage'		$ 7,500

19 / The computation is:

Inwood factor – 15%, 40 years	6.642
Inwood factor – 15%, 3 years	2.283
Inwood factor 15%, 37 years deferred 3 years	4.359

13

Final correlation and the appraisal report

I CORRELATION AND THE FINAL
ESTIMATE OF VALUE

Throughout this book we have been discussing various things which the appraiser does to develop an estimate of value. In the interests of clarity and also because our system of communication via the written or spoken work requires it, we have looked at these various matters separately. But none of the factors which influence the use (and hence the value) of real property operate in a vacuum. They are to a greater or lesser degree interrelated and so to a greater or lesser degree they can be correlated to produce a clearer overall picture than that obtained by looking at a single factor in isolation.[1] Consider for a moment a motion picture: the posters and advertisements show isolated shots, but to really know the whole story one must buy a ticket and see the show.

The appraiser's general background knowledge should extend to many of the diverse extremes of national, provincial and local history, it should include a recognition of the fact that every province, county and community has been affected differently by these historical happenings, and, of course, the difference between the effects of similar forces on property in different countries may be in direct contrast. Therefore he should be careful in applying principles developed under physical, social, economic and political conditions which vary from those with which he is concerned.

This being the case, it is natural that the appraiser should be consciously and constantly relating different matters affecting the property he is evaluating. He knows that the general background of real property in his province and city has been formed by the interplay of the same types of forces as those which are influencing it now. Therefore he must have a good general grasp of this historical background, not just as a source of factual information, but also as a means of relating causal factors with their probable effects on the present, near future and distant future use and value of individual properties and their neighbourhoods. This is correlation and all the basic 'principles' discussed in Chapter 3 should be considered.

In most appraisals the general and city background is taken as 'given' and, rather than being spelled out formally, is used as a sieve in the thought-processes of the appraiser. Certain key factors of a general nature sift through for use in the particular analysis at hand: the bulk of the general data remains in the 'hopper' of the appraisal plant, having no direct applicability at the moment. The matters of direct concern do not generally extend beyond the neighbour-hood in which the property is located and the way in which this neighbour-hood is connected to the larger community. These connections are physical (for instance, topography and transportation), social (for instance, the religious and ethnic background of the residents of the neighbourhood, relative to those of the population as a whole), economic (for instance, the median income of the neighbourhood relative to that of the city) and political (for instance, the zoning in the neighbourhood as compared to that of the city as a whole).

But while the general analysis will normally be confined to a few basic fac-tors affecting the neighbourhood, its whole purpose is to try and relate the desirability of one neighbourhood to that of another. It is an inter-neighbour-hood analysis. This is correlation, and again all the basic 'principles' should be considered.

The appraiser then goes further and considers the variations in physical, social, economic and political factors within the neighbourhood; this is an intra-neighbourhood analysis. The very concept of a neighbourhood implies only minor social, economic and political variations; major variations will gen-erally be confined to physical differences between streets and properties. How-ever a steadily increasing proportion of the appraiser's work is related to pro-perties in neighbourhoods which are changing in character: such change is generally social and economic in the first stages, then political and physical. The appraiser must analyse the evidence of such changes and tie them to-gether. This is correlation. While all the basic 'principles' should be considered, those of conformity, change, balance, substitution and highest and best use will be most important.

Next we find the appraiser inspecting and analysing the actual property. He is concerned with it both as part of the neighbourhood and as an individual property. As part of the neighbourhood it must be considered in the light of its physical, social, economic and political advantages and disadvantages rela-tive to other properties which may cause economic obsolescence.[2] This is cor-relation and the most important of the basic 'principles' to consider will be conformity, change, balance, contribution, substitution and highest and best use.

As an individual property, the analysis considers the way in which the agents in production have been combined and whether such combination is fixed or fluid. If the agents have been rigidly combined, the principles of conformity, change and highest and best use are dominant: the property can be modified in minor and superficial ways to meet changing needs, but shifts in such needs and requirements can only be met by demolishing the building and using the vacant site or rebuilding on it; locational and functional obsolescence will be unavoidable. Interior bearing-wall and/or reinforced concrete construction generally implies rigidity of plan and function.

If the agents in production have been flexibly combined, adaptation of a property to meet changing needs may be possible within a wide range of choice; the effects of functionak obsolescence can be minimized. Such flexibility is inherent in curtain wall construction, particularly when combined with the provision of open space within and around the building. The principles of balance, contribution, substitution and diminishing returns are dominant and adaptation of the property to meet the challenges of the principles of change and of highest and best use become possible. Such an analysis of the property is correlation.

From the above, it is clear that the concept of correlation permeates the appraisal process at least in the intangible thought processes of the appraiser. It takes on tangible form in the actual valuation phases.

In the market data approach:

the appraiser must consider various similar properties for which sale, rental or listing data are available and relate each to the subject property. The most important 'principles' will be change, balance, substitution and highest and best use. This entails correlation.

In the cost approach:

the appraiser must analyse and estimate the current reproduction cost of the building and also the dollar amounts of all accrued depreciation which a prospective purchaser would probably deduct from such cost, when deciding how much he would pay for the property. This entails correlation.

He must also estimate the current value of the site by one or more of the methods of valuation available to him. These entail correlation.

In the income approach:

the appraiser must have estimated anticipated and effective gross revenue, operating expenses and allowances and by subtraction have obtained an estimate of net revenue: this entails correlation.

he must select appropriate risk and recapture rates: this entails correlation.

he must select the appropriate method of capitalization to fit the pattern of the income stream in question and this automatically dictates the appropriate residual technique: this entails correlation.

if 'straight line' capitalization is appropriate, he must estimate the value of the land (or possibly on very rare occasions that of the building): this entails correlation.

So in each of the approaches to value, correlation is carried on throughout. If only one approach is either possible or relevant, then the correlation in it is also the final correlation and the estimate of value derived from the single approach is the final estimate of value. But in any single approach, there may be a number of sub-approaches. For instance, in the market data approach, separate estimates of value may have been based on direct market comparison, on the ratio of assessed values to sale prices and on the basis of market trends in value applied to an earlier purchase price of the subject property. Each of these separate value estimates must, of course, be correlated into a final estimate of value by the overall approach in question. But with many properties it is both customary and possible to use at least two approaches. In such cases three (or two) separate estimates of value will have been developed and the term 'final correlation' applies to the process of arriving at a single supportable estimate.

When correlating, the appraiser is really mentally weighing alternatives. His thoughts will be directed towards the adequacy and the reliability of the various data on which the different approaches are based and upon the purpose for which the appraisal was carried out.

Whenever the three approaches are used, it is obvious that we will have a 'bracket' including one high estimate, one low and one intermediate (unless two or more of the estimates coincide as, of course, they would in the long run under 'perfect' market conditions). The appraiser must first consider whether the 'bracket' is so wide as to indicate either mathematical error in the earlier computations or the inapplicability of one or more of the approaches to the problem in hand. For instance, if the appraisal has the secondary purpose of providing an estimate of value for fire insurance purposes with a replacement rider, then for this purpose all three estimates are irrelevant in their normal form and only the estimate of reproduction cost less physical depreciation is cogent.[3]

If the main purpose is to estimate market value, the appraiser will consider the relevance of each approach and the data used in these. He has a certain range of estimated values and within that range lies the actual estimate he will report; there is a probability distribution within which lies the 'most probable selling price.' See Chapter 16, Reference 26. Re-examination of the data and of the steps taken may disclose reasons to change the estimate arrived at by some approach to narrow the range.

The accepted theory on the mechanics of correlation has at least until recently been, that while three separate estimates based on the three approaches should be developed whenever possible, the final estimate reported should be based entirely upon one of these: in particular, the theory has taught that any averaging of the three estimates is wrong. The implication is that the final correlation, should be entirely narrative in form.

In practice·the author finds a purely narrative correlation has at least three shortcomings:

in the first place it is often impossible to explain thought processes adequately in words without using a great number of them.

secondly, a fully narrative correlation is apt to be general in character and hence relatively uninformative to the client or what is perhaps more important to his legal counsel or a court.

thirdly, many advisors of average clients are accountants and engineers whose training and experience is based to some degree on mathematical figures and computations rather than on words.

Therefore, the author combines a narrative correlation with the allocation of percentage weights to the estimates developed by each approach: he then rounds the resultant 100% weight figure and reports this as the final estimate of value. The reader is cautioned that this method of correlation may not satisfy the requirements of A.I.C. or A.I.R.E.A. and so its use in demonstration reports for these Institutes is risky; it has been included in this book for the main reason that in practice it works. The author feels that theory must work in practice and that supporting a narrative correlation with mathematical weighting of the three estimates does so, while the unsupported narrative correlation does not. It should be pointed out that A.I.C. Text, p. 266, describes a weighting procedure with approval.

II THE APPRAISAL REPORT

When the appraiser goes through the appraisal process and correlates the three estimates of value into a final estimate, he must communicate his findings to other people, by means of the appraisal report and, like all communications, this is his way of making his thought processes available to them. The particular medium of transmission is the written word and if the transmission is to be made without distortion, the appraiser must choose his words well and combine them clearly and properly. This implies a good basic vocabulary and an adequate grasp of spelling, grammar and syntax. It also implies self-restraint; it is sometimes simpler to say nothing in a hundred words than to say something in twenty.

The report is the visible evidence of the appraiser's efforts to resolve a problem. It should therefore be the best such evidence which the individual practitioner can produce. And by 'best' we mean 'best' for the job in hand. Just as the variety of real property problems is infinite, so is the variety of methods of reporting. The appraiser will do well to give considerable thought to his reporting techniques and to be constantly on the look-out for ways in which he can better these. It has been the experience of the author that such betterment normally arises from the elimination of non-essential matter rather than from the inclusion of essential. If the practitioner is experienced, keeps an open mind, and is well versed in the underlying theory, he will rarely omit much essential material: the very character of the appraisal process guards against this. The difficulty arises rather in the fact that many appraisers seem to hate to throw out anything that is even remotely connected with the problem at hand.[4] The report is meant to paint a word picture of the appraiser's conclusions and his reasons for reaching these. The clearer and more concise the picture, the better it will be understood by all concerned.

Many texts imply that the report should lead the reader to the same conclusions as that reached by the appraiser. It has been the experience of the author that in practice it is often impossible to get the client to share the appraiser's conclusions, particularly in expropriation matters; therefore, one of the important jobs the report must do is to jolt the client out of some preconceived notions. This is sometimes done best by analysis and conclusions highlighting the key unfavourable factors. For example, in one expropriation the client kept saying that under the zoning his property could be redeveloped with a 12-storey office building (it was a corner site in a run-down central area of a western city). Part of the appraisal consisted of a series of land residual techniques with hypothetical new buildings of various sizes. Such analyses showed the client and his lawyer that redevelopment under the 'highest and best use' permitted by the zoning, was, in fact, not indicated by the market.

Reference to Chapter 1 will show that an appraisal report has five essential parts. It is:

1 a written, signed opinion of the value of an
2 adequately described property made as of
3 a specified date, which evaluates the
4 property rights involved according to
5 a defined concept of value.

The practising appraiser will probably use three different types of report which in their order of length (and in inverse order of the originality of their composition) may be described as:

Form report: these are generally used for mass appraising such as assessment and mortgage assignments. The forms provided by the client contain spaces for completion by the appraiser with the appropriate information as well as his narrative comments.

Letter appraisals: these vary from a one-page statement of the appraiser's opinion of value to a fairly comprehensive seven- or eight-page letter which includes all the material found in a formal report. The appraiser, when evaluating a single family dwelling, may well decide (except in expropriation matters) that a letter is more in keeping with the requirements of the client (and, of course, the fee!) than a formal report. However, the amount of data he must gather and analyse is largely independent of the type of report: he needs all available sales data whether giving his opinion of value in a single page, a four-page letter or a 30-page formal report.

It is good practice for a busy, experienced appraiser to develop a combined 'form' and 'letter' report; the author has several to suit various needs and has also assisted clients who have mass or semi-mass appraisal requirements in developing appropriate form or letter reports for their particular needs.

Narrative reports: This is the normal form in which a professional appraiser reports to his client[5] and everything which can be said about them is applicable in lesser degree to both the form and the letter report. It is only in a fairly detailed report that the appraiser can hope to fully express in words his thought processes. A systematic order should be followed and the report should be broken down into the various parts which it logically contains. Everyone will set up his report differently; the following is the way the author does it.

Introduction

This includes the table of contents, the letter of transmittal, a summary of conclusions, the legal description of the property, the purpose and the effective date of the appraisal, a statement of highest and best use, and perhaps a photograph of the property. The most important of these items are:

Letter of transmittal
This is a formal letter under cover of which the report is sent to the client: it should include the amount of the final estimate of value, although if a number of estimates are relevant, then a page can be inserted following the letter in which important conclusions are summarized. The author includes his certificate in this letter.

Legal description of property
As noted earlier, there is only one valid description and that is the one found in the appropriate title registration office. In addition to the legal description, physical dimensions can also be set out as can details of assessment, ownership, acquisition and so forth. The author in practice leaves the physical description to a later stage.

Purpose, effective date and highest and best use
Formal definitions of the 'purpose' and 'highest and best' use are essential as is a statement of the effective date. The key to the whole appraisal process is the highest and best use.

Descriptive data

This includes the description of the city, neighbourhood and property. It should contain such of the information mentioned in earlier chapters as appears relevant in light of the purpose of the appraisal.

The valuation

This includes a narrative and mathematical description of the various approaches used.

Conclusion

This includes the correlation of the individual estimates by the different approaches into a final estimate of value.

It also includes a statement setting out any underlying assumptions or contingent conditions; the appraiser must be careful not to so restrict the admissibility of his findings as to render the report useless to his client. The author's practice is to sign this final page of the report proper; some appraisers prefer to sign the correlation page immediately below the final estimate of value.

Appendices

The report proper should be kept free of digressions such as detailed descriptions, analyses, explanations of techniques. Such detail and even tables of sales and rentals can go in appendices, summarized for inclusion in the body of the report. Diagrams and surveys can also be put in appendices, but a photograph of the subject property is often included in the introductory phase. Qualifications of the appraiser may form an appendix or be put in the introduction.

The format

It is obvious that if a good report is prepared, its impact will be greater if it is well typed on regular report paper and dressed up in an attractive cover. The author uses two embossed covers joined by a continuous plastic circular binding which permits the report to be fully opened at any page. If a 'pin-type' binding is used, care must be taken to leave adequate space on the bound side of the page so that all the typing is visible. Regular report paper has a wide margin on the left side for this reason; the appraiser should probably have his name printed at the foot of each page.

III A CONDENSED APPRAISAL PROBLEM – 484 C. Street, City

The property is a well-located 3-storey and basement apartment with 20 bachelors (1½ rooms), 12 one-bedrooms (2½ rooms) and 1 two-bedroom (4 rooms). Asking price is $250,000, 25% down and 75% in a 9½%, 25-year amortizing mortgage. Appraisal as of May 1, 1971 under normal appraising assumptions and also as if the property is sold in 10 years and appreciated 20% over that period. Investors require 12% on real property equities with such financing which is typical.

A.C.E. Investments, Ltd., federally incorporated and holding a valid licence in mortmain, acquired the site (Lot 15, Plan 1064, City), April 15, 1946, and erected the existing improvements. The original mortgage has been discharged; the above-described financing is available.

Zoning permits apartments covering 50% of a site to a density of 2.5 and 1 parking space per suite on the vacant 50%. New buildings cost $10,000 per suite (average 575 sq. ft.) which rent for $175 plus $8 parking per month; demand for parking is strong. Expenses run at 40% of effective gross (5% vacancies), but are less in lower-rent buildings with less demanding tenants. Risk rate for new buildings is 9% with recapture over 50 years.

Existing building is a legal non-conforming use under the zoning covering all the 45' x 122' site except for two concrete walks 120' long, one 3' and the other 2'6" wide; it is 41'6" high (including basement). Doors give access directly to the living rooms, a deficiency which together with inadequate kitchen cupboards and counters, results in a rental loss of $8.00 per suite. A dairy also a non-conforming use, occupies an L-shaped site next to and behind the subject and results in a rental loss of $15 per month per suite.

Unit costs for subject building are $1.70 per cu. ft., with about 30% of total cost being in the bone structure. Concrete walks cost $9 per lineal foot, 3' wide. New stoves and refrigerators have been put in 30 suites and this must be done for the other 3; halls and suites must also be redecorated at about $190 per suite, including maintenance work on the plaster, floor surfaces, etc. This scale of decorating must be done every 3 years, while stoves and refrigerators should be replaced every 20 years.

The owner-corporation manages the building but an allowance of 2.5% is indicated. A new roof was installed in 1968 as a promotion to introduce a new product; it is bonded for 30 years. New bathroom fixtures, boiler and burners and floor covering were recently installed. These renovations with 20-year normal lives, and those still required for stoves, refrigerators and redecorating should ensure occupancy at current rental levels which are consonant with those reflected in the market.

The owner's operating statement shows:

Gross rental revenue	$38,386
Expenses	
Municipal taxes	$ 3,106
Heat (average, 5 years)	2,163
Power and water (average, 5 years)	387
Insurance (3 years)	1,350
Janitor wages	900
Maintenance and repairs (average, 5 years)	536
Miscellaneous (average, 5 years)	95
Bathroom renovations	9,664
Boiler and burners	11,325
Stoves and refrigerators (30 suites)	9,000
Floor covering	4,228
Mortgage P & I	9,473

Comparable land sales (for market conditions adjust: 1970 – 105%, 1968 – 130%)

Property number	Date of sale	Sale price	Dimensions	Comments
1	Jan. 1971	$45,000	78' x 125'	Location and zoning same as subject
2	Jan. 1971	25,000	44' x 125'	Location and zoning same as subject
3	May 1970	27,500	42'6" x 125'	Location as good as subject but zoning adjustment 80%
4	June 1970	30,000	48'8" x 122'	Zoning same as subject Location adjustment 80%
5	August 1968	28,000	66' x 122'	Location adjustment 105%

Sales of comparable improved properties (all are 1971 sales under normal financing terms; unit reproduction costs are similar to subject's)

Property no.	1	2	3	4
Price	$215,000	$210,000	$225,000	$220,000
No. of suites	29	30	34	33
No. of rooms	58	77	65	68
Gross rental	$33,050	$30,000	$33,595	$34,370
Expenses	$9,400	$8,800	$8,620	$9,730
Cubic feet	178,500	165,000	206,800	206,000
Year built	1945	1942	1945	1944
Lot size	53'6" x 145'	39' x 115'	51'6" x 140'	42'8" x 130'
Site value, sq. ft.	$4.40	$5.20	$4.60	$4.50
Adjust condition & plan	92.5%	110%	95%	100%
Adjust location	97.5%	115%	102.5%	100%

Appraisal Report

Contents

STEWART, YOUNG & MASON LIMITED

Real Estate Appraisers & Consultants

902, NATIONAL BUILDING
347 BAY STREET, TORONTO 1, CANADA
TELEPHONE 363-2023

May 15, 1971

A.C.E. Investments, Ltd.
484 C. Street
City

Dear Sirs:

Appraisal - 484 C. Street, City

Pursuant to your request for an estimate of the market value of the above property, I have examined same and submit herewith estimates thereon.

The accompanying report contains the results of my investigations. In submitting this report I certify as follows:

1 That the within described property has been inspected.
2 That I have no interest, present or contemplated, therein.
3 That my employment in making this appraisal is in no way contingent on the amount of my estimate of value.
4 That this appraisal has been made in conformity with the Rules of Professional Ethics of the Appraisal Institute of Canada.

In my opinion, as of May 1, 1971, the market value of the property was $235,000. It is further my opinion that on the assumption of the property being acquired now and held for 10 years, appreciating 20% in value over that period, the value is $285,000.

Yours very truly,

(signed)
JAMES INNES STEWART

Purpose of the appraisal

The purpose of this appraisal is to estimate the market value of the owner's full 'bundle of rights' in the subject property, as of the effective date of this report. Market value means 'the amount the property will bring if exposed for sale on the open market for sufficient time to find a purchaser who buys with knowledge of all the uses to which it is adapted or for which it is capable of being put.'

A further purpose is to estimate the value of the property under the terms of financing 75% of value by a 9.5%, 25-year amortizing mortgage and assuming appreciation of 20% in the ensuing 10 years and disposal at that time.

Effective date of the appraisal

This appraisal is made as of May 1, 1971.

Legal description and ownership of the property

The property is described as being in the City and being comprised of Lot 15, Plan 1064.

The registered owner is A.C.E. Investments, Ltd. which acquired title under Instrument 63749 registered April 15, 1946. No mortgaged or other indebtedness is registered against title.

Highest and best use of the property

It is the opinion of the appraiser that the highest and best use of the property will be its continued use as an apartment house.

QUALIFICATIONS OF THE APPRAISER

Member

Law Society of Upper Canada, Appraisal Institute of Canada

Professional and educational background

Lecturer in Land Economics and Law – University of Toronto

Institution	Degree received
University of Toronto	B.A., M.B.A., M.A.
Osgoode Hall Law School	Barrister-at-law

Mr Stewart has carried out appraisals and/or lecture assignments in all major communities in Canada.

MARKET DATA APPROACH (some figures rounded)

1 *Derivation of price per suite and gross income multiplier*

Property	Sale price	No. of suites	Price per suite	Gross revenue	G.I.M.
1	$215,000	29	$7,410	$33,050	6.5
2	210,000	30	7,000	30,000	7.0
3	225,000	34	6,620	33,595	6.7
4	220,000	33	6,665	34,370	6.4

Indicated G.I.M. – 6.5

2 *Derivation of 'overall' rate and net income multiplier*

Property	Sale price	Net revenue before recapture	'Overall' rate (net ÷ sale price)
1	$215,000	$23,650	11.0
2	210,00	21,200	10.1
3	225,000	24,975	11.1
4	220,000	24,640	11.2

Indicated 'overall' rate – 11%; indicated net income multiplier – 9.1

3 *Derivation of appropriate per suite value*

Property	Price per suite	Market	Location	Condition	Aggregate[6]	Adjusted price
1	$7,410	100%	97.5%	92.5%	90.1875%	$6,680
2	7,000	100%	115 %	110 %	126.5 %	8,855
3	6,620	100%	102.5%	95 %	97.375 %	6,445
4	6,665	100%	100 %	100 %	100 %	6,665

Indicated price per suite – $6,800

4 *Derivation of appropriate gross rental*

Property	No. of rooms	Gross rental	Monthly rent[7] per room	Aggregate % adjustment	Adjusted rent per room
1	58	$33,050	$57	90.1875%	$51.40
2	77	30,000	39	126.5 %	49.35
3	65	33,595	52	97.375 %	50.65
4	68	34,370	50	100.000 %	50.00

Indicated rent, $50 per room per month; indicated gross for subject $50 x 12 x 64 = $38,400

5 *Correlation*

33 suites @ $6,800 = $224,000)
$38,400 x 6.5   = $249,600)   Correlated value, say $235,000

VALUATION OF THE SITE

1 *Market data method*

Property	Sale price	Price per sq. ft.	Adjustments			Adjusted price per sq. ft.
			Market	Location etc.	Aggregate	
1	$45,000	$4.61	100%	100%	100 %	$4.61
2	25,000	4.54	100%	100%	100 %	4.54
3	27,500	5.17	105%	80%	84 %	4.34
4	30,000	5.05	105%	80%	84 %	4.24
5	28,000	3.47	130%	105%	136.5%	4.74

Indicated value of subject site $4.50 per sq. ft. x 5500 sq. ft. = say, $25,000

2 *Land residual technique*

Hypothetical new 12-suite apartment – cost $120,000

Indicated risk rate	9%
Indicated recepture rate	2%
Indicated capitalization rate	11%

Valuation

Annual gross – 12 suites @ $175 monthly	$25,200
Less vacancies @ 5% of gross	1,260
Effective gross revenue	$23,940
Less expenses – 40% of $23,940	9,570
Estimated annual net rental revenue	$14,370
Parking revenue – $8 x 12 x 12	1,150
Estimated total net revenue	$15,520
Less income attributable to building $120,000 x 11%	13,200
Residual income attributable to land	$ 2,320
Capitalized @ 9% – indicated land value, say	$25,750

3 *Correlation*

a Two approaches have been used:

Market data approach indicates	$25,000
Income approach indicates	$25,750

b The available market data are adequate, so this approach is given sole emphasis, the other estimate implying no gross error in interpreting the market data.

Indicated site value   – $25,000

4 *Indicated land/building ratio*

Of the total value of the property of $235,000 estimated in the market data approach about $25,000 appears to be represented by land so the indicated land/building relationship is about 11% to 89% or, say, 1 to 7.

COST APPROACH

I *Estimated current reproduction cost*

Building proper

200,000 cu. ft. @ $1.70 = $340,000		
Quantity survey (see App. A)	$339,024	
Stoves & refrigerators – 33 @ $300	9,900	
Sidewalk – 220' @ $9.00	2,016	
Total estimated reproduction cost		$350,940

II *Less accrued depreciation*

1 *Observed condition schedule*

a Rehabilitation
   Decorate suites & halls $ 6,191

b Physical deterioration
   i Age life schedule – Appendix A = $41,092 $ 41,092
   ii 'Bone structure' method
       30% of building cost is in bone structure
       i.e. 30% x $340,000 = $102,000
       Actual age as % of optimal age = $\frac{24}{60}$
       $102,000 x $\frac{24}{60}$ = $ 40,800
   iii Correlation
       Bone structure method shows no gross error in
       age life schedule. Place full reliance on latter

c Functional obsolescence curable
   Replace stoves & refrigerators = 3 x $300 $ 900

d Functional obsolescence incurable[8]
   Poor entrance and kitchen facilities
   Rental loss, $8 per suite per month
   Annual rental loss = $3168 x 9.1 = $ 28,828

e Locational obsolescence
   Rental loss, $15 per suite per month
   Annual rental loss = $5940 x 9.1 = $54,054
   Land building ratio = 1 to 7
   Economic obsolescence to building $54,054 x $\frac{7}{8}$ = $ 47,297
   Total estimated accrued depreciation $124,308

2 *Market data interpretation*

The following table indicates the amount of depreciation in the eyes of the
purchaser in each of the comparable sales used in the market data approach
and how it can be applied to the subject property.

This table shows how much each purchaser implicitly depreciated the buildings in the comparable sales used in the Market Data Approach and applies this information to the subject.

Property	Current cost	Sale price	Land value	Building sale price	Acc'd Dep'n	Acc'd Dep'n % of cost	Age	Acc'd Dep'n per year
1	$303,500	$215,000	$34,000	$181,000	$122,500	40.4%	26	1.57%
2	280,500	210,000	23,500	186,500	94,000	33.5%	29	1.15%
3	351,500	225,000	33,200	191,800	159,700	45.4%	26	1.73%
4	350,000	220,000	25,000	195,000	155,000	44.2%	27	1.63%

It appears that purchasers tend to depreciate this type of building at about 1.6% per year. Indicated amount of accrued depreciation of subject building:

24 years x 1.6% = 38.4% x $340,000 = <u>$130,560</u>

Notes: 1 Building sale prices are obtained by deducting land value from sale price.
2 Accrued depreciation is obtained by deducting building sale price from cost.
3 As cubic foot costs are used for comparable, this is used for the subject.

3 *Correlation*

Full reliance is on the estimate developed by the observed condition schedule, the market data analysis disclosing no gross error therein.

III *Valuation*

Estimated reproduction cost	$350,940
Less estimated accrued depreciation	124,308
Estimated depreciated building cost	226,632
Add estimated value of the site	25,000
Estimated value by the cost approach, say	$250,000

INCOME APPROACH

Introduction

The Building Residual Technique is the appropriate capitalization method using straight capitalization plus straight line depreciation. Income attributable to the value of the site at the risk rate is deducted from net revenue; the remaining income which is attributable solely to the building indicates building value when divided by the capitalization rate; to this building value is then added the value of the site. This process with the risk and recapture rates used herein permits a decline of approximately 2% per annum and recaptures the investment in the building over 40 years.

Gross revenue

1 The owner's statement shows annual gross revenue of $38,386.
2 The market data analysis shows annual gross revenue of $38,400.
3 Correlation – The owner's figure of $38,386 is for a year in which there were no vacancies and it is confirmed by the estimate of potential gross from market data, so the owner's figure is used herein. It is felt that to earn this rent the whole building must be redecorated and the suites not already fitted with new stoves and refrigerators must have these installed.

Gross revenue		$38,386
Less 2.5% vacancy allowance		959
Effective gross revenue		$37,427

Expenses[9]

Municipal taxes	$3,200	
Heating	2,200	
Power and water	400	
Insurance	450	
Janitor's wages	900	
Maintenance and repairs	550	
Miscellaneous	100	

Allowances

Decorating	2,060	
Stoves & refrigerators	495	
Bathroom fixtures	240	
Floor covering	100	
Roof	65	
Boiler & burners	280	
Management – 2.5% of effective gross	935	
Total expenses and allowances		11,975
Estimated net revenue		$25,452

Capitalization rate

I *Recapture rate*

The remaining life of the building is about 40 years, so the appropriate recapture rate is 2.5% (i.e. $100 \div 40$).

II *Risk rate*

   1 *Market data analysis*

   This indicates an 'overall' rate of 11% and as this includes both risk and recapture it must be reconstructed to remove any recapture of land. The land/building ratio has been found to be 11% (land) to 89% (building).

Overall rate found	11.0%
Less 'true recapture' rate – 89% x 2.5%	2.2%
Indicated true risk rate	8.8%
Add recapture rate	2.5%
Indicated capitalization rate	11.3%

   2 *Competitive analysis*

   Returns on first mortgages are about 9.5% while those on common and preferred shares are about 4.0% and on real estate equities, about 12%. As real property is a combined debt-equity investment, the indicated risk rate of 8.8% seems to be consonant with general conditions.[10]

3 Projected 10-year disposal

The appropriate overall rate is developed in Chapter 14 as being 8.9%

Processing the net revenue

Estimated net revenue	$ 25,452
Less income attributable to site %25.000 x 8.8%	2,200
Residual income attributable to building	$ 23,252
Capitalized at 11.3%	205,769
Add value of site	25,000
Estimated gross value	$230,769

Less: rehabilitation	$6,191	
curable obsolescence	900	7,091
Estimated value by income approach, say		$224,000

Estimated value under projected 10-year disposal

Estimated net revenue	$ 25,452
Overall rate	8.9%
Estimated value ($25,452 ÷ 089)	$285,000

CORRELATION AND FINAL ESTIMATE OF VALUE

1 The estimate of $235,000 by the Market Data Approach is based on cogent data.
2 The estimate of $250,000 by the Cost Approach is based on comprehensive cost and depreciation analyses.
3 The estimate of $224,000 by the Income Approach is based on careful analysis of income, expense and the appropriate risk and recapture rates.
4 The appraiser is of the opinion that the estimates should be rated as follows:

Approach	Value	Rating	Value x rating
Market	$235,000	40%	$ 94,000
Cost	250,000	20%	50,000
Income	224,000	40%	89,600
		100%	$233,600

5 In the opinion of the appraiser the market value of the property as of May 1, 1971, is $235,000.

It is further the opinion of the appraiser that the value, based on disposal of the property by the purchaser in 10 years, assuming a 20% appreciation in value over that period is $285,000.

UNDERLYING ASSUMPTIONS AND CONTINGENCIES

1 That the title is good with no unregistered encumbrances or defects.
2 That management and maintenance will be adequate.
3 That no liability is assumed for legal matters.
4 That, except as indicated, separate land and building value apply only under the present use of the property.
5 That building and site dimensions and area may not be completely accurate.
6 That heating, electrical, plumbing and other systems, while not tested, are in good order.
7 That no part of this report may be republished without consent.
8 That no testimony before any tribunal will be given.

This is the last page of this report.

(signed)
JAMES INNES STEWART

APPENDIX 'A'

Schedule of physical deterioration incurable

Item	1971 Cost new	Normal life expectancy	Actual age	%	Depreciation
Excavation & backfill	$ 5,321	Indefinite	–	–	$ –
Foundation	4,152	400 years	24	6	249
Basement floor	2,000	300	24	8	160
Exterior walls	61,922	350	24	7	4,334
Sash & doors	3,805	150	24	16	609
Roof framing	9,683	200	24	12	1,162
Roof covering	2,582	30(special bond)	3	10	258
Floor framing	29,049	250	24	10	2,905
Finish floor	16,572	150	10	7	1,160
Painting and decorating	6,191	3	–	–	–
Partitions	50,019	250	24	10	5,002
Interior door & trim	5,170	175	24	14	724
Cabinet work	4,832	100	24	24	1,160
Stairs	2,718	200	24	12	326
Sheet metal	1,359	60	24	40	544
Plumbing					
Bathroom fixtures	9,654	20	–	–	–
Piping etc.	19,426	75	24	32	6,216
Lighting & wiring	13,590	75	10	13	1,767
Heating					
Boiler, burners, etc.	11,325	20	–	–	–
Radiators, piping, etc.	31,196	75	24	32	9,983
Floor covering	4,228	20	–	–	–
	$294,804			(12.4)	$36,559
	44,220 x depreciation of 12.4%				
Overhead and profit	$339,024				4,533
					$41,092

REFERENCES

1 / Webster defines the noun 'correlate': 'Either of two related things, esp. things so connected that one directly implies the other.' The verb 'correlate' is defined (inter alia): 'To establish a mutual or reciprocal relation.' In an imperfect market such as that for real property, rarely will one 'thing' directly imply another 'thing.' This is all the more reason why appraisers must 'correlate' data.

2 / Once our analysis is narrowed to a single property, the last three factors are largely given.

3 / Also in expropriations of buildings uniquely suited to their owners' uses.

4 / An extreme example is a report with a detailed description of accrued depreciation concluding: 'as the site is vacant, this concept is not applicable.'

5 / In expropriations or other litigious matters, the author reports to the lawyer not the client. A report to a lawyer in contemplation of litigation is 'privileged' and need not be produced in any preliminary examination for discovery unless the relevant expropriation statute so requires; as noted earlier some such statutes require parties to exchange reports.

6 / Percentage adjustments are multiplied; we can investigate the mathematical problem explained in Chapter 7, Reference 4. If the subject is said to be 7.5% inferior to Property 1 for condition and plan and 2.5% inferior for location the adjustment would be:

$$100 \div 92.5 = 1.0810 \qquad \$7410 \div 1.0810 = \$6854$$
$$100 \div 97.5 = 1.0256 \qquad \$6854 \div 1.0256 = \$6682$$

This final adjusted figure compares with $6680 in the earlier computation; they would coincide with sufficient decimal places.

As noted the base may be erroneously changed. A.I.C. Text, p. 83, using subject as the 100% base and the comparable 5% superior, shows two ways of factoring (we insert a price of $1000 to illustrate):

$$\$1000 \times 95\% = \$1000 \times .95 = \$9500$$
$$\$1000 \times \frac{100\%}{105\%} = \$1000 \times .95238 = \$9524$$

The text notes this difference in results not realizing that a change of base is the cause

$$\$1000 \times \frac{100\%}{95\%} = \$1000 \div 1.0527 = \$9500 \text{ (i.e. 100 is 5\% less than 105.27)}$$

It should be obvious that, if we use the same base, we must get the same answer from the same inputs. Mathematical mistakes are difficult to surmount and may be fatal to an appraisal, so it is difficult to understand why A.I.C. Text would justify the use of multiplication on incorrect reasoning since it results in the correct answer as shown above.

7 / A 'per-room' unit rental is not as common as 'per-suite' but has advantages: firstly suites need not be reduced to an average size for comparison and secondly, the number of rooms is what yields utility to a tenant.

8 / The net multiplier is used; if the deficiencies did not exist no extra operating expenses would be incurred.

9 / Major changes for owners statement:

    a Insurance premiums on annual basis
    b Major renovating costs on annual basis
    c Remove mortgage payments
    d Include allowances for vacancies and management

The major replacements have 20 year lives, but annual allowances are over 40 years so they will only be replaced once in the building's life. Since tastes and technology change faster re stoves and refrigerators, allowances are over 20 years.

10 / A normal Band of Investment would show

$$
\begin{array}{llll}
\text{Mortgage} - 75\% \text{ x} & 9.5\% & = & 7.12\% \\
\text{Equity} \quad - 25\% \text{ x} & \underline{12 \ \%} & = & \underline{3.00\%} \\
& 100 \ \% & & 10.12\%
\end{array}
$$

See Rene Baby, *The Inversion Phenomenon,* A.I.M., Summer 1970. Such rates may not reflect market behaviour in inflation so the method was not employed.

14

Mortgage-equity capitalization

INTRODUCTION

As has been noted, traditional appraisal process conceives of value as being estimated as though the property in question was free and clear of mortgage, with
the implication that no consideration need be given to the terms of financing
unless these are at considerable variance from those normally prevailing for the
particular type of property being appraised. Also the implications of income
tax and corporation tax laws and regulations on real property as an investment
are ignored; one of the results of this is that in the commonly used methods of
capitalization use is made of the concept of economic life which in general
stretches into the future for many years.

In real world markets, financing terms are of major concern as are tax considerations. A typical investor tries to acquire an equity position in real property with as large and as long-term an amortizing mortgage as possible because
this gives him maximum leverage for capital appreciation of his equity investment, since the mortgage is a fixed-sum debt.[1]

The investor also considers his tax position in determing how long to retain
his equity investment as he can deduct both interest on the mortgage and depreciation on the building (this latter at a straight line rate which probably exceeds considerably the actual rate of depreciation[2]) from the net revenue produced by the property in computing his taxable income. An amortizing mortgage
generally requires a monthly level-sum payment of blended interest and principal
payments, which over the period for which the loan is written will fully retire
the debt. Clearly the portion of the monthly payments needed to pay the interest will decline regularly as time goes on[3] and this results in progressively smaller
deductions from net revenue, which, of course, causes progressively higher taxable income.

Similarly, the annual allowable deductions for depreciation of the building
gradually decline as time goes on, being based each year on the value of such

building after all earlier such deductions. This too results in progressively smaller deductions from net revenue and progressively higher taxable income.

During the years of ownership of many types of investment properties, the combined effect of the allowable deductions for mortgage interest and building depreciation on the net revenue produced by a property is to reduce the taxable income therefrom, initially to a negative amount which gradually becomes less negative, proceeds through zero and then becomes positive in increasing amounts. Investors recognize this progression of events by perhaps using negative taxable revenues (i.e. losses) to offset other positive taxable revenue sources for which they are liable and then disposing of (or refinancing) the property in question when its taxable revenue approaches zero or becomes positive. It appears that the most favourable term for an investor to retain his equity ownership, in light of the above considerations, rarely exceeds ten years.

Mortgage-equity capitalization techniques in their more refined versions reflect the above conditions, but before proceeding to an analysis of these techniques mention must be made of what may be called:

Direct mortgage-equity capitalization[4]

Suppose the property to be appraised is of a type which typically can be financed with a 25-year first mortgage at 9.5% to 75% of the total value and that equity holders of this type of property typically hope for a 12% yield. Reference to a table of monthly amortized mortgage payments[5] discloses that the required monthly payment for such a mortgage is $8.61 per $1000 principal amount and hence the required annual payment is $8.610 x 12 = $103.32 and the annual constant percentage is $\frac{\$103.32}{\$1000.00}$ = 10.332%.

We can now develop an overall rate R_O using the band of investment principle discussed earlier.[6]

	% of value	x	Rate	=	Fractional rate
Mortgage	0.75		0.10332		0.0774
Equity	0.25		0.12000		0.0300
Total	1.00			=	0.1074

R_O = 10.74%

If the property being appraised has a net revenue of $17,800 before allowing for mortgage payments, depreciation, or income tax, its estimated value would be $17,800 ÷ 0.1074 = say $165,000.

Dividend rate

Now the above develops a very crude form of an overall rate as it does not reflect the recovery or growth of equity as the mortgage is gradually repaid; it can be refined by substitution for the 12% rate on equity what is called the dividend rate which A.I.C. Text, p. 229 points out is computed by relating the annual cash flow (i.e. net revenue after allowing for the required mortgage payments) to the original cash equity investment. For instance, if the property being appraised can be acquired for $200,000 with 25% in cash and 75% in a 25-year amortizing first mortgage at 9.5% and its net income is $17,800, the dividend rate is found to be approximately 4.7%[7] and the overall rate R_O is found to be:

	% of value	x	Rate	=	Fractional rate
Mortgage	0.75		0.10332		0.0774
Equity	0.25		0.0470		0.0117
Total	1.00				0.0891

R_O = 8.9% and the estimated value of the property would be $17,800 ÷ 0.0891 = $200,000

Even the above refinement is not very sophisticated as it contains neither a time horizon, except that inherent in the assumed 25-year mortgage, nor any recognition of possible changes in the value of the property in future years. These refinements could be included directly in further steps of the band of investment, but as this has already been formalized in the Ellwood technique we will turn now to analyse this in very general terms.

The Ellwood technique[8]

In its simplest form, this technique provides an overall rate which reflects the major differences between the traditional capitalization methods of appraisal theory and what happens in real world markets for investment properties; in so doing it also simplifies some perhaps insurmountable problems of the accepted theory which have been referred to above and which can be briefly summarized:

	Accepted theory	Ellwood
1 Equity-mortgage position	Property treated as free and clear of mortgage as long as financing terms are 'normal'	Investors buy with as little equity and as much mortgage as possible
2 Effect of mortgage terms on value	Value unaffected unless mortgage terms are not 'normal' for the sector	Mortgage terms affect value as shown by band of investment to develop

		Accepted theory	Ellwood
		of the market in question	composite overall rate. Such terms vary as between properties and sectors of the market.
3	Remaining economic life	Must be estimated and often extends as far into the future as 40 or 50 years	Need not be estimated at all as reliance is placed on income projections for relatively short periods of time
4	Period for which investors hold equity positions	Assumed plan to hold for period of remaining economic life is inherent in the theory. Could be handled by varying the recapture rate	Recognizes that investors can advantageously dispose of equity once period of tax-shelter by mortgage interest payments and depreciation allowances has expired, say, 8 to 10 years
5	Period for which future net income estimates must be made	Estimate must be valid for the full period of assumed economic life	Estimate must be valid for only the relatively short period of assumed equity holding
6	Provision for recapture of capital	Does not reflect growth in investors equity position as a mortgage is gradually amortized	Composite rate reflects the growth in the investors equity due to the mortgage amortization
7	Probable future changes in the value of a property	Appreciation or depreciation can be built into accepted technique, but in the strict theory this is not done. If appreciation is anticipated, the risk rate would be smaller and the reverse is true for an anticipated decline in value	Allowances for expected appreciation or depreciation are inherent parts of the composite overall rate
8	Splitting net income between land and buildings	Required unless the property residual technique is used	Income recognized as flowing from whole property

To fully understand how the Ellwood technique accomplishes its objectives requires a careful study of the tables and their supporting text; this is beyond the scope of the present analysis particularly since the basic premises of the technique can be explained in simple terms using tools which are commonplace to practitioners of the appraisal, mortgage and real estate vocations. The task can be handled in two alternative ways which are summarized below under the following underlying assumptions:

The property to be appraised is a walk-up apartment house in an area suitable for this type of use and general maintenance and construction of the property is good and it appears that an average net income of $17,800 can be earned annually for at least the next 10 years. This type of property typically can be financed with a 9.5% amortizing 25-year mortgage for 75% of value and a market analysis indicates that equity holders of such properties typically require a 12% yield on their equity investments and plan on holding their equity positions for about 10 years. Market trends indicate an increase in value of about 2% per year over this 10-year period.

Required	Obtained from mortgage tables and sinking fund tables[9]	Obtained from Inwood tables (Inwood is $a_{\overline{n}|}$)[10]
1 Annual constant % relevant for particular mortgage, 25 years, 9.5%	Monthly payment per $100 of mortgage times 12, expressed as a percentage $0.86102 x 12 = $10.3320 = 10.332%	Take reciprocal of appropriate Inwood factor, i.e. $\dfrac{1}{a_{\overline{25}|}}$ $\dfrac{1}{9.678} = 10.332\%$[11]
2 Unpaid balance of principal of mortgage at end of period of income projection, i.e. 10 years as a percentage of the original principal amount	Refer to loan progress schedule $16.67 has been paid off i.e. 16.67%, so that 83.333% of principal remains unpaid	Divide reciprocal of Inwood for the full mortgage term by reciprocal of Inwood for balance of term after the end of the period of income projection $\dfrac{1}{a_{\overline{25}|}} \div \dfrac{1}{a_{\overline{15}|}} = \dfrac{a_{\overline{15}|}}{a_{\overline{25}|}} = $ $\dfrac{8.065}{9.678} = 83.333\%$, so 16.667% of the loan will have been paid off

Required	Obtained from mortgage tables and sinking fund tables	Obtained from Inwood tables (Inwood is $a_{\overline{n}|}$)
3 Sinking fund factor at equity yield rate for period of income projection – i.e. 10 years, 12%	Annual factor = 0.056984 say = 0.057	Relationship between Inwood and the sinking fund factor $\dfrac{1}{S_{\overline{n}|}}$ is: $$\dfrac{1}{a_{\overline{n}|}} = \text{rate} + \dfrac{1}{S_{\overline{n}|}}$$ $$\dfrac{1}{a_{\overline{10}|}} = 12\% + \dfrac{1}{S_{\overline{10}|}}$$ $$\dfrac{1}{S_{\overline{10}|}} = \dfrac{1}{a_{\overline{10}|}} - 0.12$$ $$= \dfrac{1}{5.650} - 0.12$$ $$= 0.177 - 0.12$$ $$= 0.057$$
4 Reduction in the overall rate to reflect anticipated appreciation in value of 20% over the 10 years of equity holding	0.20 x 0.057 = 0.014	0.20 x 0.057 = 0.014

The appropriate Ellwood Composite Overall rate, R_0 can now be built up using a band of investment:

Basic rate = r_O

Step 1

Position	% of value	x	Rate		Fractional rate
Mortgage	0.75		0.103320	=	0.0774
Equity	0.25		0.12000	=	0.0300
Total	1.00				0.107400

Step 2

Deduct for equity recovery over 10 years[12]

16.67% of mortgage will have been paid off
0.056984 12% sinking fund factor 10 years
75% of value is represented by mortgage

0.75 x 0.1667 x 0.056984	=	0.007133
Basic rate	r_O	=	0.100367

Step 3

Deduct for anticipated appreciation
in value of 20% over the next 10 years[13]
0.056984 is the sinking fund factor
The appreciation applies to 100% of the value

1.0 x 0.20 x 0.056984	=	0.011396
R_O	=	0.088971
	= say	8.9%

Step 4

Estimate of value

Capitalized estimated net annual income
i.e. $17,800 ÷ .089   = $200,000

   Owing to the American practice of compounding interest monthly, the Ellwood and other rates as tabulated differ from appropriate Canadian rates.

The Ellwood notation

Under the Ellwood premise and the notation thereof, the proper overall capitalization rate will be

$$R_O = r_O + \text{dep}\ \frac{1}{S_{\overline{n}|}} \ \text{ or } R_O = r_O - \text{app}\ \frac{1}{S_{\overline{n}|}},$$

where $r_O = Y - MC$

   y = Equity yield expressed as a composite annual rate reflecting both equity cash flow and equity growth or recovery.

M = ratio of mortgage to total value

C = mortgage co-efficient or multiplier. It is a band of investment factor which includes both amortization and interest.

dep = anticipated loss in value over projected income period, as a percentage.

app = anticipated increase in value over projected income period as a percentage.

$1/S_{\overline{n}|}$ = the standard sinking fund symbol.

Using the results of our earlier analysis:

Step 1 Develop r_o = Y - MC

Y - 0.12 - 0.00713 (see step 2 above)	= 0.112867
M = 0.75	
C = 0.12 − 0.103320 = 0.01668 MC = 0.75 x 0.01668	= 0.012500
Therefore r_o	= 0.100367

Step 2 Allow for anticipated appreciation of 20% over 10 years

minus app $\dfrac{1}{S_{\overline{n}|}}$ = 0.20 x 0.056984	= 0.011396
Therefore R_o	= 0.088971
	= say 8.9%

The place of Ellwood in appraisal theory [14]

As the Ellwood analysis is strictly market oriented, there should be no question of its acceptance both in appraisal theory and in practice. Since the existence of courses to teach the principles and techniques indicated that these are recognized by both A.I.C. and A.I.R.E.A. as being worthy of study, presumably the theory has been accepted. But these courses and this acceptance have come only slowly; L.W. Ellwood first published his tables in 1959, while the courses, at least in Canada, have been presented only in the past very few years.

With regard to practical application of the Ellwood analysis, the acceptance has also been slow. But it took an interesting turn once it became part of several appraisers' stock of techniques. As noted earlier, some practitioners seem to dislike not using everything they know in every appraisal, and as the mortgage-equity concepts, when linked to an income projection over relatively short time horizons can be worked up into an exotic-looking package, they present it to the client in every report.

This proliferation of the use of a very worthwhile analysis in situations where it has no place has caused considerable misgiving among a large number of appraisers and individuals who are required to review appraisal reports. And along with this is the seeming tendency in the appraisal field to be satisfied with the status quo.

The analysis is a very important tool in that it interprets the market behaviour of certain types of investors. Also it makes it possible for an appraiser to test the reasonableness of all his assumptions and conclusions such as the various rates, the income projection period and the estimate of value itself. So it stands the tests of good theory, namely that it accurately represents the relevant sectors of the market, and is a basis for reliable prediction: this latter aspect of good theory is well illustrated in Dr Ratcliff's works referred to in Chapter 16.

REFERENCES

1 / Even apart from considerations of capital appreciation the following brief analysis shows the effect of alternative financing on the yield to the equity owner and hence on value.

Assume
A new 10,000 sq. ft. industrial building which cost, in total, $100,000 and rents for $1.20 per sq. ft. net.

$$\text{Natural constant} = \frac{\text{Net rent}}{\text{Cost}} = \frac{\$12,000}{100,000} = 12\%$$

Alternative financing available
A $75,000 at 9¾%, 15-year amortization – annual mortgage constant – 12.58%
B $60,000 at 10¼%, 25-year amortization – annual mortgage constant – 10.94%

Which financing produces highest value?
1 Natural constant should be greater than mortgage constant.
2 Scheme B maximizes value due to greater leverage.

	Scheme	
Proof	A	B
Cost	$100,000	$100,000
Mortgage	75,000	60,000
Equity	$ 25,000	$ 40,000
Net income	$ 12,000	$ 12,000
Annual mortgage payments		
A $75,000 x 12.58	9,435	
B $60,000 x 10.94		6,564
Cash flow	$ 2,565	$ 5,436
Return on equity		
A $\frac{\$2,565}{25,000}$	10.2%	
B $\frac{\$5,436}{40,000}$		13.6%

2 / The Income Tax Act, R.S.C., 1970, Ch. I, 5 actually prohibits deductions from income for depreciation (Sec. 12(1)(b)) and allows them for capital cost allowances; the term 'depreciation' is used in the text as it is one which commonly appears in appraisal literature and for the present purposes the concepts are similar.

3 / Reference to a mortgage progress schedule will make this precise.

4 / In the remainder of this analysis of mortgage-equity capitalization the data used are based on those in the example of the Canadian text. Note that the symbol R_O and r_O are used herein to designate an overall rate and a basic rate respectively.

5 / See the A.I.C. Monthly Compound Interest Tables.

6 / Note that an overall rate is developed and this does not offend against the principle pointed out in C.I.R. Journal, March 1964.

7 /

Annual net revenue	=	$17,800
Annual payments on mortgage ($150,000 x $103.00)	=	15,450
Annual cash flow	=	$ 2,350
Initial equity investment (25% of $200,000)	−	50,000
So the dividend rate ($2,350 ÷ $50,000)	=	4.7%

8 / A full appreciation of all the underlying assumptions and the many applications and ramifications of the Ellwood technique can only be obtained from a careful perusal of Ellwood Tables for Real Estate Appraising and Financing, A.I.R.E.A., 1967. Apart from the ready availability of rates and factors appropriate to a wide range of assumptions, a most interesting and useful graphic analysis is developed to show clearly what various assumptions entail and the ranges within which they and the conclusions based on them may validly vary.

Not all appraisers and appraisal theorists feel that the Ellwood technique improves the capitalization process: for instance, see the Appraisal Journal, July 1966, p. 339, William W. Torrey, 'The Ellwood Tables: A critique.' Mr Torrey's criticisms are summarized on p. 351 of the article as follows:

'The Ellwood concept over-all rate is a new refinement of the investor's method, but the degree of refinement is not significant in the range of appraisals most adapted to the concept.

'The graphic analysis is bound by its arithmetic to show such similarity from case to case as to be unsound as a basis for judging the capitalization rate.

'The virtue of the short-term projection, if you believe it is indicated by market behavior, is cancelled by the de-emphasizing of futures inherent in compound discounting, which acts alike in all capitalization techniques. The mathematics of the concept contain no direct tie to the motives behind short-term ownership.

'Effective use of the concept would require that all comparables be broken down and analyzed for a yield rate by its principles, and the mortgage market and terms be included for each item. The indirect effect of the money market in a world of equity-buying on capitalization rates is impossible to measure.

'The Ellwood technique for handling depreciation is not an improvement over old appraisal methods. Neglect of separate consideration and statement of land value has not been justified. Its relative complexity does not result in better appraisals.

'These factors should discourage sponsorship of the Ellwood concept by the American Institute of Real Estate Appraisers.'

It is too early for one to make a definite statement as to the validity and usefulness of Ellwood. It seems to be a valuable addition to appraisal thinking under certain circumstances. However, the practice of some appraisers of inserting an Ellwood-based analysis in practically every report has little merit.

9 / Tables of Mortgage Payment are available from most large corporate mortgagees. A sinking fund table appears as Tabe IV of this book; more complete tables are readily available and if desired in monthly form can be obtained from A.I.C. It should be noted that under the provisions of the Interest Act, R.S.C., 1970, Ch I, 18, Sec. 6, interest on mortgage repayable on the sinking fund plan or on any plan requiring blended payments of principal and interest in Canada will be compounded annually or semi-annually, not in advance even though payable by monthly payments of blended principal interest. In the United States, interest on mortgages can be compounded monthly and so the resultant composite overall rates developed using Canadian tables may differ somewhat from those appearing in the Ellwood tables.

A detailed analysis of the procedure and its underlying rationale will be found in the Appraisal Journal, July 1970, Charles B. Ackerson, 'Ellwood Without Algebra.'

10 / The resultant answer using annual Inwood factors will vary somewhat from that obtained from using the mortgage and sinking fund tables if these latter are monthly, semi-annual, etc. For an explanation of the relationship between various compound interest tables, reference should be made to N.E. Sheppard and D.C. Baillie, *Compound Interest,* University of Toronto, 1960; a limited analysis will also be found in the Appraisal Journal of January 1963, p. 35, Robert S. Arnold, 'Inwood – Friend or Foe.'

11 / Canadian Monthly Tables show the annuity factor for 25 years at 9.5% to be 116.140291; reducing this to an annual factor by dividing by 12 gives 9.678. The 9.5% annual factor for 15 years of 8.065 in the subsequent step is obtained in the same way from the monthly factor of 96.784232 divided by 12.

12 / If the equity holder invested the annual reductions of mortgage principal inherent in the amortization process in a sinking fund at this required equity rate of 12%, he would in 10 years have accumulated $1.00 for every $0.057 so invested.

13 / As R_O is the denominator in the basic value equation $V = \dfrac{1}{R_O}$, an appreciation in value must be reflected by a reduction in R_O, while a depreciation in value will be reflected by an addition to R_O.

14 / William N. Kinneard, Jr, 'The Ellwood Analysis in Valuation: A Return to Fundamentals,' the Real Estate Appraiser, May 1966.

15

Economics of real property[1]

Appraisal techniques are basically applications of demand and supply analysis to the problem of valuing a specific piece of property, but the laws of economics cannot determine precisely what a particular buyer will pay for a particular property at a particular time. Similarly, economic reasons can help decide whether one use of land will be more profitable than another; and it can suggest to what intensity the land can be most profitably developed in a particular use. But how a parcel of land is actually used depends in part on government policy, on the ideas of individual developers, and on many other circumstances.

To say that economics is not designed to give specific answers to particular questions is not in the least to detract from its importance. A road map is indispensable on a long journey precisely *because* it does not show every house, every tree, every bridge along the way. Economics is a map which one ignores at his peril; without it one will surely lose his way.

GENERAL ECONOMIC TRENDS,
CONSTRUCTION AND HOUSING

Trends in housing, like trends in the markets for other goods and services, respond to the ground swells that develop in the economy as a whole. We are thinking of two things: the long periods of alternating advance and stagnation (or regression) that seem to characterize economic development, and the shorter waves in business life that we call 'industrial fluctuations' or 'business cycles.'

Much ink has been spilled in the analysis of these economic movements but it cannot be claimed that they are yet satisfactorily understood. The long waves in economic life, covering 20 or 30 years or even longer, seem to be associated with things like the rate of population growth and the development of important inventions. We live in a period of advance. The pace of population growth in the Western world has quickened perceptibly in the last fifteen years, and in Canada large scale immigration has supplemented natural increase to give us a particularly rapid rate of growth. In the realm of technology, the maturing of the internal combustion engine and of the electrical age, new developments in mining and metallurgy and atomic technology, all mean that we live in an era which from the viewpoint of change is fully comparable to the great Industrial Revolution of the nineteenth century. With these things in mind, most observers think that our economy is in the upward phase of a long wave of development, and feel confident that the outlook for housing over the next generation, like the outlook for most other parts of the economy, is bright. They may be wrong; there is no way of proving anything about the future, but on the basis of what can be learned from economic history, growth prospects, especially in Canada, appear to be good.

The shorter waves in economic life have a duration of 5–10 years, and seem to be associated mainly with changes in the balance between how much businessmen want to invest and how much people as a whole want to save. It should be noted, however, that many economists believe that the duration of cycles in construction and related real estate activities is two or three times the length of cycles in other economic activities. Nevertheless, the housing market cannot fail to be affected by the general economic situation. Movements in real estate need not follow precisely movements in the rest of the economy; housing construction and the demand for housing may remain fairly strong for some time after other sectors of the economy show weakness; the reverse may also happen. But no one would expect a booming market in real estate when the rest of the economy is seriously depressed, or a seriously depressed market for houses when the rest of the economy is booming.

The largest and most dramatic changes in the fortunes of a particular market are frequently reflections of these ups and downs of the whole economy. And since it is impossible to forecast these movements with scientific accuracy, all an individual businessman can do is to keep informed about economic developments and try to judge how they will affect his own business. The intelligent businessman, or investor, reads regularly some journal giving the latest financial and economic intelligence. He keeps an eye on such important government statistical series as National Income, Employment, Prices, and so on. The Bank of Canada's monthly *Statistical Summary* or the D.B.S. monthly, *The Canadian Statistical Review*, are convenient sources for this sort of information. He also consults special statistical information that is of particular relevance to his own business or investments which for our present purposes is *Canadian Housing Statistics*, published monthly and annually by CMHC. Reports on housing and related matters in the decennial censi and quinquennial mini-censi are also available with a considerable time lag. Reference can also be had with benefit to the various annual and special reports of the Economic Council of Canada; the *Fourth Annual Review* (1967) is particularly illuminating in its discussions of population (Chapter 3) and urban growth (Chapter 7).

THE HOUSING MARKET

Introduction

Trends in the general economy are not the only factors that explain changes in individual markets. We have noted above that the real property market does not always follow general economic trends, either as to direction or intensity. Basically, like other markets, it responds to its own particular forces of supply and demand.

But in real property matters the basic economic concepts of 'price,' 'product' and 'industry' are very hard to define. The term 'real property' covers many types of properties; even if we add the adjective 'residential,' we are still left with many classes of dwelling. In order to make analysis possible we must narrow our concept still further; in what follows we shall deal only with middle-income housing, and think of the 'typical' house as being a 6- or 7-room dwelling. Also, housing as an economic good is a 'consumer durable' not a consumption good like bread and not an investment good like a machine. This means that the rate of interest plays an important part in the analysis.

There are also other difficulties; the housing market is anything but perfectly competitive.[2] True, there are many sellers and many buyers of houses, so that we are not dealing with a monopoly market either. But the product is not homogeneous; every house is different if only because of its unique location. The word 'industry' is often ambiguous; for some purposes it is sensible to speak of the 'automobile industry' but for others we have to think of a Pontiac industry, a Ford industry, and so on. In such a case we refer to the industry as being 'imperfectly competitive,' a phrase which indicates that the market comprises elements of both competition and monopoly. Housing is a special case of an imperfectly competitive industry because, as we have said, every unit of the 'product' is different from every other unit. It is generally considered to be monopolistically competitive and becomes a bilateral monopoly when a prospective buyer is bargaining for a specific property with its owner.

Among other things this means that, when we speak of the 'price of housing,' we are thinking of some 'average' price that a 'typical' house will sell for – just as when we speak of the 'price of cars,' we have in mind some average price for a particular quality of automobile. But the 'price of housing' raises still another problem. It is well known that the same house will usually sell for a different price depending on whether the payment is made in cash, cash and first mortgage, or cash and two mortgages; and, of course, mortgages vary as to repayment terms and interest rate. Adequate exposure to the market and advertising can also influence price. The very meaning of the word 'price' in connection with housing is therefore vague. The best we can do is to think of price as some average 'financial sacrifice' for the buyer and 'financial gain' to the seller. Thus a seller may be indifferent between two offers, one for $7000 cash and an $8000 mortgage, and the other for $5000 cash and an $11,000 mortgage. In one case the 'price' is $15,000, in the other $16,000, but these may very well represent the same 'financial sacrifice' to the two prospective buyers and the same 'financial gain' to the seller.[3]

DEMAND

Since everyone needs shelter, the demand for housing taken as a whole at any moment is probably quite inelastic; that is, the number of houses sold is probably not very responsive to changes in the price of housing. However, the demand is by no means completely inelastic. If the price of housing falls in relation to other goods and services more housing will be demanded. It is not, of course, that as prices fall a single buyer buys more houses – as he buys more steaks when their price falls – for one house is usually all that a single purchaser wants at one time (once he has a satisfactory house, his demand does not enter into the market at all). But if he doesn't buy any more houses he may buy 'more house'; as the cost of housing falls people often 'upgrade' their living accommodation by buying houses that in some way are superior to the ones they have been occupying. Also, some people who didn't own a house before will now become homeowners. The reverse proposition is also true; if housing becomes more expensive in relation to other goods and services, people will make do with lower quality houses, or smaller houses, or rented rooms. Thus housing, as a whole, conforms to the general law of demand that 'the lower the price, the greater the amount demanded.'

The relationship between price and quantity becomes stronger when we consider not all housing but a particular class thereof. The demand for a particular class of housing is likely to be a good deal more elastic than that for housing as a whole. That is to say, a fall in the price of a particular class of housing, the prices of all other houses remaining constant, will probably lead to a relatively large increase in the purchases of that type of housing. The sales of a particular class of housing will depend on the price of those classes of housing as compared with the prices of other classes of housing. But it is generally felt that the number of houses sold depends less on price (i.e. on the shape of the demand curve) than on other factors which determine the position or level of the demand curve; the factors which affect the volume of sales at a given price. These will be discussed under the headings of: Income, Population, Tastes, Liquid Assets and Mortgage Money. Reference should be made to relevant statistics in C.H.S.

Income In most markets the volume of sales depends to an important extent on people's incomes. It is mainly through changes in income that the influence of economic trends in the whole economy are transmitted to the housing market. As in the case of changes in the price of housing, the adjustment in the housing market to income changes is not made by people changing the number of houses they buy, but by 'upgrading' or 'downgrading' their living accommodation. Changes in the distribution of the National Income are also of importance to the demand for different types of housing. Trends in National Income (and thus in the average individual's income) are of major importance to the demand for housing; but studies indicate that there is a lagged reaction to income changes.

Population The relationship between the demand for housing and population is much more subtle than the bald proposition that as population grows the demand for houses will also grow. It is not only the size of the population that affects the demand for housing; the composition of the population is equally important. Age composition, marital status, and average family size are characteristics of the population that are of especial importance for housing.

Age composition and average family size are closely related. If a population contains an unusually large proportion of people under 20, that is to say, if the average family size is large, the demand for large houses is likely to be heavy. Average family size in Canada has increased considerably since the 1930s and the demand for three or four bedroom houses was very brisk in the 1950s and until 1965. Since then this demand has declined somewhat, as has the number of births (see Tables 77, 115, C.H.S. 1970). Architects may also have had growing family size in mind when they began to design houses with a room that can be changed from sitting room to bedroom as the need arises. The proportion of people under 20 is expected to remain about the same between now and 1980, according to the population projection made for the Gordon Commission on Canada's Economic Prospects; the numbers in this group are expected to almost double to a total of over 10 millions by 1980. See also Economic Council of Canada, *Fourth Annual Review* 1967, Chapter 3 for recent statistics and projections on this and other population characteristics.

If the population contains an unusually large number of old people, at retirement age or beyond, this will also affect the demand for housing. Canada today has a rapidly growing number of old people. People over 60 are expected to make up about 13% of a much larger population by 1980; by 1980 we will probably have about 3.5 million people over 60. How will this affect housing? Will we need an increasing number of small houses for retired couples, or will older people prefer for the most part to live in low-rent apartments? Much thought will be devoted to the problem of adequate housing for the aged during the next decade or so.

Marital status is of obvious importance to housing since married people normally want to live in their own homes while single people usually live either at home or in rented quarters. Thus 'net household formation' (see Table 117, C.H.S. 1970), new families formed by marriage less old families dissolved by death or divorce, plus net non-familial households is one of the most important factors in the demand for housing.

Two other general points must be made before we leave the subject of population. First, it is important to realize that although we have discussed population and income under different headings they are by no means unrelated factors. General economic conditions, prosperity or depression, obviously affect such things as the marriage rate and the birth rate. The rate of immigration is also much influenced, particularly by relative economic conditions in Canada and other countries; our immigration has historically been push-oriented.

Secondly, a study of the connections between population and housing demand is particularly interesting and important because many changes in the composition of population can be forecast with a good deal of confidence. The babies born this year will be in the housing market twenty years hence; the number of people who will reach age 60 five years hence can be confidently predicted by taking the number of people aged 55 today and subtracting the number of expected deaths in this group during the next five years. In brief, it is quite easy, by looking at the size of particular age groups today, to form a fairly clear picture of the size of those groups 5, 10 and 15 years hence. This is what is done in population projections; see the *Fourth Annual Review* (1967), E.C.C. Tables 3–8 and 3–9.

Tastes Ideas about what constitutes desirable housing change over time and vary between one part of the country and another. Toronto demands solid brick houses; Montreal prefers brick veneer; Prairie houses are often frame; the Trend house is popular in Vancouver. Bungalows, split levels and storey-and-a-half houses all vary in popularity from time to time. Also apartments are much more popular in many urban areas than they were prior to World War II, and the condominium competes with both rental units and single family dwellings. See Table 10, C.H.S. 1970. Over long periods, houses vie not only with each other but also with other goods for a high position in the consumer's scale of preferences. In our grandfather's day an expensive house was the main mark of social distinction; today, perhaps, most people rate automobiles and coloured television sets above housing as a form of conspicuous consumption. Apart from pointing out their effect on demand curves there is not much the economist can say about changes in tastes; hopefully the psychologist or the sociologist will someday develop a theory of consumer preferences. Tastes do change more slowly than incomes, and are probably for that reason less important than either income or population change as a factor leading to changes in the demand for different types of housing.

One matter of taste that is of especial significance is the average homeowner's idea of where he wants to live. Even if the total demand for housing remains the same many people want to change their location – from rural to urban areas, to new areas in the city, or to the suburbs, or back to old residential areas (or new apartment areas) in the city – and this 'switching,' of course, creates a demand for real estate. Canadian families are very mobile, moving on the average once every 4 or 5 years, yet there is little statistical information available on this very important aspect of the demand for housing, although C.H.S. 1970, Tables 113 and 114 provide general data on migrating families and elderly persons. Reference has already been made to the discussion of urban growth in the *Fourth Annual Review* 1967, E.C.C., Chapter 7.

Liquid assets A house is the most expensive thing that most people ever buy: it usually costs three, four or more times a person's annual income. To make the down payment on a house a purchaser must have available either cash or liquid assets that he can easily turn into cash.

A person's 'capital' is to some extent the result of past savings built up over a number of years. Saving habits in the past, however, cannot explain the rather large and sudden fluctuations in people's *liquid* resources; and it is liquid resources that are so important in determining people's ability to buy houses. Past savings are no guarantee that a person will at all times be in a liquid financial position. Savings may have been lost through unwise, or unlucky, investment; more often they may be temporarily 'lost' or unavailable if the stock, or the bond, or the house, in which they were invested cannot be sold (turned into cash) except at an unreasonable sacrifice of the original investment.

The availability of cash is much more a reflection of general economic conditions and government monetary policy than of individual thrift. When the economy is prosperous, two important factors conspire to make liquid funds readily available. First, markets are active, so that it is usually easy to transform existing investments (in property or securities) into cash, and frequently capital gains are realized in the process. Second, incomes are high as a result of good employment, overtime wages, high profits, fat fees, and perhaps stock market 'winnings'; and money savings are therefore likely to be unusually high for a few years. In depression, the reverse is the case.

Special circumstances also affect the availability of liquid funds. The most important example in recent times was the effect of the war on savings. People during the war earned high incomes, but because the supply of things to buy was limited, an unusually high proportion of these incomes flowed into savings of one kind or another – war bonds, forced savings, bank accounts, and so on. This highly liquid position of the population, and the 'backlog' of demand from the war years, resulted in high postwar demand for most goods and services, including houses. There are also seasonal changes in the supply of liquid funds – the flow of cash to the Government at Income Tax time is one example – but it is doubtful whether these changes have any significant effect on the demand for housing.

We shall not go further into this matter of the availability of liquid funds. Suffice it to understand that the supply of such funds at any particular time is not so much a matter of personal saving habits (as implied in the loanable funds theory of interest) and individual economic behaviour as it is a matter of those general movements in the economy which in one way or another affect us all. Reference to C.H.S., 1963, Table 87, indicates that as the down payments on N.H.A. houses was noticeably higher in the years 1955 to 1960 than it was in 1961-62, there may have been a drawing down of accumulated assets in the period; C.H.S. 1970, Table 103 can be used to update the analysis.

Mortgage money Most houses are paid for in part with borrowed money, and the availability and cost of such money exerts an important influence on the demand for housing. To some extent a good supply of mortgage money may reduce the average size of down payment required and thus the need for liquid funds. Actually, however, these two factors are in practice complementary. In times of brisk demand and rising prices an increased volume of both liquid funds and mortgage money are required to finance the increased volume of business. The upper limit to private first mortgages is often 60%-66% of the estimated value of the house, so that an increase in the volume of sales is ordinarily made up of increases in both cash payments and mortgage lending. The maximum is much higher for N.H.A. mortgages (up to 95% of value) and the practice of institutional lenders of blending first and second mortgages to make available over 80% of value affects the need for liquid assets to buy a house. It must also be noted that as virtually all mortgages are now amortized, an owner in effect accumulates a net asset every month by simply repaying some of the principal on his mortgage. (This latter point is developed further in Chapter 14 in the discussion of the Ellwood premise.)

SUPPLY

The supply of housing on the market consists of old houses offered for resale and newly completed houses offered for sale for the first time. The total number of already built houses is much greater than the supply of either old or new houses coming onto the market at any given time but little information is available on the relative importance of the two groups making up the supply side of the market, and we know very little about the major part of the supply side of housing, namely, the offerings of old houses.

The supply of new houses coming on the market on which we have quite detailed statistical information, will depend on the relationship between the 'price of housing' and cost of constructing new houses. If the price is below the cost of construction new houses will not be built and old houses may not even be properly maintained, in which case the total stock of housing will decline. If the price is somewhat near the cost of construction, just enough new houses will be built, on the average, to replace losses from fire and demolitions, and thus the total stock will remain constant. When prices are higher than costs, new housing will be built and the total stock of housing will be increased. The rate at which new building takes place will depend mainly on the size of the excess of prices over costs; if profit margins are very good new housing starts will mount rapidly; if they are only modest construction will proceed at a lower rate. C.H.S. 1970, Table 85 gives data concerning N.H.A. housing costs while Table 81 covers prices of these houses.

The flow supply curve for housing may be very elastic over a fairly wide range – that is, starting from a fairly low volume of construction, we can probably increase our volume of new housing construction quite considerably without raising costs very much. But if we try to build too rapidly, inefficient and inexperienced contractors are drawn into the industry; inexperienced labour is used as bottlenecks develop in the labour market; material and land costs rise. When this happens, marginal builders can only make a profit (and even then perhaps not a very large one) if the price of houses rises considerably. Thus at a high rate of construction the supply curve probably becomes quite inelastic; a further increase in the rate of construction could then only be maintained on the basis of sharply increased prices. As buyer resistance develops, or mortgage money for new houses dries up, the high-cost builders leave the industry (perhaps in a wave of bankruptcies) as rapidly as they entered it. Another important characteristic of the supply of real property is that it cannot be reduced quickly in response to a slackening of demand; it is almost wholly inelastic if we consider the stock of real property at any given moment.

Cost factors

We have already mentioned labour and material costs. At some point, as construction increases, bottlenecks will develop in these markets and the level of costs will increase. How soon the bottlenecks will be encountered depends on the strength of the demands exerted by the rest of the economy for the materials and labour required. Pressure will develop sooner in a rapidly growing, prosperous economy than in a depressed economy where there may be many idle resources of both materials and labour. The level of construction in non-housing fields may be of particular importance to the housing market, since the resources of labour and materials used in the building of industrial and commercial structures are in many cases the same as those required in building houses.

Land costs are peculiar in that they may rise abruptly for purely speculative reasons. When housing construction is high in a particular locality something like a 'land fever' may sweep over the area and inflate land prices by several hundred per cent.

The question of technique is a complex one in the housing market. In spite of some technological advance in the house-building field the rate of advance has been slower in this sector than in most other sectors of the economy. House building has, to a large extent, been unaffected by the Industrial Revolution and is still a stronghold for small scale contractors and for manual labour. Machinery seems to play a larger part in heavy construction and in industrial construction than in house building. The result is that housing tends to become more costly relative to most other goods and services, and this helps to explain why housing has become a social and political problem of some significance; as housing becomes more expensive relative to income, subsidies of one form or another seem necessary if everyone is to live in dwellings that come up to a minimum standard that is deemed socially adequate.

In some cases the introduction of new techniques which would lower costs may be prevented by government and municipal building codes, which are often described as 'anachronistic'; certainly an attempt should be made to keep these codes up-to-date in terms of new materials and new methods of construction; and the more uniformity that can be introduced within and between codes the healthier will be the situation. If trade unions are strong and if they engage in 'feather-bedding,' we obviously have another factor which retards better techniques and militates against lower cost housing. On the brighter side of the 'techniques' picture we have the prospect of more prefabrication of the whole house, or at least of parts thereof. See Chapter 5, Reference 2 re System Building.

Finally we must note that the rate of interest and the availability of mortgage money – which, as we saw above, affect the demand for housing – are also important factors on the supply side of the housing market. Builders can only build houses if they can get mortgages on them. The whole question of the rate of interest is so important that it will be discussed as a separate topic later on as well as in Chapter 11.

PRICE AND QUANTITY

The stock supply of housing

The study of demand and of supply are designed to answer two of the great questions of economics; what determines the price? what determines the amount produced and sold? In our case, what determines the price of housing and the rate of housing construction?

We must always keep in mind that the quantity of any commodity can be thought of in terms of either the stock which is available at any moment of time or the additions to or depletions from that stock which would be made at various costs and prices prevailing in the market in question. In economic language we call this latter concept of the price-quantity relationship a 'flow' and it is important to distinguish it from a stock.

In normal examples of downward sloping demand and upward sloping supply curves the assumption is made that if the price fell (or rose) the amount supplied would be decreased (or increased) and the amount demanded increased (or decreased) and there would be a change in the 'flow' of a commodity or service due to the change in its price (see Chapter 3, Reference 13). This would change the total stock in existence but as the analysis is concerned with commodities, the supply of which could be either increased or decreased readily, the question of how this change in the stock occurs is of little importance and so is in general omitted from the analysis.

When we consider the 'commodity' housing (or any building or improvement to land), it becomes apparent that changes in its stock as a result of changes of the flow into and out of the market, as depicted by normal demand and supply curves, is for all practical purposes a one-way street except over a very long time. Once a site has been improved by the erection of a building, a relatively permanent addition to the stock of improved properties has been made. The only way this stock can be reduced is to call in the bulldozers or wait until buildings are at least largely depreciated. And when we think about the great variety of the demand for accommodation in buildings it should be obvious that many people can only afford to occupy those buildings which for most uses would be taken as fully depreciated.[4]

What this implies is that at any moment of time the total stock of improved properties in any given area is completely fixed and will not be reduced in response to reductions in price. In diagrammatic terms the stock of improved properties at any given moment can be represented by a vertical line erected from the horizontal (quantity) axis at the point thereon measuring the total stock.

We will from now on discuss only the question of 'housing'; we are thinking of some sort of composite of size and quality. The same sort of analysis can be applied to any type of real property. The economist would say that this supply is completely inelastic. If we can consider two not too different periods of time, it should be clear that the existing supply of housing will be either the same on the two dates, or it will be greater on the later date than on the earlier. It cannot be noticeably smaller unless the two dates are far apart, as the stock of housing is not readily reducible in response to a change in prices. Whether it will be equal to or greater than an earlier stock of housing depends upon what has happened to the demand for housing in the interim. One further point: we cannot really speak of a 'supply curve' for housing as the units are not homogeneous; they are all different. We must recognize this but assume that we can think of some sort of 'average' unit which we can call 'housing' and which is supplied and demanded, this isn't stretching the point too much, as housing units of various types are fairly close substitutes for each other as are two identical houses in different locations.

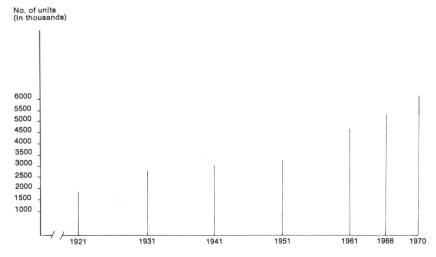

Figure 1 Stock of Housing at different times.
Sources: Censi; C.H.S. 1970, Table 8.

The flow supply of housing

The amount of a commodity supplied is a function of two things: market prices
and whether at these prices a producer can cover his costs of production (including, of course, normal profits). Therefore in considering the 'supply curve'
for housing in the sense of the amount thereof that would be produced and offered at various prices, we have to consider market prices for housing and its
costs of production. And we must always remember that this 'supply' of housing will be an addition to a fixed stock (and relative to this an extremely small
addition) at any given moment and is for our present purposes irreversible in
the sense that once a house is built we cannot shift the whole curve to the left.

Under the institutional arrangement of the house-building industry, it is relatively easy for a person (or corporation) to enter the building business when demand and prices are high, and to leave it when demand slackens and prices fall.
Also, as already noted, the building-supply industry can increase production
fairly readily in response to an increase in demand for its products. But both
these things are true only so long as there is unused capacity in these sectors of
the economy. If there is full employment of the human, natural and capital resources used by the construction and building-supply industries, then it becomes difficult to increase production.

Information on the actual stock of housing units, as reported in the decennial censi for the year 1951 and 1961 and the 1966 mini-census plus the total
number of dwelling completions in Canada and the average square foot costs

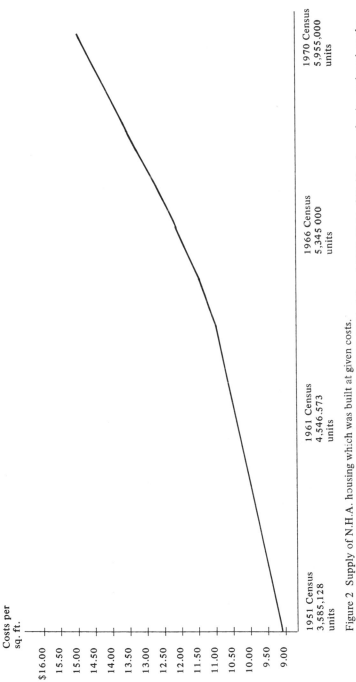

Costs per
sq. ft.

$16.00
15.50
15.00
14.50
14.00
13.50
13.00
12.50
12.00
11.50
11.00
10.50
10.00
9.50
9.00

1951 Census
3,585,128
units

1961 Census
4,546.573
units

1966 Census
5,345 000
units

1970 Census
5,955,000
units

Figure 2 Supply of N.H.A. housing which was built at given costs.
Cost figures are taken from Canadian Housing Statistics, 1963 (Table 15) and 1970 (Table 85). Numbers of units are based on the
1951 Census plus annual completions of all types of dwelling units as reported in C.H.S. 1963, Table 15 and C.H.S. 1970, Table 8.
Some figures rounded.

of construction as reported in C.H.S. 1963 and 1970 for N.H.A. houses can be put in diagrammatic form. As N.H.A. financed homes represent a very substantial proportion of all new dwelling units constructed it probably does not distort the actual situation greatly to represent the whole increase in the stock of housing as having been added under approximately the same cost structure as that prevailing for N.H.A. dwellings.[5]

The 'curve' in Fig. 2 is not a supply curve in the sense economists use the term as showing the relation between market prices and the amounts that producers are willing to supply. No market price information is shown. The figure indicates that in the years 1954-70 the average costs of N.H.A. houses increased from $9.61 per square foot to about $14.97. The 1964 cost was $11.01 and so the curve relating unit costs to output and time could be drawn almost horizontally without distorting the facts until that year (the absence of consistency in scale in the diagram may distort the slope). Costs rose more rapidly after 1964 and the curve reflects this. C.H.S. 1963, Table 15 and C.H.S. 1970, Table 8 show that the number of new housing units of all types built in Canada between 1958 and 1970 has been well over 100,000 annually (except in 1960 when it was 94,000); it was nearly 200,000 in 1969. In the diagram these increments of newly constructed houses are added along the horizontal axis to the existing 1951 stock of 3.6 million units with relatively little increase in unit costs at least until 1964. So on the supply side of the market, production of new units would not force prices up much because of increasing costs, and it will be recalled by many readers that the years 1958-64 were ones in which there was a considerable degree of unemployed resources (including labour) in Canada. This confirms our earlier discussion of the construction industry. But as noted, bottlenecks will eventually develop and costs may be pushed up sharply. This occurred in the later years of our analysis with per square foot N.H.A. costs, rising from $11.01 in 1964 to $14.97 in 1970 (C.H.S. 1970, Table 85); however, in 1970, with heavy unemployment in the economy, unit costs rose much less than in the years 1964-69. It should be noted that the square foot areas of N.H.A. dwellings were on the average somewhat larger in the years 1962-67 than in earlier or later years; minor distortions in comparing unit costs may be introduced when such areas vary.

The demand curve for housing

Here we must 'lump' the demands for various types of housing together into an overall aggregate. The demand for the existing stock of housing at any given moment must be quite inelastic. Most of the housing will be occupied and owing to the costs (social and monetary) of moving it will require fairly substantial price decreases to induce people to move, and as these would probably affect most dwellings, even then there may be no incentive to move. However, as already noted, there has been great mobility of families (particularly in metropolitan areas and between rural and urban areas) in Canada, since 1871 and even more so since the end of World War II (C.H.S. 1970, Tables 113, 114).

There are quite a few reasonably similar types of dwellings from which a Canadian purchaser can choose and such a high degree of substitutability implies that the overall demand curve for housing will have a considerable degree of price elasticity. Of the various types of dwelling accommodation it is felt that only in the market for luxury dwellings (including luxury apartments and condominia) will demand be quite price-inelastic. In the medium and low price (and rent) sectors of the market the demand for new housing will almost certainly be quite price-elastic, except for a family having no shelter, in which case it would be completely inelastic.

The housing market

We must now combine the supply and demand curves into a single diagram to obtain the type of market depiction which economists use, and we must reflect

Year	Number of dwelling completions	Average construction cost per sq. ft. N.H.A. (S.F.D.)
1951	81,310	$ 9.13
1952	73,087	9.37
1953	96,839	9.45
1954	101,965	9.61
1955	127,929	9.81
1956	135,700	10.22
1957	117,283	10.41
1958	146,686	10.56
1959	145,671	10.78
1960	123,757	10.65
1961	115,608	10.61
1962	126,682	10.56
1963	128,191	10.68
1964	150,963	11.01
1965	153,037	11.62
1966	162,192	12.56
1967	149,242	13.04
1968	170,993	13.68
1969	195,826	14.62
1970	175,827	14.97

Table shows underlying statistics on which Figure 2 is based.
Sources: Canadian Housing Statistics, 1962 (Table 96), 1970 (Tables 1 and 85).

not only the price and quantity of housing but also ajustments to the housing stock over time. In illustrating this latter concept we relax our earlier assumption that the housing stock could not be reduced, to take account of possible demolitions when the price of housing is low relative to the cost of construction. This is reflected by the steeply falling left hand portion of the net rate of construction, curve CC in Figure 4. (Net rate of construction means the number of new units built less the number demolished each year and note that the origin and the vertical axis are not at the end of the horizontal one as in Figure 3.) Such demolitions have recently been much less important than those carried out to provide sites for new construction and roadways.

In Figure 3 supply is in equilibrium with demand at price P which in Figure 4 yields a zero net rate of construction and the stock of housing (S in year 0 of the analysis) would be maintained at the level indicated, year after year. If for one of the reasons already mentioned demand increases, the demand curve shifts to D_1 and the increased demand for the existing fixed stock of houses pushes the price up to P_1, at which price new construction is possible, so the net rate of construction becomes Q_1 in Figure 4. The stock of housing is slowly increased as new houses are built and the supply curve in Figure 3 shifts to the right to S_1 in year 1; this reduces the pressure of demand on price which gradually falls to P_2 also in year 1. With the lower price, the rate of new construction falls in Figure 4 to Q_2 at price P_2 during year 2, and this is reflected in the shift in Figure 3 from S_1 to S_2, which latter is the stock at the end of year 2. As long as some new net construction continues, the stock of housing will grow and prices will fall until a new equilibrium position is reached with the stock at S_2 and price back at the original level P in Figure 3, and the net rate of construction back to zero in Figure 4. (The analysis assumes this happens in 2 years.) Of course, if demand continues to rise, keeping pace with the rising stock of housing, the price will stay above P and there will continue to be new net construction. In the real world the reactions are neither as smooth or certain as is implied in the analysis; in fact, we can never tell whether the market is precisely in equilibrium or not. But it is clear that insofar as Figure 3 reflects the demand – supply mechanism of the market, the *stock* supply has no effect on price; price is determined entirely by the position of the demand curve. This is one reason why many writers feel that the cost approach is not a very useful tool for estimating market value.

The things to keep in mind are that if any particular change affects demand, the D curve in Figure 3 moves and we follow through the effects in this diagram and in Figure 4; if the change affects construction costs the CC curve in Figure 4 moves up or down and the effect is reflected in price changes as the changing stock of housing moves the S curve in Figure 3. The only change which could start with a movement of the S curve in Figure 3 would be a natural or man-caused disaster which suddenly reduces the existing stock of housing. Note also that the demolitions phase of the CC curve may not move at all in response

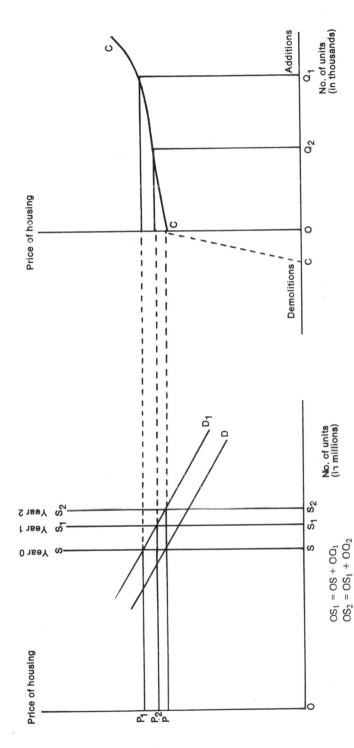

Figure 4 Flow of net new construction.

Figure 3 Existing Stock of Housing.

to changes in construction costs; for instance, if wages increase, there is no reason to feel that demolition will also increase.

This concludes the analysis. It will be appreciated that while it has been based
on 'housing' it could be repeated for other types of real property and then aggregated to show the picture for the whole real property market.[6] It will also be
appreciated that the analysis is in general terms only and no attempt has been
made to include the multitudes of detail which would have to be recognized
in any rigorous market analysis.

To summarize the argument in narrative rather than diagrammatic terms, we
may say that an economic analysis of the housing market essentially provides
an orderly way of thinking about the price of housing and the rate of housing
construction. We have tried to set out and discuss the chief factors affecting
the demand for and the supply of housing. If we could strike an exact balance
between all these factors, we could say precisely what the price of housing
would be, and what the rate of new construction would be, in any given circumstances. But economics is not designed to give exact answers to these questions. It does help us to think clearly about probable future trends. If other factors remain approximately as they are at present, and the marriage rate increases,
we may expect higher prices for houses and an increased rate of construction. If
incomes rise, we will probably sell more houses at the present or at somewhat
higher prices. If techniques improve, and nothing else changes, we would expect
lower prices and higher sales, and so on. This is far from perfect knowledge, but
it is much better than the purely intuitive approach taken towards economic
questions by the layman. Economics is merely reason applied to the problems
of price and quantity and the allocation of resources; the person who takes an
orderly, rational, reasoned approach to business problems will in the long run
win out over the person who acts only on the basis of hearsay or hunch.

It may appear that the analyses in the various diagrams do not reflect the
considerable increase in housing prices which has actually occurred since 1951.
Remember that the unit costs in Figure 2 are for the building only, so a good
deal of the increase in overall price must be related to increasing land value.
(C.H.S. 1970, Table 112 shows that using 1961 as 100 average land costs for
N.H.A., single family dwellings were 40.3 in 1951, 123.7 in 1966 and 164.5 in
1970.) Comment has already been made on how land costs rise in periods of
buoyant economic activity and to this must be added the effect of the increasingly onerous servicing and other requirements of local government.

THE INTEREST RATE, GOVERNMENT POLICY AND HOUSING

The rate of interest

We have already stressed the importance of the rate of interest to the housing
market; it affects both the demand and supply sides of the market. High interest

rates and 'tight money' will cut down both the demand for and the supply of housing and 'easy money' will have the opposite effects. The theory of the rate of interest is one of the most controversial questions in economics (and also in appraisal where the capitalization rate is a vital variable in the income approach). We can give no rounded treatment of the subject here, so let us content ourselves with a few basic ideas – expressed dogmatically, in the interests of clarity and brevity.

First, the rate of interest can be thought of in two general ways:

as being the price of borrowed money. Its level therefore depends partly on the demand for and the supply of loanable funds; as always, increased demand, supply remaining constant, will raise the price; increased supply, demand remaining constant, will lower the price.

As reflecting the liquidity[7] *and time preferences* and expectations of lenders and borrowers. This aspect of the theory of interest is one of Lord Keynes's major contributions to economic theory and is based on the inverse relationship between the rate of interest and the price of interest-paying securities; if a $1000 bond was originally issued with a 5% coupon paying $50 interest per annum, and the level of interest rates doubles, this bond will sell on the market at about $500 if it still has a considerable number of years to run until its maturity since newly issued $1000 bonds will have to bear a 10% coupon and hence will buy $100 interest per annum; a bond paying only $50 interest per annum will be worth only about one-half of these new bonds. Of course if the 5% bond was maturing in a relatively short time it would sell at little if any discount as on maturity it will be paid off at $1000.

Households and firms when they receive their pay cheques or other income must set aside sufficient to cover expenses to be paid between now and their next income payments and may also set aside a small extra amount to cover unexpected contingencies; these decisions relate to their propensities to consume. If they have any income left over they must decide, in light of their propensities to save, in what form to hold this 'speculative balance,' as Keynes called it (the other two parts of income described above he called the 'transactions' balance, and the 'precautionary' balance and the sum of these three balances is the demand for money). If the prices of securities are very high (the rate of interest very low), individuals will hold their speculative balances in money which is non-interest bearing, for two major reasons:

first, security prices are more likely to fall than to rise further and so an investment in a security could result in a capital loss;

second, as interest rates are very low, the sacrifice of not earning interest on the money held is not great.

Conversely, if the price of securities is very low (the rate of interest is very high), individuals will hold their speculative balances in securities for two main reasons which are just the opposite of those set out above.

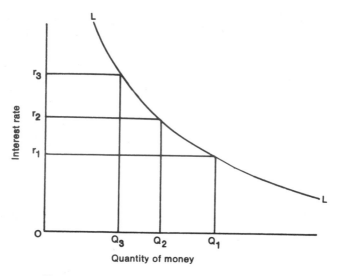

Figure 5 Equilibrium Rate of Interest: Liquidity Preference

So decisions of all income recipients on the form in which they hold their speculative balances, either in fully liquid money (general purchasing power) the unit price of which is always constant ($1 always equals $1) or in securities which while liquid in the sense that they can be disposed of at *some* price, may entail capital losses or gains, determine the level of interest rates. In terms of G.N.P., which can be thought of as aggregate National Income, this and the rate of interest must each be at a level which permits the total supply of money in the economy to be such that it equals the total demand therefor which, as pointed out above, consists of the sum of the transactions, precautionary and speculative·balances for each household and firm aggregated for the whole economy.

It is generally felt that the supply of loanable funds is not affected as much by the rate of interest as by the feelings of lenders as to what the future holds and whether they should be holding cash or financial assets which bear interest. So we can see that interest as a 'price' is very different from the normal sort of 'price.' It affects demand more than it does supply. The demand for loans reflects the general trends in the economy. When the economic outlook is good everyone wants to borrow money: businessmen for expansion of plant and equipment; governments for roads and other necessary public works; municipalities for sewers and water systems; individuals to buy goods on credit or to play the stock market on margin. In a rapidly growing economy the demand for loans will be high and this will keep an upward pressure on the interest rate.

The supply of loanable funds is peculiar. It comes in part from personal savings, and these may react inversely to changes in the rate of interest; 'target' savers need only half as much savings to produce the same revenue, if the interest rate doubles. It comes also from corporate savings – retained earnings. It comes in part from abroad – foreign investment in the country. An important part of it comes from bank loans, and here also a peculiarity arises. Under our fractional reserve banking system, banks can create or destroy money; they can, therefore, create or destroy loanable funds. Also, the Central Bank (in Canada, the Bank of Canada, in the United States, The Federal Reserve) has especially strong powers to create or destroy loanable funds since it can fix the amount of chartered bank reserves, and thus their ability to lend. It can also fix what is called the Bank Rate which is generally considered to be an important indicator of government attitudes. Here, then, government policy enters the interest rate picture; but we shall leave our discussion of monetary policy temporarily.

Secondly, while we speak about *the* rate of interest, there are in reality many rates of interest. These rates form a rough hierarchy from Treasury Bills to say 5th mortgages on speculatively acquired land – 'the rate of interest' is simply some sort of 'average' price of borrowed money. Generally speaking, if the interest rate is higher, the riskier the loan and the longer the period for which the loan is made. Ordinarily (but there are exceptions) a long-term government bond has a higher interest yield than a short-term bond, merely because it is a loan of longer duration.[8] And a private mortgage for 20 years carries a higher interest rate than a 20-year government bond because the former is a riskier loan. This multiplicity of interest rates would cause no problem if the differentials between interest rates were always constant, but this is not so: we have purposely spoken of a 'rough' pattern or hierarchy of interest rates, as the relationships between different interest rates are not constant.

The main reason for this is that the market for loanable funds is by no means 'perfect' in the sense that lenders immediately switch to different investments when relative yields change slightly. By tradition, and often by law, important lending institutions like banks, insurance companies and trust companies develop certain investment habits and often try to keep their investments in different types of securities in a fairly stable ratio to each other. The supply of funds to different markets may, therefore, not be 'even.' Mortgage money may still be flowing smoothly from the insurance companies at the same time as banks find their supply of funds reduced.[9] Or bonds may be selling well at the same time as mortgages are hard to place. The result is that interest rates may rise or fall more rapidly in some markets than in others; changes in mortgage rates, as we all know, usually lag behind changes in rates in the bond markets and on bank loans.

Another result of the imperfect market in loanable funds is that borrowers may be unable to obtain loans in the quantity they want at the going rate, or even at a somewhat higher rate. If bond yields are very attractive, insurance companies may channel most of their funds into bonds and be very sticky about lending on mortgages; builders may get accommodation if they are prepared to pay considerably higher interest, but they may be reluctant to do so until they are sure that the demand for housing is sufficiently strong to absorb this increased cost. The Canadian picture is further complicated by the rigidities built into the interest rate structure by means of arbitrary ceilings above which certain rates cannot rise; these may well prevent the rate from performing its proper function as a rationer of credit. For instance, the rate on N.H.A. loans is tied to the long-term average yield on Government of Canada bonds and the borrower or builder will not be able to offer a higher rate than that so set and will simply not get the loan. It is for these reasons that in previous discussions we have referred to the rate of interest and the availability of mortgage money. In perfect markets a thing is always available at some price. In the imperfect market for mortgages we have to consider not only the price, i.e. the interest rate, but also the 'availability,' i.e. the ease of obtaining the funds.

Theories of value and of interest can be related to some extent: having in mind the peculiarities of the supply side of the market, the loanable funds theory of interest is analogous to a cost theory of value in that interest is considered as the cost to the borrower of having the use of funds while the owner of the funds abstains from using them. But clearly the rate of interest cannot be a reward for abstaining from spending; i.e. for saving. An individual who hoards his savings in cash earns no interest, yet he abstains from spending.

The liquidity preference theory of interest is analogous to a market theory of value in that the principle of substitution is at work in creating a market in which demands for general purchasing power (i.e. money) vie with demands for things money will buy and so establishes a value or price of liquidity. When individuals prefer to hold money the rate of interest will rise and when they prefer to hold other assets (and particularly securities) the rate of interest will fall.

One further point requires note. Canada is an exporting (i.e. 'open') economy and the lower the value of the Canadian dollar relative to the U.S. dollar (in terms of which international prices of goods and services are generally quoted), the cheaper will be our exports in foreign countries, but the more expensive will be imports to Canada from these countries. If Canada imports foreign capital, this must be converted into Canadian dollars so a demand for these is created which will if substantial, either force the price of our dollar up relative to the U.S. dollar or require the government and/or central bank to keep this pressure from developing by buying the foreign capital and holding it in reserves. One reason for an inflow of capital is to finance investment in Canada, while another is to take advantage of considerably higher interest rates which may prevail in Canada relative to those in the capital-exporting countries. Both of these capital flows may force the value of our dollar upwards and so harm our exporting industry. And as one of the major tools of cyclical control centres on the level of the Bank Rate, it is obvious that to some extent at least, Canada cannot control inflationary tendencies by increases in this, as well as she could if our economy was not quite so 'open.'

GOVERNMENT MONETARY POLICY AND HOUSING

All modern governments pursue monetary and fiscal policies designed to promote economic stability – i.e. to prevent either excessive inflation or excessive deflation. Monetary policy is an attempt to maintain stability by varying the interest rate and the amount of money in the economy from time to time. If inflationary tendencies are in evidence, the Central Bank restricts the supply of money and raises the interest rate rapidly; if depression threatens, the reverse policy is followed. The Central Bank governs the money supply and affects interest rates by open market operations, changes in Bank Rate, and in Legal Reserve Ratios of the Chartered Bank and other techniques.

Fiscal policy is one of promoting stability by varying the balance between government tax revenues and expenditures. If depression threatens, purchasing power is 'pumped into' the economy by the government spending more than it receives in taxes; it thus incurs a deficit. If inflation is the problem the government attempts to arrange its affairs so that tax receipts are higher than expenditures; it then has a surplus which has the effect of 'drawing' or 'sucking' purchasing power out of the economy.

Monetary policy has a strong effect on the rate of interest, although it does not completely determine it; take the example of 'tight money' designed to reduce inflationary pressures. The Central Bank will increase its Bank Rate: this has a direct effect in increasing interest rates on short-term government bonds. The Central Bank will also engage in open market operations, selling some of its holdings of medium and long-term government bonds. This has the effect of forcing bond prices down and so increasing their yields. It also decreases chartered bank reserves (as either the banks or their customers in buying the bonds must issue cheques and thus reduce their deposits to pay for them), and so they must reduce their loans to comply with the required reserve ratio. This puts an upward pressure on interest rates on bank loans, and also on stockbrokers' loans.

Then the effects of these changes begin to spread throughout the whole hierarchy of interest rates. Insurance companies begin to restrict mortgage lending as they find that they can earn higher yields on government bonds. Companies floating bond issues find that they, too, have to offer higher rates to compete with the higher yields on government bonds. Stock prices may fall until the yield on stocks is brought into line relative to the new rates on government bonds, but it must be remembered that stocks represent equity ownership, whereas bonds and mortgages are debt.[10] The effect of the policy seeps through the economy until practically every borrower – including the house builder and the house buyer – finds that it is more difficult and more expensive to borrow money. One very noticeable effect of higher interest rates on real property values results from the higher interest charges that municipalities must pay for the money required to extend sewerage, water and other facilities; this is minimized in some Provinces by the availability of Provincial funds for the purchase of debentures of municipalities and school and other boards. In brief, by a variety of channels, the effect of 'tight' money is to reduce both the demand for and the supply of housing. 'Easy' money, of course, has the reverse effect.

Inflationary forces of the 'demand-pull' type result, basically, from too much investment (and/or consumption), or, to put it another way, from too rapid development. 'Tight' money puts a brake on this development and tends to reduce investment throughout the economy, including investment in new housing. It does not, however, necessarily affect every investment sector in the same way or to the same degree. Everyone agrees that stability policy is desirable. But it is also desirable that the policy should be 'fair' or 'just' in the sense of distributing the burden of adjustment equitably among the different sectors of the economy. The 'justness' or 'fairness' of monetary policy (and, of course, of fiscal policy) will be debated as long as such policy is used. It is fair in the sense that interest rates are raised to *everyone,* across-the-board, so to speak. But the effects vary.

Because the loanable funds market is imperfect, and the pattern of interest rates not invariant, some rates are raised more than others, and, as already noted, some cannot rise above a fixed or determinable ceiling. Borrowers in markets where interest rates rise more than the average complain of high rates, and in markets where the rates rise less than the average they complain of an inability to get funds. And even if the rate increase is the same to two industries, one industry is likely to be more 'unstable' than the other, and to react more violently to the increased cost of money. The house construction industry is one of those industries that is subject to rather violent fluctuations and tight money may in some periods be so effective in curtailing housing construction that government monetary policy seems to be incompatible with government housing policy of providing adequate levels of housing for all groups in the population; accordingly, special measures may have to be taken to provide more mortgage funds.

Traditionally, inflation has been thought of as being of the 'demand-pull' type which should be amenable to attack by typical monetary and fiscal policies, as heavy unemployment cannot in theory exist coincidentally with this type of inflation.

In 1970 a new phenomenon was apparent; there was a considerable degree of inflation *together* with heavy unemployment and the application of traditional monetary and fiscal policies seemed to make the situation worse. So some economists postulated that the type of inflation being experienced was 'cost-push' and that the cure must include not only expansionary government and central bank policies but also the imposition of an 'incomes policy,' under which major types of income would be controlled as would prices.

The *Third Annual Review*, 1966 of the E.C.C. analyses the possibility of imposing such a policy in Canada as part of a set of general targets for the whole economy. After examining the situation in five other countries, the Council feels that, under certain circumstances, an income policy may have some beneficial effects on the reconciliation of price and employment goals.

But the chances of success are much greater in a unitary state with strong central powers and a tradition of considerable governmental intervention in the detailed functioning of the economy and few constitutional or other impediments preventing the government from resorting to direct controls. Also the economy would have to be comparatively self-sufficient with private economic power relatively concentrated within the country and strong centralized organizations of both union and management. Finally there would have to be mutual confidence among economic groups that no one sector or region would try to benefit more than others from the general wage and price restraints. Clearly Canada does not fit these criteria and so it does not seem to be a favourable environment for incomes policy.

Of course the two types of inflation are not independent; rather their causes and effects are inextricably intertwined and they mutually reinforce each other: 'demand-pull' implies higher rewards being paid to the agents in production and this often results in higher costs and selling prices in the product market; 'cost-push' results in higher rewards to those agents in production who have successfully extracted these from the users of their services and these higher incomes give greater purchasing power which pays the higher prices. So costs and purchasing power rise together, although increases in purchasing power are gained only by the owners of those agents in production who have been able to exert the cost-push.

ADVERTISING AND THE REAL PROPERTY MARKET

Introduction

A tremendous amount of money is spent on advertising in most businesses and certainly it is a major item of expense in the real estate field. There are many important decisions which businessmen must make concerning the advertising budget: its total amount, how to allocate it between departments, products and salesmen, on what basis it should be set, and so forth. And yet few of them have a valid basis for making these decisions and the whole field has been largely neglected by researchers.

We will outline a few concepts which should assist, if not in solving the problem, at least in making it clear that there is a problem which is capable of solution by consideration of a few basic principles.[11]

A clear understanding of a few economic concepts will assist materially in attaining a better understanding of the advertising problems:

1 First, the concept of 'costs': obviously advertising is a cost of doing business and therefore it encounters some of the same economic problems as do other costs.

2 Secondly, the concept of market structure: any area of business in which advertising is used must of necessity be to a greater or lesser degree an area in which competition is of the 'monopolistic' or 'imperfect' type, rather than the 'perfect' type of most economic analysis. As already pointed out, many real-world markets, including that for real property, are not perfectly competitive.

3 Thirdly, the concept of 'demand' and 'elasticity of demand': advertising has as its object the 'shifting' of the demand curve, i.e. the creation of increased demand on the part of the buying public. Also it will be appreciated that the demand curve in question cannot be perfectly elastic if advertising is to be successful; this is inherent in the question of market structure raised in (2) above.

Importance of advertising in our economy

Every mature society is characterized by greater and greater refinements and specializations of products and techniques and by minor differences between what are really very similar products; generally the distinction between items is emphasized by the use of brand names. This is really what is meant when we speak of an oligopolistic, imperfectly competitive or monopolistically competitive market structure.

In order to encourage purchasers to buy Brand A instead of Brand B, advertising and promotion are used to extol its merits; in fact, without advertising it would be almost impossible to develop brand name loyalties and preferences. Certainly a large proportion of the selling costs of any business is devoted to building up consumer loyalty and preferences. However, it is a moot point as to whether advertising which seeks to foster product discrimination has the effect of increasing overall demand for products in the general field in question; if it does, then obviously there is a direct benefit to the economy; but if it does not, then the major effect is simply to raise costs and hence prices without contributing to greater productivity. This, of course, is most undesirable and could be one of the basic causes of inflation.

Economic principles of advertising

Advertising costs Such costs are pure selling expenses and are economically quite different from the production costs of a firm (i.e. rental, telephone, salaries, furniture, equipment, etc.). Selling costs are incurred to get business, while production costs are incurred to take care of business so obtained. The prime purpose of selling costs is to affect the demand for the product (in our case, real property).

From the above it will be seen that production costs are the result of sales and are functionally related to sales volume. On the other hand, selling costs are the cause of sales and have no necessary functional relationship to volume. And yet is is common practice for businessmen to base their advertising budget upon a certain percentage of sales (either past or anticipated) and hence to treat advertising not as the cause but as the result of such sales.

Of course, the principle of relating advertising expense to sales volume by means of allotting a percentage of revenue earned to such expense has the virtue of simplicity; also, since many firms follow the practice, the actual percentages used are based on experience. From this viewpoint, therefore, the procedure can be supported. However, the difficulty is that such an arbitrary base for advertising costs does not contribute to tracing the effectiveness of the money spent.

Determination of advertising budget There are a number of methods on which business people rely in order to determine how much they will spend on advertising in a given period. The most common are:

Percentage of sales or of commissions
As noted earlier, this is an illogical approach as it treats advertising as being the result of sales, not the cause. The past or current volume of sales does not itself give any guidance as to the worth of increasing volume or as to the cost of such increases.

Probably the reason for the popularity of this method is that it gives the illusion of control over what is a discretionary type of expense; it appears to be systematic. Of course, too, if experience has shown that, say, 10% of gross commission can be spent on advertising, then such expenditure is a 'safe' one; also, if competitors use the method, then advertising costs will be roughly proportional to each firm's share of the market.

This percentage of commission basis is widely used in the real estate field and therefore can be said to have stood the test of time. However, it is probably retained due to inertia, and adequate research would almost certainly disclose better bases.

All-that-can-be-afforded

This approach is an adjunct of the percentage-of-sales approach. It generally amounts.to allotting a certain percentage of profits (either past or estimated) to promotion. It has the advantage of safety and also, with income taxes being graduated and at their present high level, it enables a firm (particularly if it is unincorporated) to utilize its advertising expenses to reduce taxable income in proportion to the size of its profit. The major criticism of the method is that it may prevent a business from taking advantage of advertising opportunities to increase volume and profits or may result in spending more on advertising than the results would justify.

Return-on-investment

For a service-type business, investment in fixed assets is rarely a major item in its business operations; so this approach (which is fairly common in manufacturing, retail and transportation industries) has little appeal or practical importance. Like all arbitrary methods, it is inadequate and it also shares the fault of the percentage-of-sales approach in that it treats advertising as a result of investment rather than treating investment as being the result of effective advertising.

Objective and task

Under this approach, the advertising budget is the amount needed to attain certain decided-upon objectives. Clearly this has applicability to service businesses which are embarking on some specific project. For example, if a certain subdivision is to be disposed of, then, in consultation with advertising consultants, the necessary types and costs of advertising can be estimated in advance. This approach is straightforward and is far more logical than the others commented on above; its major weakness is that it does not relate the worth of attaining the objective to the cost of so attaining. But this can be done by means of adequate research as to the effectiveness of each method and quantity of advertising.

Conclusions

Enough has been said as to the illogical character of most approaches to the question of advertising cost. The key to the whole problem is, of course, research: this need be neither formal nor on a large scale. Each firm can, and should, carry out its own research aimed at ascertaining the effectiveness of various media. It should further give considerable thought to the implications of increasing sales volume through advertising. The principle of diminishing returns applies to increasing the amount of business just as it does to any other situation in which one of the factors of production is fixed in supply. And what is the fixed factor when we consider increasing sales volume? Clearly, it is the managerial skill of the businessman himself;[12] if he spreads this too thin, then inevitably the profitability of the business will decline and such decline once started is very rapid. Hence, the firm should think twice before attempting to increase its volume of sales too rapidly by means of advertising or other forms of promotion.

What the businessman must try to do is estimate the volume and profitability of sales with and without a given outlay on advertising. Then he can compare the results and make his decision. Our society being dynamic, we can never expect to attain exactness concerning such a nebulous type of expenditure as advertising, but through proper analysis we can do much to assure that advertising dollars do, in fact, produce profitable sales.

Advertising effectiveness

Clearly the measure of effectiveness should be profitability, and yet many firms seem to feel that the measure is volume of sales. It is simple to ascertain whether sales volume has increased and fairly simple to relate such increase to advertising expenditures. It is not so simple to ascertain whether the increased volume has, in fact, resulted in a proportionate or greater than proportionate increase in profit; if it has not, then there is doubt as to whether the advertising or other expenditure which caused the increased volume was, in fact, worth incurring. Such increases in profits depend on the elasticities of demand and supply for the service or product in question.

Of course, the relationship between volume and profit is a complex one and depends upon many more things than just advertising; but advertising is a fully controllable expense and hence it appears logical that the thinking businessman should attempt to correlate such expenses not with volume of sales but rather with profitability.

How then can a firm satisfy itself, first as to the profitability of a certain volume of sales and, secondly, as to what type and amount of advertising is appropriate to such volume? The simplest way to measure the profitability of sales at various volumes is by means of a detailed analysis of the expenses which must be incurred and the revenue to be produced at each level of sales. In making such an analysis, the businessman is cautioned to remember that expenses have a way of creeping up unpredictably and therefore should be estimated on a generous basis. On the other hand, revenue earned from sales has a habit of falling short of its estimated amount as volume increases, owing to the greater number of bad debts, collection expenses, abortive deals, and so forth. At a sales volume where marginal revenue is just equal to marginal costs, profits will be at a maximum.[13] And as in many industries the major controllable expense is advertising, what we want to do is to carry advertising to the point where its marginal cost equals the marginal revenue from the added sales. The whole problem revolves about 'control' or 'feed-back.' What is required is some system whereby the results from individual advertisements and classes of media can be tabulated and related to sales obtained, revenue earned, and the profitability of such extra revenue when contrasted with the extra costs incurred to earn them.

Now, just as sales volume may reduce profitability, so it will almost inevitably make the imposition and policing of controls more difficult. When sales volume is the master, then the important checks as to profitability are generally ignored or minimized. This is our old friend, the law of diminishing returns, at work again; the managerial skill of the businessman gets spread too thin and therefore he cannot supervise the carrying-out of the controls adequately. However, this does not imply that such checks should not be utilized. They become, of course, increasingly important in larger firms, because in them there is often a tendency to make arbitrary rules as to advertising and these can be much abused if proper controls are not also imposed.

REFERENCES

1 / The analysis derives from material developed by several individuals for the Division of Extension, University of Toronto; credit for the stock-flow analysis is believed to be due to David Winch, sometime professor of economics at the University of Alberta. The omission of credit to any unknown contributors is unintentional.

2 / The table at the end of the chapter summarizes important characteristics of various types of market structure encountered in economic theory and the real world.

3 / In economic theory this can be analysed with indifference curves from which can be developed approximate demand curves. See Bellan and Chapter 16, Reference 19.

4 / Bernard J. Frieden, *The Future of Old Neighborhoods,* M.I.T. 1964. The 'filtering' process of the market is illustrated in the context of old, centrally located urban neighbourhoods. The demand curve for a family with no shelter would have zero elasticity.

5 / The average cost of N.H.A. dwellings may have no counterpart in the actual cost of any individual property and, of course, has none in non-residential properties.

The historical or current cost of a building would be represented by a single point vertically above the 'quantity' of the building. Obviously such a point would have no effect on price and one must conclude that the cost approach will have little relevance in the short-run real property market.

6 / H.A.J. Green, *Aggregations in Economic Analysis,* Princeton 1964. The problems of aggregation are discussed.

7 / Both the A.I.C. and A.I.R.E.A. texts ignore the liquidity preference of the theory of interest in their theoretical treatments of risk rates which means closing the door on theoretical advances of the 20th century; this reinforces the Ricardian and Classical biases of the accepted appraisal theory. Of course, in the practical aspects of the texts, liquidity is recognized. Lord Keynes's liquidity theory of interest evolves from Bohm Bawerk's concept of time-preference. See Chapter 16, Reference 24. One problem with a loanable funds-based theory is that it stresses time preference to the virtual exclusion of liquidity preference.

8 / Bank of Canada statistics released late in May 1971 shows that the long-term average yield on Government of Canada bonds was 7.2% whereas the average rate on 91-day Treasury Bills was 2.96%. See also Chapter 11.

9 / Reference to C.H.S. 1970, Table 29 shows that the total amount of residential mortgage lending approved by chartered banks has in recent years ranged from $23,000 to $338,189,000. As of April 21, 1970, the accumulated total of such loans was $1,665,000,000, of which $200 million had been advanced since January 1, 1970. Prior to the 1967 amendments to the Bank Act, chartered banks could only lend on real property in N.H.A. insured mortgages; they can since that date make any type of real property mortgage loan.

10 / This point does not seem to be clearly recognized in the accepted appraisal theory of risk rates. In the example of the summation approach on p. 200 of the A.I.C. Text, the safe rate component is said to be the yield on Federal Government bonds, i.e. debt securities. One should recall that the yields on very short term government securities may be much lower than that on such bonds having several years to run until maturity. The only true 'safe' rate at any given moment surely is reflective of the yield on very short-term government securities, such as treasury bills. The principles on which the approach is based may well be valid, but it must be considered as pure theory in the appraisal context.

11 / A particularly good analysis is to be found in Joel Dean, *Managerial Economics,* Prentice Hall.

12 / In economic theory there is always one entrepreneur, no more no less, for each firm.

13 / The rule of producing, where MC = MR, for optimal profit is fully analysed in Bellan. Note has already been made of the differences between concepts used by appraisers and accountants; one of the major problem of accounting records from the economist's viewpoint is that they are based on average and total costs and revenues, whereas for economic analysis the marginals to these are relevant.

Addendum

Reference has been made to the effect of speculation on land values but there is good reason for feeling that this does not per se raise the demand-determined price. If 2 adjoining parcels of land owned one by a speculator and the other by a long-time owner, are acquired by the same developer, the price paid will be identical for each parcel assuming adequate knowledge on the part of both vendors. Hence, the conclusion that speculation per se does not affect the demand-determined price. Of course if one (or more) speculator-developer owns a very considerable proportion of the buildable land in or near a centre of economic activity, this may influence the supply side via monopolistic power which will force prices up; but this effect is due to the scale of ownership rather than to the speculator's intervention.

ANALYSIS OF VARIOUS TYPES OF MARKET STRUCTURE

	Characteristic considered	Perfect competition	Monopolistic competition	Oligopoly
1	Many buyers	Yes	Yes	Yes
2	Many sellers	Yes	Yes	Very few
3	Buyers relatively small so cannot affect price	Yes	Yes	Yes
4	Sellers relatively small so cannot affect price	Yes	Limited control over price	Very large
5	Homogeneous product	Yes	Differentiated	Differentiated
6	Buyers knowledge of market and of alternatives	Perfect	Confused by promotion and inertia, loyalties	Confused by promotion of seller
7	Freedom of entry and exit to and from market by suppliers	Yes	Yes	Large capital investment limits freedom
8	Availability of financing	Yes	Yes	Yes
9	Agency intervention	No	Yes	Strong and complex
10	Advertising	No	Limited and local	Vigorous and national
11	Reaction of competitive suppliers to price changes	None	Some, but limited	Reaction is key to behaviour
12	Supply curve	Upward slope for firm	None for industry, up slope for firm	None for industry, up slope for firm
13	Demand curve	Horizontal	Downward slope, fairly elastic	Downward slope, fairly inelastic
14	What is an example?	Individual wheat farmer	A corner grocer in well populated neighbourhood of a large urban area	Automobile manufacturers

Monopoly	Monopsony (buyer's monopoly)	Bilateral monopoly	Real property market (residential)
Usually	Only one buyer generally buying some specialized good or service. Often an oligopolist in product market	Only one	Yes
Only one	Usually many, selling services of agents in production	Only one	Yes
Usually	Always large relative to market in question	Buyer relatively strong	Yes
Generally large, price is regulated	Price often fixed	Seller relatively strong	Yes
Yes, but use of price discrimination	Close substitutes	Yes: only one good or service is bargained for	Close substitutes
No true alternatives; seller knows this	Only one buyer who knows its requirements	Good	Fair
Large capital investment limits freedom	Few limits on freedom except need to sell services	Freedom is limited by need to settle eventually	Yes
Yes	Yes	Yes	Discrete price changes. Down payment important
Based on sole means of transmission, sale outlets, etc.	Often union/management intervention	Often union and management associations	Generally organized with standard fees
Generally institutional	Limited in buying market	Not needed once this stage is reached	Vigorous and local
No close competitors	No close competitors for buyer	Price indeterminacy	Considerable and often irrational
None in strict sense. Average cost curve may slope down for large range of output	Marginal factor cost curve; upward slope	Marginal factor cost curve; steep up slope; may be vertical	Stock is vertical; flow – none for industry, usually elastic and upward sloping for a firm
Downward slope, generally quite inelastic	Downward slope, MRP curve	Downward slope, generally quite inelastic	Downward slope; fairly inelastic
Public telephone utility, provincial liquor sales system	A single large employer in a relatively small community	An offeror – purchaser of a house facing the offeree-owner-vendor	Initially all potential purchasers and sellers. May become a bilateral monopoly

16

An economist looks at appraisal theory

The matter of the relationship between economic and appraisal theory does not appear to have been the subject of much or any study by professional economists and hence the explorer must rely largely on his own resources. A consideration of the conditions under which our Appraisal Theory was developed should make it obvious both why Appraisal Theory and Economic Theory may not agree and why so little thought has been given to the discrepancies. Arthur Warner has admirably outlined the origin of the appraisal theory in its first systematic presentation in 1932 when Frederick M. Babcock wrote the 'Valuation of Real Estate.'[1] Others who have recognized the problems include Charles F. Louie,[2] Paul Wendt,[3] Laura Kingsbury,[4] Sanders A. Kahn[5] and Richard U. Ratcliff.[6]

While any attempt to make rigorous some abstruse practical applications (which in effect is what Babcock did in 1932) is worthy of the highest praise, the reactions (one could more properly say lack of reactions!) of the appraisal institutes, societies and their members to the scheme he propounded is inexplicable. Also, it is suggested that there could not be a worse economic theory on which to base appraisal theory than that which has been developed by the Institutes out of Babcock's original treatise.

We can consider our topic under several headings as follows:

.1 The Source of the Economic Theory on which Appraisal Theory claims to be based.
2 The Type of Market Structure visualized by the Economic Theory on which Appraisal Theory is based.
3 The relevance of the concept of the Agents in Production for Distribution Theory on which Appraisal Theory is based.
4 Miscellaneous matters such as capitalization rates.

The literature implies that the source from which Appraisal Theory springs is Alfred Marshall's 'Principles of Economics'[7] and, in a sense, this is correct,

but largely only as Marshall was a follower of the Classical School of Economists of David Ricardo and John Stuart Mill. That Marshall didn't really feel
'real property economics' was similar to normal theoretical economics is clear
from the inclusion in his 'Principles' of certain Appendices which explain more
fully his ideas on special problems of economics including that of land valuation which is particularly referred to in Appendix G. Also Marshall in Chapter
XI of Book V discusses the question of marginal costs in relation to urban
land values. At no place in any of the recognized appraisal texts does the word
'marginal' appear with reference to either cost or revenue. And yet how, since
the 'marginal revolution' of 1871,[8] can any theory be given serious consideration which doesn't at least consider the implications of the marginal concept?
Of course strict marginal analysis is based on minute changes in the various
variables whereas in the real estate market, the changes are of finite size. But
techniques to handle finite differences have been developed and also adaptations of the differential calculus have been made in other fields.

It is therefore suggested that accepted appraisal theory is based largely on
the distribution theory Classical economics, of which the chief exponents were
David Ricardo[9] and John Stuart Mill[10] and that Marshall contributed only insofar as he was the direct successor of the Classicists as well as their bridge to the
marginal school.

The key problem of the Classical school was not that of Value but rather
that of Distribution: in other words, the concern was not with how big the
pie was but rather with how the pie was divided among the various contributors to its making. These contributors were called agents in (or factors of) production. Certainly this problem of distribution was what concerned Ricardo
and that it was a major concern of Mill is to be assumed from the opening portion of his chapter 'Of Value' where (in 1848 remember!) he wrote, 'Happily
there is nothing in the laws of value which remains for the present or any
future writer to clear up; the theory of the subject is complete ...' And yet in
1871 this 'complete theory' was in large part rendered obsolete. The chapters
on Distribution in both Ricardo's and Mills' Principles precede those on Value;
this order has, of course, been reversed in most subsequent texts.

So this is the economic theory on which appraisal theory is based! A theory
which since 1871 has had little validity in the everyday world and which caused
Lord Keynes, one of the 20th century's most important economists to write.
'But it was Ricardo's more fascinating intellectual construction which ... con-
strained the subject (economic theory) for a full hundred years to an artificial
groove.'[11] Jevons some years earlier had written 'I am beginning to think very
strongly that the true line of economic science descends from Smith through
Malthus to Senior while another branch through Ricardo to Mill has put as
much error into the science as they have truth'[12] ... 'that able but wrong-
headed man David Ricardo shunted the car of economic science on to a wrong

line ... on which it was further urged to confusion by his equally able and wrong-headed admirer John Stuart Mill.'[13]

Why in the middle of the 20th century appraisers would adhere to an off-shoot of economic theory which most other applied and theoretical econo-mists had discarded as an 'historical curiosity'[14] is hard to say. Ricardian rent theory (for that is what appraisal theory is based on) is simple and this has its appeal. But it relies for its validity on certain basic assumptions, the chief of which are that all 'land' is capable of only one use, namely growing 'corn'; that labour and capital are always applied as equi-proportionate doses to land; and that wages of labour are kept at a psychological subsistence level by popu-lation pressures. Such assumptions probably had few, if any, applications even in the England of the early 19th century and certainly have none in our mod-ern urban, industrialized society. Also the Classical theory is basically a long-run one which is not too concerned with short-run market equilibrium; and yet it has been said that in economics the long run is the time which never comes! Certainly in appraisal practice the concern is the short-run market period.

If all that was wanted was a theory of rent which was ancient, there were several available to choose from which are not only older than the Classical, but also more logical. Ricardo said that the rent of land was due to the exist-ence of poor land; i.e. to the *niggardliness* of nature. In the field of real estate appraisal, we more correctly think of rent as being due to the productiveness of the property; i.e. to the *bounty* of nature. And this latter far more accept-able idea was inherent in the writings of many economists prior to Ricardo, of whom the best known are the Physiocrats,[15] Adam Smith[16] and Thomas Ro-bert Malthus.[17] And we must not forget the remarkable insight shown by J.H. von Thuenen, who in 1826, constructed an economic model to show how rent was influenced by the distance of land from the market.[18]

And if what was wanted was a more applicable and modern theory of price determination, reference could have been made to either the mathematical concepts of Edgeworth[19] or to the theory of Chamberlin,[20] or that of Isard.[21] The former developed what is now a common diagrammatic tool of economic theory, one function of which is to illustrate the indeterminacy of price deter-mination in a market in which both buyer and seller are to some degree mono-polists, and, of course, this is what the real estate market is like; it becomes a bilateral monpoly when one potential buyer faces the owner of a certain pro-perty to negotiate purchase and sale; prior to that it is generally monopolisti-cally competitive. Chamberlin refined a theoretical concept which had been touched on by several earlier theorists, namely that most markets are neither perfectly competitive nor fully monopolistic on either the buyer's or seller's side but rather are a combination of competitive and monopoly elements. Isard stresses the point that economic phenomena have both time and space dimensions and that orthodox economic theory in general ignores the latter.

Of course it is easy to see why from a practical point of view a theory of appraisal once defined and appearing to have impeccable economic forebears should not be challenged by appraisers. The courses offered by various appraisal bodies have not been primarily educational in character, but rather are of a trade training nature. They emphasize 'how' things are done and not 'why' they should or should not be done. Obviously trade training is a poor vehicle for theoretical analysis and this added to the inertia of the institutes, societies and their lecturers and what appears to be a vested interest in the status quo is sufficient reason why despite its obvious theoretical and practical shortcomings, Appraisal Theory should not be subjected to rigorous examination.[22] And there is no reason to doubt that in the actual real estate market something rather like what is described as the Appraisal Process does, in fact, take place and hence perhaps even if adequate theory were developed, it wouldn't make very much difference to the practice of appraising. But as has been the case in many other fields, good theory makes possible the refinements of both theory and practice and bad theory makes such refinements impossible.

Ricardo was both a theorist and a practical businessman who wished to influence governmental policies. As a theorist, he worked largely on problems of long-run equilibrium, while as a businessman he was concerned with short-run market problems. In these latter he was very 'anti-landowner,' whereas in the former he was not. It is interesting, then, to note that his basic theory which has been adopted (but not, it is suggested, 'adapted') to real estate appraisal, has no reference to actual market conditions but only to the state in which the market would arrive in the long run. And also that this great adversary of the land-owning class has in the 20th century become the founding father of the quasi-profession whose endeavour is to estimate such landowner's interests in land!

Ricardo has been thought to have held a labour theory of value and certainly this is the aspect of his thoughts which appealed to Marx and which forms the basis of the economic theory of communism. However, from the point of view of what we would call market value, Ricardo and all Classical economists were cost-of-production theorists. Perhaps this is why the Cost Approach is so much emphasized in Appraisal theory when, in fact, cost per se has little to do with market value being a long-run, not a short-run concept, as a price determinant.

To understand Ricardo's theory of rent, one must first understand what he was attempting to show by it. If we accept that all production is made possible by a combination of the efforts of labour, land and capital, then several questions must be answered, of which two are: what will be the value of the product, and how will the total proceeds from the sale of the product be distributed between the co-operating factors? The first question Ricardo answered by saying that the value would equal the cost of production. But remember that, as a theorist, he was thinking only of the long-run; in the short-run market, he would feel that the interaction of demand and supply would determine price (value); whereas in the long-run, price (value) would be determined solely by supply: i.e. by the cost of production. And even in the short-run he seems to feel that cost of production was the main value-determinant. In contrast, the stock-flow analysis of Chapter 15 shows that, in the short-run real property market, demand is the sole determinant of price.

It has already been pointed out that Ricardo's real task in economics was to determine the laws of distribution and not the laws of value. How was the price (value) of the product to be distributed between the co-operating agents in production? If we think back to our high school mathematics, we will remember that, if we have three unknown quantities, we must use three equations containing these unknowns, to find a unique value for each unknown. This was Ricardo's problem and he decided to dispose of it by dissolving away two of the unknowns by assumptions. What he wanted to end up with was an equation showing that in the short-run the price (value) of a product was received by the capitalist (who was also the entrepreneur) after paying for the labour and land used in production. The entrepreneur was the residual recipient in the short-run; this is ignored in the accepted appraisal theory. So he disposed of labour and land as follows.

Labour he said was always paid a 'corn' wage equal to the minimum psychological subsistence wage necessary to maintain the work force at a constant level. And he relied on the Malthusian theory of population to show that, if the wage level rose above the necessary subsistence level, population would increase to force wages back down to subsistence. This then disposed of the 'unknown' labour; it was paid a 'given' wage.

Land he disposed of in an equally artful fashion. He said that price (value) was always determined by production on land which was at the 'margin of cultivation.' He assumed that all land had just a single use, namely to grow 'corn' and that at any given price (value) of 'corn' there was some quality of land which would produce just enough 'corn' to pay the wages of labour and profits of capital employed thereon but leave nothing over to pay rent on land. And if price (value) is determined by the costs of production on this marginal, rent-free land, then the rent of land doesn't enter into price (value). Rent entered into the costs of production on all supra-marginal land but didn't affect price (value) as this was determined on marginal, rent-free land. Hence the 'unknown' land disappeared. It must be recognized that Ricardo's definition of land as being 'the original and indestructible powers of the soil' is vital to his analysis as land so defined has no cost of production.

As far as capital goods were concerned, Ricardo treated them as stored up labour and his model of the economy consisted of applying combined doses of labour and capital to land, the product in the short-run being divided among the three agents in accordance with the above principles: namely that labour was paid a subsistence level of wages, marginal land received no rent and so capital received the surplus after paying wages. On supra-marginal land, capital still got the same surplus, but the landlord also got a surplus in the form of rent. As illustrative of his attitude towards demand, Ricardo said that the amount of the surplus earned each year (i.e. the short-run) in the production of 'corn' determined how much the capitalist would set aside as a 'wage-fund' to support labour over the next year of production; demand for labour depended solely on the size of this fund, and not at all on the productivity of labour.

Let us now consider the question of market structure. What this depends on is the shape and elasticity of the demand and supply curves. We can summarize the various structures as follows (see Table in Chapter 15):

> Perfect competition – infinitely elastic demand curve
> Monopolistic competition – downward sloping demand curve
> Pure monopoly – zero elastic supply curve

The author is not certain what assumptions Ricardo made as to the demand curve for land but in his model it is clear that he assumed that with even a minor increase in the price of 'corn,' inferior grades of land would be brought into production and in modern terminology, we would say that this implied that the demand was very elastic.

On the supply side, Ricardo took the total supply of land to be fixed and so we have a supply curve with zero elasticity. We can set out these assumptions in a diagram and contrast it with what is probably a close approximation of the real estate market taken as a whole.

Clearly the Ricardian model is extremely limited in its application and has no relevance for the everyday real estate market, which is of the bilateral monopoly or monopolistic competition type. As noted earlier, this theory pays no attention to the marginal analysis and yet, as soon as we have sloping (as opposed to horizontal and/or vertical) curves the whole mechanism for determining price and quantity, depends not directly on the demand and supply curves but indirectly on them through the curves marginal to them.

One further matter should be clarified at this stage. As Ricardo was theorizing about the economy as a whole and as he treated the land in that economy as a gigantic farm capable of producing only a single crop, 'corn,' it is obvious that all the revenue earned by land could be treated as a surplus which was not a necessary cost of production. And this revenue Ricardo called 'rent' and it soon came to be called 'economic rent.' But what is true of the whole is not true of the part and so to any actual farmer or other land user, the rent he paid for land which had alternative uses (say, growing 'corn' or potatoes or as a building site) was a cost of production that must be met if the land wasn't to be lost to him and put to its next best alternative use.

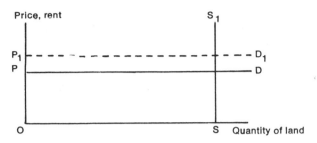

Ricardo's model

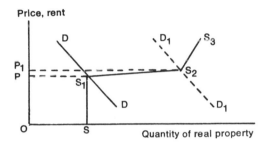

Real property model   (23)

Appraisal theory has inexplicably adopted the idea of 'economic rent' to mean the total rent which a parcel of real property would earn on the open market if it wasn't already under lease. This is an improper use of a term which has an ancient and definite meaning in economic theory completely different from that in which it is employed by appraisers. Rent definitely enters into the cost of production of an individual land user and cannot be thought of as a costless surplus, except when we are considering all land of a given type and capable of only a single use. In this latter case, all the rent paid for the use of the land is a pure surplus which could be taxed away without reducing the supply of land. But in a modern society, practically all land has alternative uses, so obviously some or all of the rent paid for land is a necessary cost of production if the land is to be prevented from being put to some other use. And even if we consider only the actual use of improved real property, clearly most of this has a definite cost of production, unlike Ricardian land which was defined so as to be costless. And therefore only that portion of the rent which exceeds the minimum amount needed to keep the land in its present use can be considered as a surplus. Why can't what appraisers call 'economic rent' be called what it is, namely 'market rent?' See also Chapter 12, Reference 13.

In appraisal theory, the concept of the agents in production is used in the same way in which Classical economists used it, namely to show how the gross product was distributed between the co-operating agents who produced the product. But there the similarity ends. Ricardo was thinking of the economy as a whole at a time in history when there were three fairly distinct classes of people who had to be paid out of the proceeds of production, namely labourers, capitalists (who were often also what we would call entrepreneurs) and landowners. So in his day and under his assumptions one could use the idea of the three agents in production in both the theory of production and the theory of distribution.

In a modern economy it is suggested that the concept has validity (and then merely in general terms) only in a theory of production. It is quite true that appraisal theory does make use of the idea of agents in production in this manner, but the major application of the concept is as the nucleus of a theory of distribution as will be clear from a perusal of the diagram in Chapter 3, Reference 20; but remember that the appraisal distribution ends with 'land.' In the land and building residual techniques, the earnings attributable to the various factors are distributed between them so that we can arrive at a residual income to capitalize. And in the basic theory, the implication is that land is always residual. But when the point of application is reached in the actual residual techniques, appraisal theory suddenly realizes that land in a modern society is rarely residual. This is obvious when we recognize that in 95% of all actual appraisals of income-producing properties, the building residual technique is considered to be the appropriate method to use simply because the terms of the rental contract or the age, condition and utility of the building do not warrant the assumption that the land beneath the building is the residual recipient of the revenue earned by the property.

This leads one to the inevitable conclusion that the whole idea of the agents in production is inapplicable in a modern society as far as distribution theory in a fixed and definite order is concerned. No longer are there three distinct social classes whose incomes can be classified solely as wages, interest or rent. Rather, we observe that wage earners frequently own real property (and hence earn at least implicit rent) and stocks and bonds. What is true of the wage earner is even more true of the capitalist and landowner; they generally have a variety of sources of income. So the only logical way in which we can talk about the agents in production is as part of a theory of production. In any type of society there must be productive contributions from labour, capital and land. But in an advanced society of the 20th century there is no validity in the idea that these agents must be paid in some definite, unchanging order, as has become one of the dogmas of appraisal theory.

Reference to the diagram in Chapter 3, Reference 20, will show that the appraiser thinks there are not three but four agents in production, the fourth being 'co-ordination.' As noted in that chapter, this largely ignores the entrepreneur. The entrepreneur is a risk-taker in the face of uncertainty; only if he guesses right will he be paid and then only if labour, co-ordination, capital and land have been paid first. What he earns is called 'profit' and it is unfortunate that this is often confused in appraisal literature with the 'interest' of capital. Interest is a necessary cost of production whereas profit is strictly a surplus and in terms of our earlier diagrams the entrepreneur has a receptacle to the right of that designated as land (as pointed out this is not included in the appraisal scheme); profit, if any is always residual in the short-run market period. Only in the long run is land residual. In the perfectly competitive model of economic theory only 'normal' profits can be earned except in the form of 'rent' to one of the agents in production and this will be competed away in due course.

It is obvious from what has been said so far that the serious shortcomings in appraisal theory may have an effect in practice. The accepted appraisal theory concerning the rate of interest is that the preference of investors as to safety, marketability, denomination, collateral, duration, management and capital appreciation are the desiderata. At no point does a serious attempt seem to have been made to make use of the theory developed by Bohm-Bawerk[24] or Fisher.[25] And as for the theories of Keynes and the more recent writers, these might just as well have never been developed for all the impact they have had on appraisal dogma. Certainly in Canada with its legal interest-rate ceilings and rigidities much more must be considered than the matters stressed in appraisal theory. Chapter 15 discusses this in greater detail.

Now there is no question that any given rate of interest is based on the above-noted investor preferences. But it would be expected that appraisal theory would devote a good deal of space to the theory of interest. Instead, all it does is describe several methods by which the appropriate risk and recapture rates can be developed. This, of course, is perhaps all that can be expected in a trade training course, but in a true educational programme it is essential that students and practitioners should know not only how to decide upon appropriate rates but also why these rates are appropriate; and also in which of the various methods and techniques of capitalization the various types of rates are appropriate.

The accepted appraisal theory leaves much to be desired. It is suggested that the reason is the lethargy and inertia of appraisers and their Institutes. The enormous task which Babcock set himself and completed so admirably nearly 40 years ago has been largely left to stagnate, and little, if any, effort has been made to add to his foundation. There is much in economic theory that might prove helpful and in the modern world of mathematics and computers many tools exist which could be used by appraisers. Much effort is being extended by many students, teachers and practitioners in an attempt to elevate the standard of appraising and it is unfortunate that such effort is to a large extent dissipated by dogmatic adherence to inadequate theory.

It is natural that appraisal theory should be heavily slanted towards what are now called the cost approach and the residual techniques; these were the stock in trade of the Classical economists and they had little concern with the short-run market and hence with the market data approach. But surely what is really needed is to refine the market data approach so that, among other things, both the amount of accrued depreciation to use in the cost approach and the appropriate risk and recapture rates to use in the income approach can be based, not on purely theoretical computations as in the accepted appraisal theory, but on the actual behaviour of sellers and buyers in the market. This, it is suggested, would, within the limits imposed by the inapplicability of the underlying theory, lead to considerable improvements in the practice of appraising. Dr Paul Wendt in his already cited book also feels that refinement of the market data approach is extremely important. Professor Richard Ratcliff shares this opinion: it is the market data approach which should be refined and used to the exclusion (or refinement) of all other approaches to the value estimate. He also believes that statistical analysis should be used by appraisers and that their final estimate of value should often be expressed in accordance with the probabilities involved; in other words, the most probable selling price is the expected value in a distribution of all possible selling prices.[26]

REFERENCES

1 / Appraisal Journal, July 1963, p. 316. This is a particularly illuminating article! Mr Warner found that of the more than 1,400 articles which appeared in the Journal in its first 30 years (1932-61) only 48 were on theoretical topics and, of these, 44 appeared between 1932 and 1938!

2 / Charles F. Louie, 'Depreciation and the Cost Approach,' Appraisal Journal, October 1961, p. 516.

3 / Paul Wendt, *Real Estate Appraisal,* Holt 1956.

4 / Laura Kingsbury, *The Economics of Housing,* Kings Crown Press 1946.

5 / Sanders A. Kahn, 'The Entrepreneur – The Missing Factor,' Appraisal Journal, October 1962. S.A. Kahn, F.E. Case, A. Schimmel, *Real Estate Appraisal and Investment,* Ronald 1963.

6 / Dr Ratcliff has contributed many articles and texts among which are: *A Restatement of Appraisal Theory,* University of Wisconsin; *Real Estate Analysis,* McGraw-Hill 1961; *Modern Real Estate Valuation,* Democrat Press 1965.

7 / Eighth Edition, Macmillan, London 1922; First Edition 1890. See, for instance, A.I.C. Text, p. 13.

8 / Three books were published in 1871 which seriously weakened all the earlier theory of value. For English readers, the most important of these was W.S. Jevons, *The Theory of Political Economy,* Macmillan, London. Many older writers, of course, recognized the 'marginal principle,' but either didn't stress it or didn't put it in rigorous and/or understandable terms.

9 / David Ricardo, *Principles of Economics,* 1817, Everyman's Edition.

10 / John Stuart Mill, *Principles of Political Economy,* 1848. Reprint 1965, A.M. Kelley.

11 / J.M. Keynes, *Essays in Biography,* The Norton Library 1951, p. 103. In all fairness it must be admitted that Keynes seemed to have developed an overly critical opinion of most earlier economists. Also the Classical concepts, particularly in macro economics have been referred to favourably by many economists in recent years.

12 / W.S. Jevons, *Letters and Journals,* p. 344.

13 / W.S. Jevons, *Theory of Political Economy* (2nd Edition), pp. vii, 1.

14 / Mark Blaug, *Economic Theory in Retrospect,* 1962, Revised edition 1968, Irwin.

15 / See particularly F. Quesnay, *Tableau économique,* 1758, A.R.J. Turgot, *Réflexions,* 1769.

16 / Adam Smith, *Wealth of Nations,* 1776, Modern Library.

17 / Thomas Robert Malthus, *An Inquiry into the Nature and Progress of Rent,* 1815, John Murray, London.

18 / Johann Heinrich von Thuenen, *Der Isolirte Staat,* Hamburg 1826.

19 / F.Y. Edgeworth, *Mathematical Psychics,* Kegan Paul, London, 1881.

20 / E.H. Chamberlin, *The Theory of Monopolistic Competition,* Harvard 1933 (7th Edition 1956).

21 / Walter Isard, *Location and Space Economy,* Wiley 1956. Any theory which doesn't consider the question of space and location is of little use in appraising. However, appraisal theory cannot be faulted in not adapting Isard's concepts to its own needs as they are both recent and still not fully formulated. In connection with the variable of time, one of the characteristics of the real estate market is its dynamism: the orthodox economic theory on which it is based is of the static-equilibrium or at best the comparative static type: it can really have very little real implication in a dynamic market and yet it is in many ways our best tool for analysis. But it should be adapted, not merely adopted, to specific market situations.

22 / Another reason probably exists in Canada. Under the B.N.A. Act, 'education' is a matter of exclusive Provincial jurisdiction. Hence any Institute organized solely on a Federal level cannot, if it acts within its legal powers, conduct 'educational' courses or award designations based on 'educational' requirements. But under the exclusive jurisdiction in Trade and Commerce given to the Federal Government, such Institutes may well be within their rights in staging 'trade training' courses. It is significant that all true professions are chartered provincially, and only have federal organization for the purpose of co-ordination of standards, ethics, etc. on a national level. True professionalism is impossible of attainment in Canada under sole Federal jurisdiction. Note has already been made of improvements made recently in the A.I.C. curriculum.

23 / We should distinguish between the demand for 'land' and the demand for 'uses' of land. Ricardo assumed only one use for land, namely growing 'corn,' so he didn't have to make the distinction; and similarly for supply. The two diagrams are therefore not fully illustrative of identical situations, but are felt to be appropriate for the purposes of general comparisons. The diagram of the real estate market is a 'short-cut' from the 2-part one shown in Chapters 3 and 15 and is used in an attempt to make the analysis more comparable. We would need the 2-part figure to show adjustments to stock from the flow.

24 / Eugen von Bohm-Bawerk, *The Positive Theory of Capital,* Macmillan 1879.

25 / Irving Fisher, *The Theory of Interest,* Macmillan 1930.

26 / Richard Ratcliff, 'A Neoteric View of the Appraisal Function,' Appraisal Journal, April 1965. Other articles on the use of statistical inference in appraising include William C. Pendleton, Appraisal Journal, January 1965; Richard U. Ratcliff, 'Don't Underrate the Gross Income Multiplier,' A.I.M., Winter 1969-70; Theodore Reynolds Smith, 'Multiple Regression and the Appraisal of Single Family Residential Properties,' Appraisal Journal, April 1971.

TABLE I

Inwood (single rate) $a_{\overline{n}|}R$

Present worth of $1 per annum received at end of year

Formula: $PW = \dfrac{1}{R} - \dfrac{1}{R(1+R)^n}$ (R = risk rate, n = number of years)

Risk rates

Years	6%	7%	8%	9%	9.5%	10%	12%	15%
1	.943396	.934579	.925926	.917431	.913242	.909091	.892857	.869565
2	1.833393	1.808018	1.783265	1.759111	1.747253	1.735537	1.690051	1.625709
3	2.673012	2.624316	2.577097	2.531295	2.508907	2.486852	2.401831	2.283225
4	3.465106	3.387211	3.312127	3.239720	3.204481	3.169865	3.037349	2.854978
5	4.212364	4.100197	3.992710	3.889651	3.839709	3.790787	3.604776	3.352155
6	4.917324	4.766540	4.622880	4.485919	4.419825	4.355261	4.111407	3.784483
7	5.582381	5.389289	5.206370	5.032953	4.949612	4.868419	4.563756	4.160420
8	6.209794	5.971299	5.746639	5.534819	5.433436	5.334926	4.967639	4.487322
9	6.801692	6.515232	6.246888	5.995247	5.875284	5.759024	5.328249	4.771584
10	7.360087	7.023582	6.710081	6.417658	6.278798	6.144567	5.650222	5.018769
11	7.886875	7.498674	7.138964	6.805191	6.647304	6.495061	5.937698	5.233712
12	8.383844	7.942686	7.536078	7.160725	6.983839	6.813692	6.194373	5.420619
13	8.852683	8.357651	7.903776	7.486904	7.291178	7.103356	6.423547	5.583147
14	9.294984	8.745468	8.244237	7.786150	7.571852	7.366687	6.628167	5.724476
15	9.712249	9.107914	8.559479	8.060688	7.828175	7.606080	6.810863	5.847370
16	10.105895	9.446649	8.851369	8.312558	8.062260	7.823709	6.973985	5.954235
17	10.477260	9.763223	9.121638	8.543631	8.276037	8.021553	7.119629	6.047161
18	10.827603	10.059087	9.371887	8.755625	8.471266	8.201412	7.249669	6.127966
19	11.158116	10.335595	9.603599	8.950115	8.649558	8.364920	7.365776	6.198231
20	11.469921	10.594014	9.818147	9.128546	8.812382	8.513564	7.469443	6.259931

21	11.764077	10.835527	10.016803	9.292244	8.648694	7.562003	6.312462
22	12.041582	11.061241	10.200744	9.442425	8.771540	7.644646	6.358663
23	12.303379	11.272187	10.371059	9.580207	8.883218	7.718434	6.398837
24	12.550358	11.469334	10.528758	9.706612	8.984744	7.784316	6.433771
25	12.783356	11.553583	10.674776	9.822580	9.077040	7.843139	6.464149
26	13.003166	11.825779	10.809978	9.928972	9.160945	7.895660	6.490564
27	13.210534	11.825779	10.935165	10.026580	9.237223	7.942554	6.513534
28	13.406164	11.986709	11.051078	10.116128	9.306567	7.984423	6.535508
29	13.590721	12.137111	11.158406	10.198283	9.369606	8.021806	6.550877
30	13.764831	12.277674	11.257783	10.273654	9.426914	8.055184	6.565980

For payment made at beginning of year add 1.000 to factor for one fewer years. To extend table for more years multiply Inwood factor for the number of years longer than that from which the extension is required, by the deferment factor (Table III) for that year and add result to Inwood factor for that year, i.e. for 40 years @ 9%: 6.418 x .0754 i.e. Inwood, 10 years x Deferment 30 years   =   .00482

add 9% Inwood factor for 30 years   =   10.274

9% Inwood factor for 40 years   =   10.756

TABLE II

Hoskold (double rate)

Present worth of $1 per annum received at end of year (recapture reinvested at 3%)

Formula: $PW = \dfrac{(1+r)^n - 1}{R(1+r)^n - (R-r)}$ (R = risk rate, r = reinvestment rate, n = number of years)

Risk rates

Years	6%	7%	8%	9%	9.5%	10%	12%	15%
1	0.943	0.935	0.926	0.917	.913	0.909	0.893	0.870
2	1.810	1.777	1.746	1.716	1.702	1.687	1.632	1.556
3	2.607	2.541	2.478	2.418	2.389	2.361	2.255	2.112
4	3.344	3.236	3.134	3.039	2.994	2.950	2.785	2.570
5	4.026	3.871	3.726	3.592	3.529	3.468	3.243	2.955
6	4.660	4.452	4.263	4.088	4.006	3.928	3.642	3.283
7	5.249	4.987	4.750	4.535	4.434	4.338	3.992	3.565
8	5.799	5.481	5.196	4.939	4.820	4.707	4.302	3.810
9	6.312	5.937	5.604	5.307	5.170	5.039	4.578	4.025
10	6.792	6.360	5.980	5.642	5.488	5.341	4.825	4.215
11	7.242	6.753	6.326	5.950	5.778	5.615	5.048	4.384
12	7.665	7.119	6.646	6.232	6.044	5.866	5.250	4.536
13	8.063	7.461	6.943	6.492	6.288	6.096	5.434	4.672
14	8.437	7.780	7.219	6.733	6.514	6.308	5.601	4.796
15	8.790	8.080	7.476	6.956	6.722	6.503	5.755	4.908
16	9.123	8.360	7.715	7.163	6.915	6.684	5.896	5.010
17	9.438	8.624	7.939	7.355	7.095	6.851	6.026	5.103
18	9.736	8.872	8.149	7.535	7.262	7.007	6.146	5.189
19	10.019	9.106	8.346	7.703	7.418	7.152	6.257	5.268
20	10.286	9.327	8.531	7.861	7.563	7.288	6.361	5.341

21	10.540	9.535	8.705	8.008	7.700	7.414	6.457	5.409
22	10.782	9.733	8.869	8.147	7.828	7.533	6.547	5.427
23	11.011	9.919	9.024	8.277	7.948	7.644	6.631	5.530
24	11.230	10.096	9.170	8.400	8.061	7.749	6.709	5.585
25	11.438	10.264	9.309	8.516	8.168	7.848	6.783	5.636
26	11.636	10.423	9.439	8.625	8.269	7.940	6.852	5.684
27	11.825	10.575	9.563	8.729	8.364	8.028	6.917	5.729
28	12.006	10.719	9.681	8.827	8.454	8.111	6.979	5.771
29	12.178	10.856	9.793	8.919	8.539	8.189	7.037	5.810
30	12.343	10.987	9.889	9.007	8.619	8.263	7.091	5.847

For payment made at beginning of year add 1.000 to factor for one fewer years. Extension of table can be done as in Inwood but as reinvestment is at a rate lower than the risk rate, the reversionary factor must reflect this.

TABLE III

Deferment (reversion)

Present worth of $1 which will not be received until some future date

Formula: $PW = \dfrac{1}{(1+R)^n}$ (R = risk rate, n = number of years)

Risk rates

Years	6%	7%	8%	9%	9.5%	10%	12%	15%
1	.943396	.934579	.925926	.917431	.913242	.909091	.892857	.869565
2	.889996	.873439	.857339	.841680	.834011	.826446	.797194	.756144
3	.839619	.816298	.793832	.772183	.761654	.751315	.711780	.657516
4	.792094	.762895	.735030	.708425	.695574	.683013	.635518	.571753
5	.747258	.712986	.680583	.649931	.635228	.620921	.567427	.497177
6	.704961	.666342	.630170	.596267	.580117	.564474	.506631	.432328
7	.665057	.622750	.583490	.547034	.529787	.513158	.452349	.375937
8	.627412	.582009	.540269	.501866	.483824	.466507	.403883	.326902
9	.591898	.543934	.500249	.460428	.441848	.424098	.360610	.284262
10	.558395	.508349	.463193	.422411	.403514	.385543	.321973	.247185
11	.526788	.475093	.428883	.387533	.368506	.350494	.287476	.214943
12	.496969	.444012	.397114	.355535	.336535	.318631	.256675	.186907
13	.468839	.414964	.367698	.326179	.307338	.289664	.229174	.162528
14	.442301	.387817	.340461	.299246	.280674	.263331	.204620	.141329
15	.417265	.362446	.315242	.274538	.256323	.239392	.182696	.122894
16	.393646	.338735	.291890	.251870	.234085	.217629	.163122	.106865
17	.371364	.316574	.270269	.231073	.213777	.197845	.145644	.092926
18	.350344	.295864	.250249	.211994	.195230	.179859	.130040	.080805
19	.330513	.276508	.231712	.194490	.178292	.163508	.116107	.070265
20	.311805	.258419	.214548	.178431	.162824	.148644	.103667	.061100

21	.294155	.241513	.198656	.163698	.148697	.135131	.092560	.053131
22	.277505	.225713	.183941	.015905	.135797	.122846	.082643	.046201
23	.261797	.210947	.170315	.014382	.124015	.111678	.073788	.040174
24	.246979	.197147	.157699	.013023	.113256	.101526	.067882	.034934
25	.232999	.184249	.146018	.011806	.103430	.092296	.058823	.030378
26	.219810	.014561	.135202	.106393	.094457	.083905	.052521	.026415
27	.207368	.013426	.125187	.097608	.086262	.076278	.046894	.022970
28	.195630	.012392	.115914	.089548	.078778	.069343	.041869	.019974
29	.184557	.011449	.107323	.082155	.071943	.063039	.037383	.017369
30	.174110	.010586	.099377	.075371	.065702	.057309	.033378	.015103

To extend table for longer periods multiply factor for year from which extension is desired by factor for the number of years of the extension: i.e. for 40 years @ 9%: .0754 x .4224 = 0.313.

TABLE IV

Sinking fund $\dfrac{1}{S\overline{n}\rceil r}$

Amount required to be invested annually to add up to $1 at some future date

Formula: $SF = \dfrac{r}{(1+r)^n - 1}$ (r = investment rate, n = number of years)

Investment rates

Years	6%	7%	8%	9%	9.5%	10%	12%	15%
1	1.000000	1.000000	1.000000	1.000000	1.000000	1.000000	1.000000	1.000000
2	.485437	.483092	.480769	.478469	.477327	.476190	.471698	.465116
3	.314110	.311052	.308034	.305055	.303580	.302115	.296349	.287976
4	.228591	.225228	.221921	.218669	.217063	.215471	.209234	.200265
5	.177396	.173891	.170456	.167092	.165436	.163797	.157410	.148315
6	.143363	.139796	.136315	.132920	.131253	.129607	.123226	.114236
7	.119135	.115553	.112072	.108691	.107036	.105405	.099118	.090360
8	.101036	.097468	.094015	.090674	.089046	.087444	.081302	.072850
9	.087022	.083486	.080080	.076799	.075205	.073641	.067679	.059574
10	.075868	.072378	.069029	.065820	.064266	.062745	.056984	.049252
11	.066793	.063357	.060076	.056947	.055437	.053963	.048415	.041068
12	.059277	.055902	.052695	.049651	.048188	.046763	.041437	.034480
13	.052960	.049651	.046522	.043567	.042152	.040779	.035677	.029110
14	.047585	.044345	.041297	.038433	.037068	.035746	.030871	.024688
15	.042963	.039795	.036830	.034059	.032744	.031474	.026824	.021017
16	.038952	.035858	.032977	.030300	.029035	.027817	.023390	.017947
17	.035445	.032425	.029629	.027046	.025831	.024664	.020457	.015366
18	.032357	.029413	.026702	.024212	.023046	.021930	.017937	.013186
19	.029621	.026753	.024128	.021730	.020613	.019547	.015763	.011336
20	.027185	.024393	.021852	.019546	.018477	.017460	.013879	.009761

21	.025005	.022289	.019832	.017617	.016594	.015624	.012240	.008416
22	.023046	.020406	.018032	.015905	.014928	.014005	.010811	.007265
23	.021278	.018714	.016422	.014382	.013449	.012572	.009560	.006278
24	.019679	.017189	.014978	.013023	.012134	.011300	.008463	.005429
25	.018227	.015811	.013679	.011806	.010959	.010168	.007500	.004699
26	.016904	.014561	.012507	.010715	.009909	.009159	.006652	.004069
27	.015697	.013426	.011448	.009735	.008969	.008258	.005904	.003526
28	.014593	.012392	.010489	.008852	.008124	.007451	.005244	.003010
29	.013580	.011449	.009619	.008056	.007364	.006728	.004660	.002651
30	.012649	.010586	.008827	.007336	.006681	.006079	.004144	.002300

Index

Index of authors

Index of cases